CENTAUR CLASSICS

GENERAL EDITOR: J. M. COHEN

THE CHRONICLES
OF JEAN FROISSART

THE CHRONICLES
OF JEAN FROISSART

IN LORD BERNERS' TRANSLATION
SELECTED, EDITED AND INTRODUCED BY

GILLIAN AND WILLIAM ANDERSON

SOUTHERN ILLINOIS UNIVERSITY PRESS

CARBONDALE   ILLINOIS

Library of Congress Catalog Card No. 63-14937

INTRODUCTION

---

*'He saith among the trumpets Ha, ha; and he smelleth the
battle afar off, the thunder of the captains, and the shouting.'*
Job, 39.

LORD BERNERS undertook his translation of Froissart's chronicles at the high
commandment of his 'most redoubted sovereign lord King Henry the VIII,
King of England and of France, and high defender of the Christian faith, etc.' It
was printed in London by Richard Pynson, the first volume appearing in 1523
and the second in 1525. By this period the Tudors had brought ease and a measure
of unity to England after the devastations of the Wars of the Roses, and the young
Henry VIII, still significantly entitled King of France, had already made an attempt
at regaining the lost territories in France. The great days of the fourteenth century
when Englishmen won fame and victory from Flanders to beyond the Pyrenees
were a perpetual challenge to the monarchs who succeeded Edward III. Although
nothing came of the plans of Henry VIII and Wolsey to reassert England's power
on the continent, they did succeed in inspiring Berners to make this translation and
so fix the names of Crécy and Poitiers in the consciousness of succeeding generations
of Englishmen. Just as the wars between the knights of the Round Table in Mallory's
Morte d'Arthur reflect the unsettled state of England during the Wars of the Roses,
so Berners' translation is fully of the period when the young and lusty Henry VIII
was determined to be a knight as valorous as any of his predecessors, and while
he still masqueraded as the Defender of the old Faith and the old ideals.

Lord Berners' translation was probably the most important prose work to be
written in English since Malory finished *Morte d'Arthur* in 1471. Like Malory, Berners
belonged completely to the old Mediaeval world of an undivided Christianity in
the West whose highest secular ideal was that of the 'veray parfit gentil knight'.

Berners' Froissart places one immediately in Calais and Christendom, where the
most important questions are the battles in which the monarchs themselves take a
prominent part, where young men go to war wearing one eye bandaged until they
have performed some feat worthy of their ladies, and where the magnates have
little care for the people murdered, raped or left to starve in the cause of great
dynastic quarrels.

Sir John Bourchier, Lord Berners, had seen a full life of battles and intrigue by the time he came to translate Froissart. Born sometime in the 1460's, he may have been to Balliol College, Oxford. He succeeded his grandfather as Lord Berners in 1474 and three years later he was knighted. After having been involved in a plot to place the future Henry VII on the throne, he had to fly to Brittany. When Henry VII was at last successful in establishing his meagre rights, Berners entered his service. He took part in Henry VIII's French excursion in 1513, and three years later he was Chancellor of the Exchequer. In the same year as the Field of the Cloth of Gold, he was made Deputy of Calais, the last of the French possessions won by Edward III to remain in English hands. At Calais most of his literary work was done and there he died in 1533.

Although he is chiefly remembered for his translation of Froissart, his other works are of much interest. There are two romances, *Arthur of Little Britain* and *The Boke of Duke Huon of Burdeux*, and an English version of a French translation of Guevara's *Libro del Emperador Marco Aurelio* which went into fifteen editions in the course of the sixteenth century.

Only about fifty years before Berners was born, Jean Froissart had died after a lifetime of almost incredible industry with his pen. Froissart was born in Valenciennes in 1337, the year of the outbreak of the Hundred Years' War. As a subject of the Counts of Hainault from whose family came Philippa of Hainault, the wife of Edward III, he stood to a certain extent aside from the main quarrels between France and England. He was a French speaker and therefore heir to the strongly established French literary tradition. The story of his first love and his childhood are related in his poem the *Espinette amoureuse*. Froissart must already have made some reputation for himself before arriving in England for his first visit in 1361 when he was made secretary to Queen Philippa. The court of Edward III presented an admirable opportunity for meeting most of the chief actors in the wars recently ended with the Treaty of Brétigny. Froissart's sociable and obliging nature coupled with the royal favour made him a welcome guest wherever he went. He had already planned his lifework of writing a chronicle of the great deeds of his century. One of his chief sources from the earlier part of the fourteenth century was the chronicle of Jean Le Bel, a canon of Liége, and he took great pains to verify Jean's remarks even to the extent of visiting Scotland in 1365.

There he accompanied King David Bruce on a tour of the greater part of Scotland which resulted in the remarkable description of the Scots, partly included in these selections, and also in his romance *Meliador* which is laid for the most part in Scotland. Until the death of his patroness in 1369, Froissart spent much of his time in England. He was present at Bordeaux when the future Richard II was born just before the Black Prince set out to Spain to win the battle of Najera for Pedro the Cruel. After Philippa's death Froissart returned to his native country where he found a new patron in the lively and cultured Duke Wenceslas of

Luxemburg, a son of the blind King of Bohemia who met his death at Crécy. His researches and journeys to get information involved him in considerable expense and it was only in 1373 when he was appointed to the living of Les Estinnes, which he held for ten years, that his money troubles had some relief. The same year probably saw the composition of the first book of his chronicles. Froissart later became chaplain to his patron Guy de Blois and in 1388 set out to visit the much admired Gaston de Foix at Orthez, a journey which was extremely fruitful in gaining information about the wars in Spain and Portugal. In 1395 he made his last visit to England, a journey which must have stirred many old emotions in him. There he was well received by Richard II to whom he presented a copy of his chronicles. This is the incident with which we have ended this selection. In fact the chronicles continue until the murder of Richard II, an event which Froissart recorded with much dismay. It is not known when Froissart died, but it was some time after 1404.

Froissart is often spoken of as though he were a diffuse writer, scribbling down whatever news came to him, and it is a pity perhaps that a mere selection from his chronicles such as this will add to that impression. However, he, like many of his contemporaries, saw the whole governance of the external world as being in the hands of Fortune. Nearly all the people who enter into his pages are consumed by worldly ambitions, by desire for the praise of others, by love of the glittering armour and the hopes of victory in war. One vast sweep of the Wheel of Fortune in the chronicles describes a complete turn in the fortunes of the House of Plantagenet from the murder of Edward II to the murder of Richard II. This figure of Fortune came originally from Boethius' *Consolation of Philosophy*, which extended its influence in the fourteenth century through the translations of Jean de Meung in France and Geoffrey Chaucer in England. Froissart would have learned from a study of that work not to expect the intervention of God in matters conducted by men who thought entirely of things of this world. All is under the rule of Fortune whether it be the great King of France captured at Poitiers or the poorest of the women and children slaughtered by the Scots at Durham. In one of his poems Froissart describes Fortune thus:

> . . . elle met un homme en haut
> Ne l'en chaut
> Comment voist, puis le renverse
> Et le berse
> A un trop villain bersaut.

(She raises a man up; it does not matter to her how he goes; then she overthrows him and casts him down with a rude blow.) This conviction that worldly life is the result of accident, lends to his view of history a mordant detachment, especially when he has to speak of those who meet misfortune as a result of overweening pride.

The Hundred Years' War gives many splendid examples of the reversals of

Fortune. Froissart remarks on the alternation of good and bad monarchs in English history and thus we are shown England just recovering from the civil wars of the reign of Edward II. As Edward III begins to rise in fortunes with his early successes against the Scots, so France starts on the path which will lead to her abasement. Edward is checked by the choice of Philip of Valois as King of France in 1328, despite the latter's more distant connection with the direct royal line. There then follows a long and uneasy period of balance which ends with Philip's confiscation of Gascony in 1337 and Edward's attempts to build up a grand alliance of the Empire against France. This alliance in fact comes to nothing and it is not until the dispute over the Breton succession that Edward is finally able to make his power felt against the Valois. After the battle of Morlaix in 1342 Brittany becomes an important foothold for the English and continues thus for about forty years. The wheel of Fortune then raises Edward up with the victory of Crécy, followed ten years later by that of Poitiers and the capture of King John of France. After the Treaty of Brétigny, the fortunes of the English begin somewhat to decline and France finds an effective counterbalance in the brilliant and crafty monarch Charles V. Then both countries lie under kings who are minors and the wheel comes full circle in England with the murder of Richard II.

Another aspect of the fourteenth century made vivid by Froissart is the series of popular movements. These vary between well organized and successful risings, such as those under men like James van Artevelde in Flanders, the discontented English peasantry asserting their rights in 1381, or the pointless butchery of the Jacquerie. In these, guided by his strict mediaeval sense of order and degree, Froissart is largely on the side of the knightly classes but this disapproval, as for example of John Ball, does not prevent him from describing the common peoples' aims and desires clearly. The sufferings of the unwilling victims of this almost ceaseless warfare only rarely arouse his pity. But for the most part he shares the attitude of the English army when news was brought to them at Tornehem of the death of Queen Philippa: 'whereof every creature was sore displeased and right sorrowful, and specially her son the Duke of Lancaster. Howbeit there is no sorrow but it behoveth at length to be borne and forgotten: therefore the Englishmen left not their order, but remained a long space before the Frenchmen . . .' Even such a catastrophe as the Black Death—which is not mentioned in the version translated by Berners—only receives a short mention from Froissart in another revision of the chronicles.

Where Froissart does show his heart, is when he speaks of Philippa of Hainault. The passages describing her intervention on behalf of the burgesses of Calais and later, her own death, are among the most affecting of the whole work. Froissart's sociable nature which enabled him to coax first-hand reports from several of the chief actors in his history is shown best by his visit to the court of Gaston de Foix. The grisly story of the death of Gaston, the Earl of Foix's son and heir, is told simply and without a word of judgement on the father. It is too much for modern taste if taken in isolation as it is here, but in the full version of the chronicle one gets a better idea of the sinister King of Navarre and of why any emissary or gift from him was to be dreaded and feared. Even so Froissart's unqualified praise of the Earl is hard to swallow.

One of the most revealing passages is the narration of the Bascot of Mauléon, with its long recital of wars and sieges, changing sides, ransoms and all the concerns of a professional soldier of the time. We are reminded of the famous words attributed to Sir John Hawkwood, the Essex soldier who fought in Italy and still rides his charger in Florence cathedral, 'Do you not know that I live by war and that peace would be my undoing?' War was the trade of a whole class. Clausewitz's dictum that war is an extension of diplomacy scarcely applies here. In fact diplomacy was what happened in the winter when the weather put an end to most expeditions. One cannot hope to find in Froissart any significant details of the wool trade which bound England economically to Flanders, of the French taxation system which made Gascony prefer the less demanding English rule, or of the great constitutional problems which remained unsettled in both countries. What Froissart does bring to life is the practice of a knightly code, rarely entirely fulfilled, by men who were brought up from their cradle to regard war as their right and proper business, nourished on stories of the Arthurian heroes and taught to follow their feudal lords wherever they might be led. There were certainly the strongest political and economic reasons for the war and the social unrest during this period. For example, Edward III by leading his turbulent barons to war in France gained a respite for most of his reign from the constitutional problems which had plagued his grandfather and brought his father to a dreadful death. We are not shown the Edward who murdered his mother's lover before locking her up, who caused the bankruptcy of two of the greatest banking houses in Florence, who attempted in vain to disgrace Archbishop Stafford for his own bad management and who ended his days in senile decay totally dominated by a scheming mistress.

Instead we learn how Edward III looked to the generality of men in England and abroad: the warrior king of a warlike race, successful, open-handed, with a flair for ceremonial and public occasions. We see him not with the intellect but as his contemporaries did. Being men mostly of heart and hand rather than of head, they judged him according to their own driving forces of pride and the desire for honour, of the needs of greater material comfort and gain rather than by his success in any closely reasoned policy. Edward III's long-term policies in fact ended in disaster after his death. As France grew strong again under Charles V, the English nobility could no longer make their fortunes by ransoms and raids on the continent and they turned upon Richard II who failed to redress their grievances. All this we can only infer from Froissart; this sort of reasoning was foreign to him. What we do find in him is the stuff of history; we can feel we are there and we know what it felt like. This is the healthiest experience a study of history can give: to set not only the mind thinking but also to guide it rightly by imaginative truth.

C. S. Lewis in an admirable passage on Berners' translation in his *English Literature in the Sixteenth Century excluding Drama* (Oxford 1954) points out that youthfulness is the chief characteristic of Froissart and his world. It is the immediacy of the emotions and the feeling for physical action which transmits this. An example of the first is the Countess of Montfort's cry of joy as the English fleet appears to relieve the siege and the exuberance with which the English knights sally out to attack the besiegers. Froissart's ability to transmit the sensation and speed of physical action is communicated by his description of Sir John Chandos, felled to the earth at the battle of Najera: 'And on him there fell a great big man of Castile called Martin Ferrant, who was greatly renowned of hardiness among the Spaniards, and he did his intent to have slain Sir John Chandos, who lay under him in great danger. Then Sir John Chandos remembered of a knife that he had in his bosom and drew it out and struck this Martin so in the back and the sides, that he wounded him to death as he lay on him. Then Sir John Chandos turned him over and rose quickly on his feet . . .' It is so admirably graphic and what is most remarkable, as fresh in Berners' translation as it is in the original.

This is because in translating Froissart Berners had the good taste to stick to the style of the original. Instead of indulging in 'facundious rhetorike', which he eschewed, he employed words as though they were clear windows into understanding. It is difficult to compare this style with that of any of his prose-writing contemporaries because for the most part they did not write of his subjects. An earlier editor (Utterson of the 1812 edition) praised his style thus: ' . . . we cannot but feel admiration at the manner in which his task was completed. The simple, yet not altogether unpolished, manners of the age of chivalry, are painted with a fidelity and propriety which is not lessened by the phraseology appearing so appropriate to the facts and customs which it relates. The language is at once nervous, yet plain; elegant, yet impressive; it is very often affecting, but never tame.'

Once a modern reader has made the necessary adjustment to archaic words and phrasings, he can surrender himself utterly to the writing. What is perhaps most remarkable about Berners' version is that it never has the taste of a translation. He actually makes many mistakes as a translator but this hardly ever makes his reader want to turn to the original because he feels he is missing something. Even when Berners goes so far astray as to introduce an eclipse at the battle of Crécy instead of a flash of lightning, he never loses that easy confident manner of style without which many short books seem twice as long as all the chronicles of Froissart. It is hard to think of many translations into English which give this illusion of being original works. Urquhart's Rabelais is one and Malory another but Urquhart was out to beat Rabelais in a way that Berners has no desire to do, and Malory's originals have either disappeared or been overshadowed by the brilliance of his version. Berners differs from them as he does from other lesser translations because he was an interpreter of the passing middle ages to the new era that had just begun.

This translation of Froissart may be seen as a high point in an antiquarian movement in English thought and literature which began with Malory. It is present in works such as Leland's *Itinerary*, and it was to continue after Berners' death in the work of scholars like Camden and Stow. Berners' motives for undertaking this mighty task to a large extent aimed at instructing men of all ages with examples from which they might profit and improve their lives, and especially at arousing in the youth of England a desire to emulate the noble deeds of their ancestors. 'What pleasure shall it be to the noble gentlemen of England to see, behold and read the high enterprises, the famous acts, and glorious deeds done and achieved by their valiant ancestors?' The age of the feudal knight had long passed. What had lasted longer and still survives into our own day is the knightly ideal. This ideal received a new impulse during Berners' lifetime from Castiglione's *Il Cortegiano*, a work which is largely taken up with descriptions of knightly exercises and only at the end of which comes the description of the stages of Platonic love for which it is famous. When the Platonic ideal met and fused with the old western knightly ideal as exemplified by Berners, a new model was created for English literature and education.

Another reason why we feel so confident in Berners is that he was a man completely at home in the society and the methods of war described by Froissart. He was familiar with the English, French, Spanish and Imperial courts and Fuller describes him as a 'martiall man, well seen in all military discipline.' He had experience of all types of men and his dramatic sense was sufficiently developed to grasp the exact tone of whoever is speaking. Thus whether it is the deputations of the Flemish towns persuading Edward III to assume the title of King of France, or the Douglas uttering his last words at Otterburn, or the Bascot of Mauléon telling his long tales by the fireside at Orthez, all these widely differing tones of speaking are exactly represented. Conversation and direct speech are the downfall of most translators and it is here that Berners shows his greatest skill.

There is an exceptional interest in those works which interpret a period of history passing away to the age which succeeds it. Just as Boethius interpreted ancient learning to generations which knew no Greek, and Castiglione preserved the freedom of spirit of the Renaissance for a Europe about to be plunged into the wars and controversies of the Counter-Reformation, so Berners was one of the many men who preserved the old knightly ideal and at the same time added a new aspect to it: that of patriotism. It was at last becoming a matter of pride for an Englishman to write in English and not in French or Latin. One of the chief inducements to the poet Wyatt to introduce the new metres was that English

poetry should equal that of Italy.   The English court was now entirely English
speaking, unlike that of Edward III where French was the language of the king
and his associates.   Lord Berners' lifetime covers the period in which the new
nation states arose in Europe and finally put an end to the old Christendom.

In England great changes have often been preceded by an archaising period.
Coke and the Puritan lawyers in the early seventeenth century read into Magna
Carta their own ideas of individual liberties; the Levellers saw the Norman
Conquest as the crushing of Anglo-Saxon freedoms which must be restored; and
William Morris and the early Socialists created a dream of a Mediaeval England
which never existed; and so, before the Reformation in England men were creating
their own vision of the past.   Whether they were out to preserve the Arthurian
epics, to hand down the famous deeds of the past or to restore the Church to its
pristine ways, their efforts had an effect upon the coming changes far greater than
they could realise or even desire.   This does not mean that Berners mistranslated
Froissart, but that he saw in the chronicles an opportunity to fan the flames of a
patriotism which was new in his day and which had not existed in Froissart's time.

Like Thomas Wyatt and his father, and the Howard family into which he
married, Lord Berners had founded his fortunes on his early association with the
Tudors.   He played a large part in putting down opposition to their rule and for
the most part he seems to have been in agreement with the policies introduced by
Henry VII and carried on by Henry VIII.   His life was largely devoted to the
royal service and to increasing the royal power.   Therefore another reason for
using the period of the fourteenth century as an example for Englishmen to emulate
was the fact that Edward III was the last king of England to rule with undisputed
right of succession and with a power increased by military success.   His reign was
looked upon by succeeding generations as 'the good old days' of Edward III,
rather as Cromwell invoked the golden age of Elizabeth and a present day Tory
sighs for Palmerstonian diplomacy.   It was this kind of prestige that Henry VIII
coveted and in Berners' translation he could shine in the reflected glory of a
vanished age.

Thus Berners' Froissart stands in the noble line of English sixteenth and seventeenth century patriotic literature which extends as far as Shakespeare's historical
plays and Drayton's *Barons' Wars* and *Poly-Olbion*. It is difficult to over-estimate
the extent to which mediaeval customs and modes of thought extended into
Elizabethan times. To a large extent, as in the case of heraldry, they were con-
sciously preserved and jealously guarded.   At few other periods has such respect
been shown to ancient blood and past achievements. 'Where is Bohun? Where
is Mowbray? Where is Mortimer? Nay, which is more and most of all, where is
Plantagenet? They are intombed in the urns and sepulchres of mortality.' Thus
rings Chief Justice Crewe's lament for the vanished heroes of English history in

1625. One of the chief means whereby their names have not been forgotten has been through Berners' translation.

* * * * * * * *

The selection we have made from Berners' *Froissart* only covers about a third of the original version. This has meant some drastic pruning and, in the later stages, total omission of some very interesting material. But we felt that if we gave the Crécy and Poitiers wars more or less in full it would give an idea of the grandeur of scale upon which the whole work is constructed. If a wider selection giving shorter extracts of all the subjects chronicled by Froissart had been attempted, this might have appeared too episodic and fragmentary and one of the great virtues—its ability to hold the reader's attention over great length—might thus have been lost. Berners himself translated the work for its English interest and therefore the concentration in this selection is on the English successes in France. The rest, like the visit to the Earl of Foix, the description of the Scots, the madness of Charles VI of France with whom we meet again in Shakespeare's *Henry V*, are given either for their inherent dramatic quality or the light they throw on life in the fourteenth century.

To make these selections as comprehensible as possible to the modern reader we have changed the punctuation and the spelling of those words which are still in circulation. Most of the unfamiliar words will be found in the glossary at the back. Sometimes we have inserted a word in square brackets where its omission seemed to confuse the understanding. The chief difficulty in an edition of this work is the names. The same name varies from page to page. Froissart made innumerable mistakes and these Berners followed without attempting to correct them. W. P. Ker in his introduction to the Tudor Translations edition (1901) has this to say, after a diatribe against early Tudor spelling: 'Unhappily to this grievance, if such it be, Lord Berners has added considerably—partly through the fault of the French text, partly through the original and acquired ineptitude of the printer, but with more than can be fairly put down to their discredit—by his unqualified neglect of the historical names. It is beyond all language of complaint. The man who has been led into the intricate fallacies of the names in Berners' *Froissart* is only too glad to escape in silence.'

As this is only a selection and not a full version of the translation the best thing to do seemed to be to change whatever names were wrong or antiquated according to modern usage. Rather than overburden the text with notes it appeared better to alter the names in the text. We have been much helped by the suggestions in the 1812 reprint of the first edition from which these selections were taken, the Tudor Translations edition mentioned above and G. C. Macaulay's selections in the Globe edition (1895). However there were many names which they had missed and there are many more with which we could do nothing. As one example of the difficulties encountered in these names, at one point the counties of Kent and Essex appear lumped together under the single appellation of 'Brendpest'.

To show how far we have departed generally from the original here are two extracts, the first in the old spelling and the second in our version:

'And in the towne of Gaunt, there was a man, a maker of honey, called Jaques Dartvell. He was entred into such fortune and grace of the people, that all thynge was done that he dydde; he might commaund what he wolde through all Flaunders, for ther was non, though he were never so great, that durst disobey his commaundment. He had alwayes goyng with hym up and downe in Gaunt lx or fourskore varlettes armed, and amonge them, there were thre or foure that knewe the secretnes of his mynde; so that if he met a parsone that he hated, or had him in suspectyon, incontynent he was slayne . . .'

'And in the town of Ghent there was a man, a maker of honey,* called James van Artevelde. He was entered into such fortune and grace of the people, that all thing was done that he did: he might command what he would through all Flanders, for there was none, though he were never so great, that durst disobey his commandment. He had always going with him up and down in Ghent sixty or four-score varlets armed, and among them there were three or four that knew the secretness of his mind, so that if he met a person that he hated, or had him in suspicion, incontinent he was slain . . .'

Richmond, Surrey   G. A.
1963   W. A.

---

* A mead brewer.

The Preface
of John Bourchier, Knight
Lord Berners
Translator of this
present chronicle

WHAT condign graces and thanks ought men to give to the writers of histories, who with their great labours have done so much profit to the human life. They show, open, manifest and declare to the reader, by example of old antiquity, what we should enquire, desire and follow, and also what we should eschew, avoid and utterly fly: for when we, being unexpert of chances, see, behold and read the ancient acts, gests and deeds, how and with what labours, dangers and perils they were gested and done, they right greatly admonish, ensign and teach us how we may lead forth our lives. And farther, he that hath the perfect knowledge of others' joy, wealth and high prosperity, and also trouble, sorrow and great adversity, hath the expert doctrine of all perils. And albeit that mortal folk are marvellously separated, both by land and water, and right wondrously situate, yet are they and their acts, done peradventure by the space of a thousand year, compact together by the histographier, as it were the deeds of one self city and in one man's life. Wherefore I say that history may well be called a divine providence; for as the celestial bodies above complect all and at every time the universal world, the creatures therein contained and all their deeds, semblably so doth history. Is it not a right noble thing for us by the faults and errors of other to amend and erect our life into better? We should not seek and acquire that others did, but what thing was most best, most laudable and worthily done, we should put before our eyes to follow. Be not the sage counsels of two or three old fathers in a city, town or country, whom long age hath made wise, discreet and prudent, far more praised, lauded and dearly loved than of the young men? How much more then ought histories to be commended, praised and loved, in whom is included so many sage counsels, great reasons, and high wisdoms of so innumerable persons of sundry nations and of every age, and that in so long space as four or five hundred year.

The most profitable thing in this world for the institution of the human life is history. One, the continual reading thereof maketh young men equal in prudence to old men, and to old fathers stricken in age it ministereth experience of things. More, it yieldeth private persons worthy of dignity, rule and governance: it compelleth the emperors, high rulers and governors to do noble deeds to the end they may obtain immortal glory: it exciteth, moveth and stirreth the strong, hardy warriors for the great laud that they have after they be dead, promptly to go in hand with great and hard perils in defence of their country. And it prohibiteth reprovable persons to do mischievous deeds for fear of infamy and shame.

So thus through the monuments of writing, which is the testimony unto virtue, many men have been moved, some to build cities, some to devise and establish laws right profitable, necessary and behoveful for the human life, some other to find new arts, crafts and sciences, very requisite to the use of mankind. But above all things whereby man's wealth riseth, special laud and cause ought to be given to history: it is the keeper of such things as have been virtuously done, and the witness of evil deeds; and by the benefit of history all noble, high and virtuous acts be immortal. What moved the strong and fierce Hercules to enterprise in his life so many great incomparable labours and perils? Certainly nought else but that for his merit immortality might be given to him of all folk. In semblablewise did his imitator, noble Duke Theseus, and many other innumerable worthy princes and famous men whose virtues be redeemed from oblivion and shine by history. And whereas other monuments in process of time by variable chances are confused and lost, the virtue of history diffused and spread through the universal world hath to her custos and keeper it (that is to say, time) which consumeth the other writings. And albeit that those men are right worthy of great laud and praise, who by their writings show and lead us the way to virtue, yet nevertheless the poems, laws and other acts that they found devised and writ be mixed with some damage, and sometime for the truth they ensign a man to lie. But only history, truly with words representing the acts, gests and deeds done, complecteth all profit. It moveth, stirreth and compelleth to honesty; detesteth, irketh and abhorreth vices. It extolleth, enhanceth and lifteth up such as be noble and virtuous; depresseth, poistereth and thrusteth down such as be wicked, evil and reprovable. What knowledge should we have of ancient things past an history were not, which is the testimony thereof, the light of truth, the masters of the life human, the president of remembrance and the messenger of antiquity? Why moved and stirred Phalerius the King Ptolemy oft and diligently to read books? Forsooth for none other cause but that those things are found written in books that the friends dare not show to the prince.

Much more I would fain write of the incomparable profit of history, but I fear me that I should too sore torment the reader of this my preface; and also I doubt not but that the great utility thereof is better known than I could declare; wherefore

I shall briefly come to a point. Thus, when I advertised and remembered the manifold commodities of history, how beneficial it is to mortal folk, and eke how laudable and meritorious a deed it is to write histories, fixed my mind to do something therein; and ever when this imagination came to me I volved, turned, and read many volumes and books containing famous histories. And among all other I read diligently the four volumes or books of Sir John Froissart of the country of Hainault, written in the French tongue, which I judged commodious, necessary and profitable to be had in English, since they treat of the famous acts done in our parts, that is to say in England, France, Spain, Portugal, Scotland, Brittany, Flanders and other places adjoining; and specially they redound to the honour of Englishmen.

What pleasure shall it be to the noble gentlemen of England to see, behold and read the high enterprises, famous acts and glorious deeds done and achieved by their valiant ancestors? Forsooth and God, this hath moved me at the high commandment of my most redoubted sovereign lord King Henry the Eighth, King of England and of France, and high defender of the Christian faith, etc., under his gracious supportation to do my devoir to translate out of French into our maternal English tongue the said volumes of Sir John Froissart; which chronicle beginneth at the reign of the most noble and valiant King Edward the Third, the year of our Lord a thousand three hundred and twenty-six and continueth to the beginning of the reign of King Henry the Fourth, the year of our Lord God a thousand and four hundred: the space between is threescore and fourteen years; requiring all the readers and hearers thereof to take this my rude translation in gre. And in that I have not followed mine author word by word, yet I trust I have ensued the true report of the sentence of the matter. And as for the true naming of all manner of personages, countries, cities, towns, rivers or fields, whereas I could not name them properly nor aptly in English, I have written them according as I found them in French. And though I have not given every lord, knight or squire his true addition, yet I trust I have not swerved from the true sentence of the matter. And there as I have named the distance between places by miles and leagues they must be understood according to the custom of the countries whereas they be named, for in some place they be longer than in some other. In England a league or mile is well known. In France a league is two miles and in some place three, and in other country is more or less: every nation hath sundry customs.

And if any fault be in this my rude translation, I remit the correction thereof to them that discreetly shall find any reasonable default, and in their so doing I shall pray God to send them the bliss of heaven. Amen.

B

Here beginneth the prologue of Sir John Froissart of the Chronicles of France, England, and other places adjoining. [Ch. 1]

TO the intent that the honourable and noble adventures of feats of arms, done and achieved by the wars of France and England, should notably be enregistered and put in perpetual memory, whereby the prewe and hardy may have ensample to encourage them in their well doing, I, Sir John Froissart, will treat and record an history of great louage and praise. But, or I begin, I require the Saviour of all the world, who of nothing created all things, that he will give me such grace and understanding, that I may continue and persevere in such wise that whoso this process readeth or heareth may take pastime, pleasure and ensample.

It is said of truth that all buildings are masoned and wrought of divers stones and all great rivers are gurged and assembled of divers surges and springs of water. In likewise, all sciences are extraught and compiled of divers clerks: of that one writeth, another peradventure is ignorant; but, by the famous writing of ancient authors, all things be known in one place or another. Then to attain to the matter that I have enterprised, I will begin first by the grace of God and of the blessed Virgin our Lady Saint Mary, from whom all comfort and consolation proceedeth, and will take my foundation out of the true chronicles sometime compiled by the right reverend, discreet and sage master, Jean le Bel, sometime canon in Saint Lambert's of Liége, who with good heart and due diligence did his true devoir in writing this noble chronicle, and did continue it all his life's days, in following the truth as near as he might, to his great charge and cost in seeking to have the perfect knowledge thereof. He was also in his life's days well-beloved and of the secret counsel with the lord Sir John of Hainault, who is often remembered, as reason requireth, hereafter in this book, for of many fair and noble adventures he was chief causer, and by whose means the said Sir Jean le Bel might well know and hear of many divers noble deeds, the which hereafter shall be declared. Truth it is that I, who have enterprised this book to ordain for pleasure and pastime, to the which always I have been inclined, and for that intent I have followed and frequented the company of divers noble and great lords, as well in France, England, Scotland, as in divers other countries, and have had knowledge by them, and always to my power justly have enquired for the truth of the deeds of war and adventures that have fallen, and especially since the great battle of Poitiers, whereas the noble King John of France was taken prisoner, as before that time I was but of a young age or understanding. Howbeit, I took on me, as soon as I came from school, to write and recite the said book, and bare the same compiled into England and presented the volume thereof to my Lady Philippa of Hainault, noble Queen of England, who right amiably received it, to my great profit and advancement. And it may be so, that the same book is not as yet examined nor corrected so justly as such a case requireth; for feats of arms dearly bought and achieved, the honour thereof ought to be given and truly divided to them that by prowess and hard travail have deserved it. Therefore to acquit me in that behalf, and in following the truth as near as I can, I, John Froissart, have enterprised this history on the foresaid ordinance and true foundation, at the instance and request of a dear lord of mine, Robert of Namur, knight, Lord of Beaufort, to whom entirely I owe love and obeisance, and God grant me to do that thing that may be to his pleasure. Amen.

Here the matter speaketh of some of the predecessors of King Edward of England.   [Ch. 3]

FIRST, the better to enter into the matter of this honourable and pleasant history of the noble Edward, King of England, who was crowned at London the year of our Lord God MCCCXXVI on Christmas Day, living the king his father and the queen his mother, it is certain that the opinion of Englishmen most commonly was as then, and oftentimes it was seen in England after the time of King Arthur, how that between two valiant kings of England there was most commonly one between them of less sufficiency, both of wit and of prowess: and this was right well apparent by the same King Edward the Third, for his grandfather, called the good King Edward the First, was right valiant, sage, wise and hardy, adventurous and fortunate in all feats of war, and had much ado against the Scots, and conquered them three or four times, for the Scots could never have victory nor endure against him. And after his decease, his son of his first wife, who was father to the said good King Edward the Third, was crowned king and called Edward the Second, who resembled nothing to his father in wit nor in prowess, but governed and kept his realm right wildly and ruled himself by sinister counsel of certain persons, whereby at length he had no profit nor land, as ye shall hear after. For anon after he was crowned, Robert Bruce King of Scotland, who had often before given much ado to the said good King Edward the First, conquered again all Scotland and burnt and wasted a great part of the realm of England, a four or five days' journey within the realm at two times, and discomfited the king and all the barons of England at a place in Scotland called Stirling, by battle arranged the day of Saint John Baptist, in the seventh year of our Lord MCCCXIV. . . .

Hereafter beginneth the occasion whereby the war moved between the Kings of France and England.   [Ch. 5]

NOW showeth the history that this Philip le Beau, King of France, had three sons and a fair daughter named Isabel, married into England to King Edward the Second. And these three sons, the eldest named Louis, who was King of Navarre in his father's days and was called King Louis Hutin, the second had to name Philip the Great or the Long, and the third was called Charles: and all three were Kings of France after their father's decease by right succession each after other, without having any issue male of their bodies lawfully begotten. So that after the death of Charles, last king of the three, the twelve peers and all the barons of France would not give the realm to Isabel, the sister, who was Queen of England, because they said and maintained, and yet do, that the realm of France is so noble that it ought not to go to a woman, and so consequently to Isabel, nor to the King of England, her eldest son: for they determined the son of the woman to have no right nor succession by his mother, since they declared the mother to have no right. So that, by these reasons, the twelve peers and barons of France by their common accord did give the realm of France to the Lord Philip of Valois, nephew sometime to Philip le Beau, King of France, and so put out the Queen of England and her son, who was as next heir male, as son to the sister of Charles, last King of France.

Thus went the realm of France out of the right lineage, as it seemed to many folk, whereby great wars hath moved and fallen and great destructions of people and countries in the realm of France and other places, as ye may hear after. This is the very right foundation of this history to recount the great enterprises and great feats of arms that have fortuned and fallen. Since the time of the good Charlemagne, King of France, there never fell so great adventures.

Here the history speaketh of the manner of the Scots and how they can war.   [Ch. 17]

. . . THESE Scottish men are right hardy and sore travailing in harness and in wars; for when they will enter into England, within a day and a night they will drive their whole host twenty-four mile, for they are all a-horseback, without it be the trandals and laggers of the host who follow after afoot. The knights and squires are well horsed, and the common people and other on little hackneys and geldings; and they carry with them no carts nor chariots, for the diversities of the mountains that they must pass through in the country of Northumberland. They take with them no purveyance of bread nor wine, for their usage and soberness is such in time of war that they will pass in the journey a great long time with flesh half-sodden, without bread, and drink of the river-water without wine; and they neither care for pots nor pans, for they seethe beasts in their own skins. They are ever sure to find plenty of beasts in the country that they will pass through, therefore they carry with them none other purveyance but on their horse: between the saddle and the pannel they truss a broad plate of metal, and behind the saddle they will have a little sack full of oatmeal, to the intent that when they have eaten of the sodden flesh, then they lay this plate on the fire and temper a little of the oatmeal; and when the plate is hot they cast of the thin paste thereon, and so make a little cake in manner of a cracknell or biscuit, and that they eat to comfort withal their stomachs. Wherefore it is no great marvel though they make greater journeys than other people do. And in this manner were the Scots entered into the said country, and wasted and burnt all about them as they went and took great number of beasts. They were to the number of four thousand men of arms, knights and squires mounted on good horses, and other ten thousand men of war were armed after their guise, right hardy and fierce, mounted on little hackneys, the which were never tied nor kept at hard meat but let go to pasture in the fields and bushes. They had two good captains, for King Robert of Scotland, who in his days had been hardy and prudent, was as then of great age and sore grieved with the great sickness; but he had made one of his captains a gentle prince and a valiant in arms called the Earl of Moray, bearing in his arms silver, three oreillers gules; and the other was the Lord James Douglas who was reputed for the most hardy knight and greatest adventurer in all the realm of Scotland, and he bore azure, a chief silver. These two lords were renowned as chief in all deeds of arms and great prowess in all Scotland.

How King Edward was married to my Lady Philippa of Hainault (1328).   [Ch. 19]

IT was not long after but that the king and the queen his mother, the Earl of Kent his uncle, the Earl of Lancaster, Sir Roger Mortimer, and all the barons of England, and by the advice of the king's council, they sent a bishop and two knights bannerets, with two notable clerks, to Sir John of Hainault, praying him to be a mean that their lord, the young King of England, might have in marriage one of the earl's daughters of Hainault, his brother, named Philippa: for the king and all the nobles of the realm had rather have her than any other lady for the love of him. Sir John of Hainault, Lord Beaumont, feasted and honoured greatly these ambassadors and brought them to Valenciennes to the earl his brother, who honourably received them and made them such cheer that it were over-long here to rehearse. And when they had showed the content of their message, the earl said, 'Sirs, I thank greatly the king your prince and the queen his mother and all other lords of England, sith that they have sent such sufficient personages as ye be to do me such honour as to treat for the marriage; to the which request I am well agreed, if our Holy Father the Pope will consent thereto': with the which answer these ambassadors were right well content.

Then they sent two knights and two clerks incontinent to the Pope, to Avignon, to purchase a dispensation for this marriage to be had, for without the Pope's licence they might not marry, for [by] the lineage of France they were so near of kin as at the third degree, for the two mothers were cousins-german issued of two brethren. And when these ambassadors were come to the Pope and their requests and considerations were well heard, our Holy Father the Pope with all the whole college consented to this marriage, and so feasted them. And then they departed and came again to Valenciennes with their bulls.

Then this marriage was concluded and affirmed on both parties. Then was there devised and purveyed for their apparel and for all things honourable that belonged to such a lady who should be Queen of England. And there this princess was married by a sufficient procuration brought from the King of England. And after all feasts and triumphs done, then this young queen entered into the sea at Wissant and arrived with all her company at Dover. And Sir John of Hainault, Lord Beaumont, her uncle, did conduct her to the city of London, where there was made great feast, and many nobles of England, and the queen was crowned. And there was also great jousts, tourneys, dancing, carolling and great feasts every day, the which endured the space of three weeks. The English chronicle saith this marriage and coronation of the queen was done at York with much honour, the Sunday in the even of the Conversion of Saint Paul, in the year of our Lord MCCCXXVIII. In the which chronicle is shewed many other things of the ruling of the realm, and of the death of King Edward of Caernarvon and divers other debates that were within the realm, as in the same chronicle more plainly it appeareth: the which the author of this book speaketh no word of, because per-adventure he knew it not, for it was hard for a stranger to know all things. But according to his writing this young Queen Philippa abode still in England with a small company of any persons of her own country, saving one who was named Walter of Manny who abode still with the queen and was her carver, and after did so many great prowesses in divers places that it were hard to make mention of them all.

How Philip of Valois was crowned King of France (1328).   [Ch. 21]

KING Charles of France, son to the fair King Philip, was three times married, and yet died without issue male. The first of his wives was one of the most fairest ladies in all the world, and she was the daughter of the Earl of Artois. Howbeit she kept but evil the sacrament of matrimony, but brake her wedlock; wherefore she was kept a long space in prison in the Castle Gaillard before that her husband was made king. And when the realm of France was fallen to him, he was crowned by the assent of the twelve douze-peers of France; and then, because they would not that the realm of France should be long without an heir male, they advised by their counsel that the king should be remarried again: and so he was, to the daughter of the Emperor Henry of Luxembourg, sister to the gentle King of Bohemia; whereby the first marriage of the king was fordone, between him and his wife that was in prison, by the licence and declaration of the Pope that was then. And by his second wife, who was right humble and a noble wise lady, the king had a son, who died in his young age, and the queen also at Issoudun in Berry. And they both died suspiciously, wherefore divers persons were put to blame after privily. And after this, the same King Charles was married again the third time to the daughter of his uncle, the Lord Louis Earl of Evreux, and she was sister to the King of Navarre and was named Queen Joan. And so in time and space this lady was with child, and in the meantime the King Charles her husband fell sick and lay down on his death-bed. And when he saw there was no way with him but death, he devised that if it fortuned the queen to be delivered of a son, then he would that the Lord Philip of Valois should be his governour and regent of all his realm, till his son come to such age as he might be crowned king; and if it fortuned the queen to have a daughter, then he would that all the twelve peers of France should take advice and counsel for the further ordering of the realm, and that they should give the realm and royalty to him that had most right thereto. And so within a while after the King Charles died, about Easter in the year of our Lord MCCCXXVIII; and within a short space after the queen was delivered of a daughter. Then all the peers of France assembled a council together at Paris, as shortly as they might conveniently, and there they gave the realm by common accord to Sir Philip of Valois and put clean out the Queen Isabel of England and King Edward her son; for she was sister-german to King Charles last dead, but the opinion of the nobles of France was, and said and maintained, that the realm of France was of so great nobility, that it ought not by succession to fall into a woman's hand. And so thus they crowned King of France Philip Valois at Rheims, on Trinity Sunday next after.

And anon after he summoned all his barons and men of war and went with all his power to the town of Cassel and laid siege thereto, in making war against the Flemings who rebelled against their own lord, and namely they of Bruges, of Ypres, and of [the] Franc; for they would not obey the Earl of Flanders, but they had chased him out of his own country, so that he might not abide in no part thereof but only in Ghent, and scantly there. These Flemings were a sixteen thousand and had a captain called Nicholas Zannequin, a hardy man and a courageous. And they had made their garrison at Cassel, at the wages of divers towns in Flanders, to the intent to keep the frontiers there about. But ye shall hear how the Flemings were discomfited, and all by their own outrage.

Of the battle of Cassel in Flanders (1328). [Ch. 22]

AND on a day they of the garrison of Cassel departed out to the intent to have discomfited the king and all his host. And they came privily without any noise in three battles well ordered, whereof the first battle took the way to the king's tents; and it was a fair grace that the king had not been taken, for he was at supper, and all his company, and thought nothing of them. And the other battle took the straight way to the tents of the King of Bohemia, and in manner they found him in like case. And the third battle went to the tents of the Earl of Hainault, and in likewise had near taken him. These hosts came so peaceably to the tents that with much pain they of the host could arm them, whereby all the lords and their people had been slain, and the more grace of God had not been shown before. But in manner by miracle of God these lords discomfited all three battles, each battle by itself, all in one hour, in such wise that of the sixteen thousand Flemings, there escaped never a person: captains and all were slain. And the king and lords of France knew not one of another, nor what they had done, till all was finished and achieved, for they lay in three sundry parties one from another. But, as for the Flemings, there was not one left alive, but all lay dead on heaps, one upon another in the said three sundry places. And this was done on Saint Bartholomew's day the year of our Lord MCCCXXVIII.

Then the Frenchmen entered into the town of Cassel and set up the banners of France. And the town yielded them to the king, and also the towns [of] Poperinge and of Ypres, and all they of the castellany of Bergues, and then they received the Earl Louis their lord and sware to him faith and loyalty for ever. Then after the king and his people departed and went to Paris, and he was much honoured and praised for this enterprise and aid that he had done to his cousin Louis, Earl of Flanders. And thus the king was in great prosperity and every day increased his royal estate; for, as it was said, there was never king in France that held like estate as did this King Philip of Valois.

Of the homage that King Edward of England did to the King of France for the Duchy of Guyenne (1329).   [Ch. 24]

AND after that the King [of England] had done these two executions, he took new councillors of the most noblest and sagest persons of his realm. And so it was about a year after that Philip of Valois was crowned King of France, and that all the barons and nobles of the realm had made their homage and fealty to him, except the young King of England, who had not done his homage for the Duchy of Guyenne, nor also he was not summoned thereto, then the King of France, by the advice of all his council, sent over into England the Lord d'Aubigny, the Lord Beausault, and two notable clerks, masters of the parliament of Paris, named Master Simon of Orleans and Master Peter of Mézières. These four departed from Paris and did so much by their journeys that they came to Wissant, and there they took sea and arrived at Dover, and there tarried a day to abide the unshipping of their horses and baggages. And then they rode forth so long that they came to Windsor whereas the king and the young Queen of England lay: and then these four caused to be known to the king the occasion of their coming. The King of England, for the honour of the French king his cousin, caused them to come to his presence and received them honourably; and then they published their message. And the king answered them how that the nobles of his realm nor his council was not as then about him, but desired them to draw to London, and there they should be answered in such wise, that of reason they should be content. And so they dined in the king's chamber and after departed and lay the same night at Colebrook, and the next day at London.

It was not long after but that the king came to his Palace of Westminster, and all his council was commanded to be there at a certain day limited. And when they were all assembled, then the French ambassadors were sent for, and there they declared the occasion of their coming and delivered letters from their master. Then the king went apart with his council to take advice what was best for him to do. Then it was advised by his council that they should be answered by the ordinance and style of his predecessors, by the Bishop of London. And so the Frenchmen were called into the council chamber. Then the Bishop of London said, 'Lords that be here assembled for the King of France, the king's grace my sovereign lord hath heard your words and read the tenor of your letters. Sirs, we say unto you that we will counsel the king our sovereign lord here present that he go into France to see the king your master, his dear cousin, who right amiably hath sent for him; and as touching his faith and homage, he shall do his devoir in everything that he ought to do of right. And, sirs, ye may show the king your master that within short space the King of England our master shall arrive in France and do all that reason shall require.' Then these messengers were feasted and the king rewarded them with many great gifts and jewels, and they took their leave and did so much that at last they came to Paris, where they found King Philip, to whom they recounted all their news: whereof the king was right joyous, and specially to see the King of England his cousin, for he had never seen him before.

And when these tidings were spread abroad in the realm of France, then dukes, earls and other lords apparelled them in their best manner. And the King of France wrote his letters to King Charles of Bohemia his cousin and to the King of Navarre, certifying them the day and time when the King of England should be with him, desiring them to be with him at the same day: and so they came thither with great array. Then it was counselled the King of France that he should receive the King of England at the city of Amiens, and there to make provision for his coming. There was chambers, halls, hostelries and lodgings made ready and apparelled to receive them all and their company, and also for the Duke of Burgundy, the Duke of Bourbon, the Duke of Lorraine and Sir John of Artois. There was purveyance for a thousand horse, and for six hundred horse that should come with the King of England.

The young King of England forgot not the voyage that he had to do into France, and so he apparelled for him and his company well and sufficiently. And there departed out of England in his company two bishops, beside the Bishop of London, and four earls: the Lord Henry, Earl of Derby, his cousin-german, son to Sir Thomas, Earl of Lancaster with the wry neck, the Earl of Salisbury, the Earl of Warwick and the Earl of Hereford; and six barons: the Lord Raynold Cobham, the Lord Thomas Wake, Marshal of England, the Lord Percy, the Lord Mohun and the Lord Mowbray, and more than forty other knights; so that the king and his company were about a thousand horse. And the king was two days in passing between Dover and Wissant. Then the king and his company rode to Boulogne and there tarried one day. This was about the mid of August the year of our Lord God a thousand three hundred and twenty-nine.

And anon the tidings came to King Philip of France how the King of England was at Boulogne. Then the King of France sent his constable with great plenty of knights to the King of England, who as then was at Montreuil by the seaside, and there was great token of love and good cheer made on both parties. Then the King of England rode forth with all his rout, and in his company the Constable of France. And he rode so long that they came to the city of Amiens, whereas King Philip, and the King of Bohemia, the King of Majorca and the King of Navarre were ready apparelled to receive the King of England, with many other dukes, earls and great barons; for there was all the twelve peers of France ready to feast and make cheer to the King of England, and to be there peaceably to bear witness to the King of England's homage. There was the King of England nobly received and thus these kings and other princes tarried at Amiens the space of fifteen days. And in the meantime there were many words and ordinances devised; but as far as I could know, King Edward of England made his homage to the King of France all only by word, and not putting his hands between the King of France's hands, nor none other prince nor prelate limited for him: for the King of England would not proceed any further in doing any more concerning his homage, but rather he was determined to return again into England. And there was read openly the privileges of ancient time granted, [in] the which was declared in what manner the king should do his homage and how and in what wise he should do service to the King of France. Then the King of France said, 'Cousin, we will not deceive you: this that ye have done pleaseth us right well as for this present time, till such time as ye be returned again into your realm, and that ye have seen under the seals of your predecessors how and in what wise ye should do.'

And so thus the King of England took his leave and departed from the King of France right amiably, and of all other princes that was there, and returned again into England; and laboured so long that he came to Windsor, where his queen received him right joyously and demanded tidings of King Philip her uncle and of her lineage of France. The king showed her all that he knew, and of the great cheer and honour that he had there, and said, in his mind there was no realm could be compared to the realm of France.

And then within a space after the King of France sent into England of his special council the Bishop of Chartres and the Bishop of Beauvais, the Lord Louis of Clermont, the Duke of Bourbon, the Earl of Harcourt and the Earl of Tancarville, with divers other knights and clerks, to the council of England, the which was then holden at London, for the performance of the King of England's homage, as ye have heard before. And also the King of England and his council had well overseen the manner and form how his ancient predecessors had done their homage for the Duchy of Aquitaine. There were many as then in England that murmured and said how the king their lord was nearer by true succession of heritage to the crown of France than Philip of Valois, who was as then King of France. Howbeit, the king and his council would not know it nor speak thereof as at that time. Thus was there great assembly and much ado how this homage should be performed. These ambassadors tarried still in England all that winter, till it was the month of May following, or they had answer definitive. Howbeit, finally the King of England, by the advice of his council and on sight of his privileges, whereunto they gave great faith, was determined to write letters in the manner of patents sealed with his great seal, knowledging therein the homage that he ought to do to the King of France; the tenor and report of the which letters patent followeth:—

'Edward, by the grace of God King of England, Lord of Ireland, and Duke of Aquitaine, to them that these present letters shall see or hear send greeting. We would it be known that as we made homage at Amiens to the right excellent prince, our right dear cousin, Philip King of France, and there it was required by him that we should knowledge the said homage, and to make it to him expressly, promising to bear him faith and troth, the which we did not as then, because we were not informed of the troth; we made him homage by general words, in saying how we entered into his homage in like manner as our predecessors, Dukes of

Guyenne, in times past had entered into the homage of the King of France for that time being; and since that time we have been well informed of the troth: therefore we knowledge by these presents that such homage as we have made in the city of Amiens to the King of France in general words was and ought to be understanded this word, liege man*; and that to him we owe to bear faith and troth as Duke of Aquitaine and peer of France, Earl of Ponthieu and of Montreuil. And to the intent in time coming that there should never be discord, for this cause we promise for us and our successors, Dukes of Aquitaine, that this homage be made in this manner following: the King of England, Duke of Acquitaine, holdeth his hands between the hands of the King of France; and he that shall address the words to the King of England, Duke of Aquitaine, shall speak for the King of France in this manner: Ye shall become liege man to the king, my lord here present, as Duke of Guyenne and peer of France, and to him promise to bear faith and troth, say 'Yea.' And the King of England, Duke of Guyenne, and his successors, saith 'Yea.' And then the King of France receiveth the King of England, Duke of Guyenne, to this said homage as liege man, with faith and troth spoken by mouth, saving his right and all other. And furthermore, when the said king entereth in homage to the King of France for the Earldom of Ponthieu and of Montreuil, he shall put his hands between the hands of the King of France for the said earldom. And he that shall speak for the King of France shall address his words to the king and earl and say thus: Ye that shall become liege man to the King of France my lord here present, as Earl of Ponthieu and Montreuil, and to him promise to bear faith and troth, say 'Yea.' And the king, Earl of Ponthieu, saith 'Yea.' Then the King of France receiveth the king and earl to this said homage, by his faith and by his mouth, saving his right and all other. And after this manner it shall be done and renewed as often as homage should be done. And of that we shall deliver, and our successors, Dukes of Guyenne, after these said homages made, letters patent sealed with our great seal, if the King of France require it; and beside that, we promise in good faith to hold and to keep effectuously the peace and concord made between the Kings of France and the Kings of England, Dukes of Guyenne, etc.'

These letters the lords of France brought to the king their lord, and the king caused them to be kept in his chancery.

How the lord Sir Robert of Artois was chased out of the realm of France (1329).   [Ch. 25]

THE man in the world that most aided King Philip to attain to the crown of France was Sir Robert, Earl of Artois, who was one of the most sagest and greatest lords in France, and of high lineage extraught from the blood royal, and had to

* This should be 'liege homage'.

his wife sister-german to the said King Philip, and always was his chief and special companion and lover in all his estates. And the space of three year, all that was done in the realm of France was done by his advice, and without him nothing was done. And after it fortuned that this King Philip took a marvellous great displeasure and hatred against this nobleman Sir Robert of Artois, for a plea that was moved before him whereof the Earl of Artois was cause. For he would have won his intent by the virtue of a letter that he laid forth, the which was not true, as it was said; wherefore the king was in such displeasure, that if he had taken him in his ire, surely it had cost him his life without remedy. So this Sir Robert was fain to void the realm of France and went to Namur, to the Earl John his nephew. Then the king took the earl's wife and her two sons, who were his own nephews, John and Charles, and did put them in prison, [where they] were kept straitly, and the king sware that they should never come out of prison as long as they lived: the king's mind would not be turned by no manner of means.

Then the king in his fury sent hastily to the Bishop Raoul of Liége and desired him at his instance that he would defy and make war against the Earl of Namur, without he would put out of his country Sir Robert, Earl of Artois. And this bishop, who greatly loved the King of France and but little loved his neighbours, did as the king desired him. Then the Earl of Namur, sore against his will, caused the Earl of Artois to avoid his land. Then this earl, Sir Robert, went to the Duke of Brabant, his cousin, who right joyously received him and did him great comfort. And as soon as the King of France knew that, he sent word to the duke that if he would sustain, maintain or suffer the Earl of Artois in his country, he should have no greater enemy than he would be to him, and that he would make war against him and all his to the best of his power with all the realm of France. Then the duke sent the Earl of Artois privily to Argenteuil to the intent to see what the king would do further in the case; and anon the king knew it for he had spies in every corner.

The king had great despite that the duke should so deal with him, and within a brief space after the king purchased so by reason of his gold and silver, that the King of Bohemia, who was cousin-german to the Duke of Brabant, and the Bishop of Liége, the Archbishop of Cologne, the Duke of Gueldres, the Marquis of Juliers, the Earl of Bar, the Lord of Loos, the Lord Fauquemont and divers other lords were allied together all against the Duke of Brabant, and defied him and entered with a great host into his country by Hesbaing, and so came to Hannut, and burnt twice over the country whereas it pleased them. And the King of France sent with them the Earl of Eu, his constable, with a great host of men of arms. Then the Earl William of Hainault sent his wife, sister to the king, and his brother Sir John of Hainault, Lord Beaumont, into France to treat for a peace and sufferance of war between the king and the Duke of Brabant. And at last the King of France, with much work, consented thereto, upon condition that the duke should put himself utterly to abide the ordinance of the King of France and of his council in every matter that the king and all such as had defied him had against him; and also within a certain day limited to avoid out of his country the Earl of Artois; and to make short, all this he did.

How King Edward was counselled to make war against the French king (1337).   [Ch. 28]

IN this season, ... Sir Robert of Artois was as then in England, banished out of France, and was ever about King Edward; and always he counselled him to defy the French king, who kept his heritages from him wrongfully: of the which matter the king oftentimes counselled with them of his secret council, for gladly he would have had his right, and if he wist how. And also he thought that if he should demand his right and it refused, what he might do then to amend it, for if he should then sit still and do not his devoir to recover his right, he should be more blamed than before. Yet he thought it were better to speak not thereof, for he saw well that by the puissance of his realm it would be hard for him to subdue the great realm of France, without help of some other great lords, either of the Empire or in other places for his money. The king oftentimes desired counsel of his chief and special friends and councillors. Finally, his councillors answered him and said, 'Sir, the matter is so weighty and of so high an enterprise, that we dare not speak therein, nor give you any counsel. But, sir, this we would counsel you to do: send sufficient messengers, well informed of your intention, to the Earl of Hainault, whose daughter you have married, and to Sir John of Hainault his brother, who hath valiantly served you at all times, and desire them by way of love that they would counsel you in this matter; for they know better what pertaineth to such a matter than we do. And, sir, if they agree to your intent, then will they counsel you what friends ye may best take.' The king was content with this answer and desired the Bishop of Lincoln to take on him this message, and with him two bannerets and two doctors. They made them ready and took shipping and arrived at Dunkirk, and rode through Flanders till they came to Valenciennes, where they found the earl lying in his bed sick of the gout, and with him Sir John his brother. They were greatly feasted, and declared the cause of their coming and showed all the reasons and doubts that the king their master had made. Then the earl said, 'As help me God, if the king's mind might be brought to pass, I would be right glad thereof: for I had rather the wealth of him that hath married my daughter than of him that never did nothing for me, though I have married his sister. And also he did let the marriage of the young Duke of Brabant, who should have married one of my daughters. Wherefore I shall not fail to aid my dear and well-beloved son, the King of England: I shall give him counsel and aid to the best of my power, and so shall do John my brother, who hath served him or this. Howbeit he must have more help than ours, for Hainault is but a small country as to the regard of the realm of France, and England is far off to aid us.' Then the bishop said, 'Sir, we thank you in our master's behalf of the comfort that ye give us. Sir, we desire you to give our master counsel, what friends he were best to labour unto to aid him.' 'Surely,' said the earl, 'I cannot devise a more puissant prince to aid him than the Duke of Brabant, who is his cousin-german, and also the Bishop of Liége, the Duke of Gueldres, who hath his sister to his wife, the Archbishop of Cologne, the Marquis of Juliers, Sir Arnold of Baquehem and the Lord of Fauquemont. These lords be they that may make most men of war in short space of any that I know. They are good men of war, they may well make ten thousand men of war, so they have wages thereafter: they are people that would gladly win advantage. If it were so that the king my son, your master, might get these lords to be on his part, and so to come into these parts, he might well go over the water of Oise and seek out King Philip to fight with him.' With this answer these ambassadors returned into England to the king and reported all that they had done, whereof the king had great joy and was well comforted.

These tidings came into France and multiplied little and little, so that King Philip's enterprise of the said crusade began to assuage and wear cold; and he countermanded his officers to cease off making of any further provision, till he knew more what King Edward would do. Then King Edward ordained ten bannerets and forty other knights and sent them over the sea to Valenciennes, and the Bishop of Lincoln with them, to the intent to treat with the lords of the Empire, such as the Earl of Hainault had named. When they were come to Valenciennes, each of them kept a great estate and port and spared nothing, no more than if the King of England had been there in proper person, whereby they did get great renown and praise. They had with them young bachelors, who had each of them one of their eyes closed with a piece of silk: it was said how they had made a vow among the ladies of their country that they would not see but with one eye, till they had done some deeds of arms in France; howbeit they would not be known thereof. And when they had been well feasted at Valenciennes, then the Bishop of Lincoln and part of his company went to the Duke of Brabant, who feasted them greatly, and agreed and promised to sustain the King of England and all his company in his country, so that he might go and come armed and unarmed at his pleasure, and to give him the best counsel he could. And also, if the King of England would defy the French king, that he would do the same and enter into the country of France with men of war, so that their wages might be borne, to the number of a thousand men of arms.

Thus then the lords returned to Valenciennes, and did so much by messengers and by promise of gold and silver, that the Duke of Gueldres, who was the king's brother-in-law, and the Marquis of Juliers, the Archbishop of Cologne and Waleran his brother, and the Lord of Fauquemont came to Valenciennes to speak with these lords of England before the Earl of Hainault and the Lord John his brother. And by the means of a great sum of florins that each of them should have for themselves and for their men, they made promise to defy the French king and to go with the King of England when it pleased him, with a certain men of war; promising also to get other lords to take their part for wages, such as be beyond the river of Rhine, and be able to bring good numbers of men of war. Then the lords of Germany took their leave and returned into their own countries, and the Englishmen tarried still with the Earl of Hainault, and sent certain messengers to the Bishop of Liége and would gladly have had him on their party: but he would never be against the French king, for he was become his man and entered into his fealty. King Charles of Bohemia was not desired, for they knew well he was so firmly joined with the French king by reason of the marriage of John, Duke of Normandy, who had to wife the king's daughter, whereby they knew well he would do nothing against the French king.

How that James van Artevelde governed all Flanders (1337). [Ch. 29]

IN this season there was a great discord between the Earl of Flanders and the Flemings, for they would not obey him nor he durst not abide in Flanders but in great peril. And in the town of Ghent there was a man, a maker of honey,* called James van Artevelde. He was entered into such fortune and grace of the people, that all thing was done that he did: he might command what he would through all Flanders, for there was none, though he were never so great, that durst disobey his commandment. He had always going with him up and down in Ghent sixty or four-score varlets armed, and among them there were three or four that knew the secretness of his mind, so that if he met a person that he hated, or had him in suspicion, incontinent he was slain: for he had commanded his secret varlets, that whensoever he met any person and made a sign to them, that incontinent they should slay him, whatsoever he were, without any words or reasoning; and by that means he made many to be slain, whereby he was so doubted that none durst speak against anything that he would have done, so that every man was glad to make him good cheer. And these varlets, when they had brought him home to his house, then they should go to dinner where they list, and after dinner return again into the street before his lodging, and there abide till he came out, and to wait on him till supper-time. These soldiers had each of them four groats Flemish by the day, and were truly paid weekly. Thus he had in every town soldiers and servants at his wages, ready to do his commandment and to espy if there were

* A mead brewer.

c

any person that would rebel against his mind, and to inform him thereof; and as soon as he knew any such, he would never cease till they were banished or slain without respite. All such great men as knights, squires or burgesses of good towns, as he thought favourable to the earl in any manner, he banished them out of Flanders, and would levy the moiety of their lands to his own use and the other half to their wives and children [of] such as were banished, of whom there were a great number abode at Saint-Omer. To speak properly, there was never in Flanders nor in none other country, prince, duke nor other that ruled a country so peaceably so long as this James van Artevelde did rule Flanders. He levied the rents, winages and rights that pertained to the earl throughout all Flanders, and spended all at his pleasure without any account making. And when he would say that he lacked money, they believed him, and so it behoved them to do, for none durst say against him. When he would borrow anything of any burgess, there was none durst say him nay.

These English ambassadors kept an honourable estate at the town of Valenciennes: they thought it should be a great comfort to the king their lord, if they might get the Flemings to take their part. Then they took counsel of the earl in that matter, and he answered that truly it should be one of the greatest aids that they could have; but, he said, he thought their labour in that behalf could not prevail without they get first the good-will of James van Artevelde. Then they said they would assay what they could do; and so thereupon they departed from Valenciennes and went into Flanders, and departed into three or four companies: some went to Bruges, some to Ypres, and some to Ghent. And they all kept such port and made so large dispense, that it seemed that silver and gold fell out of their hands; and made many great promises and offers to them that they spake to for that matter. And the bishop, with a certain with him, went to Ghent, and he did so much, what with fair words and otherwise, that he got the accord of James van Artevelde and did get great grace in the town, and specially of an old knight that dwelt in Ghent, who was there right beloved, called the Lord of Courtrai, a knight banneret, and was reputed for a hardy knight and had always served truly his lords. This knight did much honour to the Englishmen, as a valiant knight ought to do to all strangers. Of this he was accused to the French king, who incontinent sent a straight commandment to the Earl of Flanders that he should send for this said knight, and as soon as he had him, to strike off his head. The earl, who durst not break the king's commandment, did so much that this knight came to him at his sending, as he that thought none evil: and incontinent he was taken and his head stricken off: whereof many folks were sorry and were sore displeased with the earl, for he was well-beloved with the lords of the country.

These English lords did so much, that James van Artevelde divers times had together the councils of the good towns to speak of the business that these lords of England desired, and of the franchises and amities that they offered them in the King of England's behalf. So often they spake of this matter, that finally they agreed that the King of England might come and go into Flanders at his pleasure. Howbeit they said they were so sore bound to the French king that they might not enter into the realm of France to make any war, without they should forfeit a great sum of florins: and so they desired that they would be content with this answer as at that time. The English lords returned again to Valenciennes with great joy. Oftentimes they sent word to the King of England how they sped, and ever he sent them gold and silver to bear their charges and to give to the lords of Germany, who desired nothing else.

In this season the noble Earl of Hainault died, the sixth day of June the year of our Lord MCCCXXXVII, and was buried at the Friars in Valenciennes. The Bishop of Cambrai sang the mass; there were many dukes, earls and barons, for he was well-beloved and honoured of all people in his life days. After his decease, the Lord William his son entered into the counties of Hainault, Holland and Zealand, who had to wife the daughter of Duke John of Brabant, and had to name Joan. She was endowed with the land of Binche, the which was a right fair heritage and a profitable; and the Lady Joan her mother went to Fontenelles on the Scheldt and there used the residue of her life in great devotion in the abbey there, and did many good deeds.

How King Edward of England made great alliances in the Empire (1338).   [Ch. 32]

AFTER this discomfiture at Cadsand, tidings thereof spread abroad in the country, and they of Flanders said that without reason and against their wills, the Earl of Flanders had laid there that garrison; and James van Artevelde would not it had been otherwise, and incontinent he sent messengers to King Edward recommending him to his grace with all his heart, counselling him to come thither and to pass the sea, certifying him how the Flemings greatly desired to see him. Thus the King of England made great purveyances. And when the winter was past, he took the sea, well accompanied with dukes, earls and barons, and divers other knights, and arrived at the town of Antwerp, as then pertaining to the Duke of Brabant: thither came people from all parts to see him and the great estate that he kept. Then he sent to his cousin the Duke of Brabant, and to the Duke of Gueldres, to the Marquis of Juliers, to the Lord John of Hainault, and to all such as he trusted to have any comfort of, saying how he would gladly speak with them. They came all to Antwerp between Whitsuntide and the feast of Saint John. And when the king had well feasted them, he desired to know their minds, when they would begin that they had promised, requiring them to despatch the matter briefly; for that intent, he said, he was come thither and had all his men ready, and how it should be a great damage to him to defer the matter long. These lords had long counsel among them, and finally they said, 'Sir, our coming hither as now was more to see you than for anything else. We be not as now purveyed to give you a full answer. By your licence we shall return to our people and come again to you at your pleasure, and then give you so plain an answer that the matter shall not rest in us.' Then they took day to come again a three weeks after the feast of Saint John. The king showed them what charges he was at with so long abiding, thinking when he came thither that they had been full purveyed to have made him a plain answer, saying how that he would not return into England till he had a full answer. So thus these lords departed and the king tarried still in the abbey of Saint Bernard; and some of the English lords tarried still at Antwerp to keep the king company, and some of the other rode about the country in great dispense. The Duke of Brabant went to Louvain and there tarried a long time, and oftentimes he sent to the French king, desiring him to have no suspicions to him and not to believe any evil information made of him: for by his will, he said, he would make none alliance nor covenant against him; saying also that the King of England was his cousin-german, wherefore he might not deny him to come into his country.

The day came that the King of England looked to have an answer of these lords: and they excused them and said how they were ready and their men, so that the Duke of Brabant would be ready for his part, saying that he was nearer than they, and that as soon as they might know that he were ready, they would not be behind, but at the beginning of the matter as soon as he. Then the king did so much that he spake again with the duke, and showed him the answer of the other lords, desiring him by amity and lineage that no fault were found in him, saying how he perceived well that he was but cold in the matter, and that without he were quicker and did otherwise, he doubted he should lose thereby the aid of all the other lords of Germany through his default. Then the duke said he would take counsel in the matter. And when he had long debated the matter, he said how he would speak again with the other lords; and he did send for them, desiring them to come to him whereas they pleased best. Then the day was appointed about the mid of August, and this council to be at Hal, because of the young Earl of Hainault, who should also be there, and with him Sir John of Hainault his uncle.

When these lords were all come to his parliament at Hal, they had long counsel together. Finally they said to the King of England, 'Sir, we see no cause why we should make defiance to the French king, all things considered, without ye can get the agreement of the Emperor, and that he would command us to do so in his name. The Emperor may well thus do, for of long time past there was a covenant sworn and sealed, that no King of France ought to take anything pertaining to the Empire: and this King Philip hath taken the castle of Crévecoeur in Cambrésis and the castle of Arleux in Palluel, and the city of Cambrai; wherefore the Emperor hath good cause to defy him by us. Therefore, sir, if ye can get his accord, our honour shall be the more.' And the king said he would follow their counsel. Then it was ordained that the Marquis of Juliers should go to the Emperor, and certain knights and clerks of the king's, and some of the council of the Duke of Gueldres; but the Duke of Brabant would send none from him, but he lent the castle of Louvain to the King of England to lie in. And the marquis and his company found the Emperor at Nuremburg and showed him the cause of their coming. And the Lady Margaret of Hainault did all her pain to further forth the matter, whom Sir Louis of Bavaria, then Emperor, had wedded. And there the Marquis of Juliers was made an earl, and the Duke of Gueldres, who before was an earl, was made a duke. And the Emperor gave commission to four knights and to two doctors of his council to make King Edward of England his Vicar-General throughout all the Empire; and thereof these said lords had instruments public, confirmed and sealed sufficiently by the Emperor.

How King Edward of England was made Vicar-General of the Empire of Germany (1338). [Ch. 34]

WHEN the King of England and the other lords to him allied were departed from the parliament of Hal, the king went to Louvain and made ready the castle for his abiding, and sent for the queen to come thither if it pleased her: for he sent her word he would not come thence of an whole year, and sent home certain of his knights to keep his land from the Scots. And the other lords and knights that were there still with the king rode about the realm of Flanders and Hainault, making great dispense, giving great rewards and jewels to the lords, ladies and damosels of the country, to get their good-wills. They did so much that they were greatly praised, and specially of the common people, because of the port and state that they kept. And then about the feast of All Saints, the Marquis of Juliers and his company sent word to the king how they had sped; and the king sent to him that he should be with him about the feast of Saint Martin. And also he sent to the Duke of Brabant, to know his mind where he would the parliament should be held: and he answered at Herck in the county of Loos, near to his country. And then the king sent to all other of his allies that they should be there. And so the hall of the town was apparelled and hanged, as though it had been the king's chamber; and there the king sat crowned with gold, five foot higher than any other, and there openly was read the letters of the Emperor, by the which the king was made Vicar-General and Lieutenant for the Emperor, and had power given him to make laws and to minister justice to every person in the Emperor's name, and to make money of gold and silver. The Emperor also there commanded by his letters that all persons of his Empire and all other his subjects should obey to the King of England his Vicar, as to himself, and to do him homage. And incontinent there was claim and answer made between parties, as before the

Emperor, and right and judgment given. Also there was renewed a judgment, and a statute affirmed, that had been made before in the Emperor's court, and that was this: that whosoever would any hurt to other should make his defiance three days before his deed, and he that did otherwise should be reputed as an evil-doer and for a villain's deed. And when all this was done, the lords departed and took day that they should all appear before Cambrai three weeks after the feast of Saint John; the which town was become French.

Thus they departed and every man went to his own. And King Edward, as Vicar of the Empire, went then to Louvain to the queen, who was newly come thither out of England, with great nobleness and well accompanied with ladies and damosels of England. So there the king and the queen kept their house right honourably all that winter, and caused money, gold and silver, to be made at Antwerp, great plenty. Yet for all this the Duke of Brabant left not, but with great diligence sent often messengers to King Philip, as the Lord Leon of Crainhem, his chief counsellor, with divers other, ever to excuse him; for the which cause this knight was often sent, and at the last abode still in the French court with the king, to the intent always to excuse him against all informations that might be made of him: the which knight did all his devoir in that behalf.

How King Edward and all his allies did defy the French king (1339).   [Ch. 35]

THUS the winter passed and summer came, and the feast of Saint John Baptist approached. And the lords of England and of Germany apparelled themselves to accomplish their enterprise: and the French king wrought as much as he could to the contrary, for he knew much of their intents. King Edward made all his provision in England and all his men of war to be ready to pass the sea incontinent after the feast of Saint John: and so they did. Then the king went to Villevorde, and there made his company to be lodged, as many as might in the town and the other without along on the river-side in tents and pavilions: and there he tarried, from Maudlin-tide till our Lady Day in September, abiding weekly for the lords of the Empire, and specially for the Duke of Brabant, on whose coming all the other abode. And when the King of England saw how they came not, he sent great messengers to each of them summoning them to come as they had promised, and to meet with him at Mechlin on Saint Giles' day, and then to show him why they had tarried so long. Thus King Edward lay at Villevorde and kept daily at his cost and charge well to the number of sixteen hundred men of arms, all come from the other side of the sea, and ten thousand archers, beside all other provisions; the which was a marvellous great charge, beside the reward he had given to the lords, and beside the great armies that he had on the sea. The French king on his part had set Genoese, Normans, Bretons, Picards and Spaniards to be ready on the sea to enter into England as soon as the war were opened.

These lords of Germany at the King of England's summons came to Mechlin and with much business. Finally they accorded that the King of England might well set forward within fifteen days after. And to the intent that their war should be the more laudable, they agreed to send their defiances to the French king: first the King of England, the Duke of Gueldres, the Marquis of Juliers, Sir Robert d'Artois, Sir John of Hainault, the Marquis of Meissen, the Marquis of Brandenburg, the Lord of Fauquemont, Sir Arnold of Baquehem, the Archbishop of Cologne, Sir Waleran his brother, and all other lords of the Empire. These defiances were written and sealed by all the lords except the Duke of Brabant, who said he would do his deed by himself at time convenient. To bear these defiances into France was charged the Bishop of Lincoln, who bare them to Paris and did his message in such manner that he could not be reproached nor blamed; and so he had a safe-conduct to return again to his king, who was as then at Mechlin.

How Sir Walter of Manny, after the defiances declared, made the first journey into France (1339).   [Ch. 36]

IN the first week that the French king was thus defied, Sir Walter Manny, as soon as he knew it, he gat to him a forty spears and rode through Brabant night and day till he came into Hainault and entered into the wood of Blaton, as then not knowing what he should do. But he had showed to some of them that were most priviest about him, how he had promised before ladies and damosels or he came out of England, that he would be the first that should enter into France and to get either town or castle, and to do some deeds of arms. And then his intent was to ride to Mortagne and to get it if he might, the which pertained then to the realm of France: and so rode and passed the wood of Blaton, and came in the morning before the sun-rising to Mortagne, and by adventure he found the wicket of the gate open. Then he alighted with his company and entered in, and did set certain of his company to keep the gate, and so went into the high street with his pennon before him and came to the great tower, but the gate and wicket was fast closed. And when the watch of the castle heard the brunt and saw them, he blew his horn and cried, 'Treason! Treason!' Then every man awoke and made them ready, and kept themselves still within the castle. Then Sir Walter of Manny went back again and did set fire in the street joining to the castle, so that there were a threescore houses burnt and the people sore afraid, for they weened all to have been taken. Then Sir Walter and his company rode back to Condé and there passed the river of Aisne. Then they rode the way to Valenciennes and coasted on the right hand and came to Denain, and so went to the abbey, and so passed forth toward Bouchain, and did so much that the captain did let them pass through by the river. Then they came to a strong castle pertaining to the Bishop of Cambrai, called the castle of Thun, the which suddenly they took, and the captain and his wife within. And the Lord Manny made a good garrison and set therein a brother of his called Sir Giles Manny, who afterward did much trouble to the city of Cambrai, for the castle was within a league of the town. Then Sir Walter Manny returned into Brabant to the king his sovereign lord, whom he found at Mechlin, and there showed him all that he had done.

How that after the said defiances made, the Frenchmen entered into England (1339). [Ch. 37]

AS soon as King Philip knew that he was defied of the King of England and of his allies, he retained men of war on every side, and sent the Lord Galois de la Baume, a good knight of Savoy, into the city of Cambrai, and made him captain there, and with him Sir Thibaud de Moreuil and the Lord of Roye: so that they were, what of Savoy and of France, a two hundred spears. And King Philip sent and seized into his hands the county of Ponthieu, the which the King of England had before by reason of his mother; and also he sent to divers lords of the Empire, as to the Earl of Hainault his nephew, to the Duke of Lorraine, the Earl of Bar, the Bishop of Metz, the Bishop of Liége, desiring them that they would make no evil purchase against him or his realm. The most part of these lords answered how they would do nothing that should be against him; and the Earl of Hainault wrote unto him right courteously how that he would be ready always to aid him and his realm against all men, but seeing the King of England maketh his war as Vicar and Lieutenant of the Empire, wherefore, he said, he might not refuse to him his country nor his comfort, because he held part of his country of the Emperor.

And as soon as Sir Hugh Quieret, Sir Nicholas Behuchet and Barbevaire, who lay and kept the straits between England and France with a great navy, knew that the war was open, they came on a Sunday in the forenoon to the haven of Southampton, while the people were at mass. And the Normans, Picards and Spaniards entered into the town and robbed and pilled the town, and slew divers, and defiled maidens and enforced wives, and charged their vessels with the pillage, and so entered again into their ships. And when the tide came, they disanchored and sailed to Normandy and came to Dieppe, and there departed and divided their booty and pillages.

How King Edward besieged the city of Cambrai (1339).   [Ch. 38]

THE King of England departed from Mechlin and went to Brussels, and all his people passed on by the town. Then came to the king a twenty thousand Germans, and the king sent and demanded of the Duke of Brabant what was his intention, to go to Cambrai or else to leave it. The duke answered and said that as soon as he knew that he had besieged Cambrai, he would come thither with twelve hundred spears of good men of war. Then the king went to Nivelles and there lay one night, and the next day to Mons in Hainault; and there he found the young Earl of Hainault, who received him joyously. And ever Sir Robert of Artois was about the king as one of his privy council, and a sixteen or twenty other great lords and knights of England, the which were ever about the king for his honour and estate, and to counsel him in all his deeds. Also with him was the Bishop of Lincoln, who was greatly renowned in this journey both in wisdom and in prowess. Thus the Englishmen passed forth and lodged abroad in the country, and found provision enough before them for their money; howbeit some paid truly and some not.

And when the king had tarried two days at Mons in Hainault, then he went to Valenciennes; and he and twelve with him entered into the town, and no more persons. And thither was come the Earl of Hainault and Sir John his uncle, and the Lord of Fagnolle, the Lord of Werchin, the Lord of Havreth and divers other who were about the earl their lord. And the king and the earl went hand in hand to the great hall, which was ready apparelled to receive them. And as they went up the stairs of the hall the Bishop of Lincoln, who was there present, spake out aloud and said, 'William Bishop of Cambrai, I admonish you as Procurer to the King of England, Vicar of the Empire of Rome, that ye open the gates of the city of Cambrai; and if ye do not, ye shall forfeit your lands and we will enter by force.' There was none that answered to that matter, for the bishop was not there present. Then the Bishop of Lincoln said again, 'Earl of Hainault, we admonish you in the name of the Emperor, that ye come and serve the King of England his Vicar before the city of Cambrai with such number as ye ought to do.' The earl, who was there present, said, 'With a right good will I am ready.' So thus they entered into the hall, and the earl led the king into his chamber, and anon the supper was ready.

And the next day the king departed and went to Haspres, and there tarried two days and suffered all his men to pass forth; and so then went to Cambrai and lodged at Iwuy, and besieged the city of Cambrai round about; and daily his power increased. Thither came the young Earl of Hainault in great array, and they lodged near to the king, and the Duke of Gueldres and his company, the Marquis of Meissen, the Earl of Mons, the Earl of Salm, the Lord of Fauquemont, Sir Arnold of Baquehem, with all the other lords of the Empire such as were allied with the King of England. And the sixth day after the siege laid, thither came the Duke of Brabant with a nine hundred spears, beside other, and he lodged toward Ostrevant on the river Scheldt, and made a bridge over the water to the intent to go from the one host to the other. And as soon as he was come, he sent to defy the French king, who was at Compiègne; whereof Leon of Crainhem, who had always before excused the duke, was so confused that he would no more return again into Brabant, but died for sorrow in France.

This siege during, there were many skirmishes. And Sir John of Hainault and the Lord of Fauquemont rode ever lightly together, and burnt and wasted sore the country of Cambrésis. And on a day these lords, with the number of five hundred spears and a thousand of other men of war, came to the castle of Oisy in Cambrésis, pertaining to the Lord of Coucy, and made there a great assault: but they within did defend them so valiantly that they had no damage, and so the said lords returned to their lodgings. The Earl of Hainault and his company on a Saturday came to the gate toward Saint-Quentin and made there a great assault. There was John Chandos, who was then but a squire, of whose prowess this book speaketh much, he cast himself between the barriers and the gate, and fought valiantly with a squire of Vermandois called John of Saint-Disier; there was goodly feats of arms done between them. And so the Hainaulters conquered by force the bails, and there was entered the Earl of Hainault and his marshals, Sir Berard of Werchin, Sir Henry d'Antoing and other, who adventured them valiantly to advance their honour. And at another gate, called the gate Robert, was the Lord Beaumont and the Lord of Fauquemont, the Lord d'Enghien, Sir Walter of Manny and their companies, made there a sore and hard assault. But they of Cambrai, and the soldiers set there by the French king, defended themselves and the city so valiantly, that the assaulters won nothing, but so returned right weary and well beaten to their lodgings. The young Earl of Namur came thither to serve the young Earl of Hainault by desire, and he said he would be on their part as long as they were in the Empire, but as soon as he entered into the realm of France, he said, he would forsake them and go and serve the French king, who had retained him. And in likewise so was the intent of the Earl of Hainault, for he had commanded all his men, on pain of death, that none of them should do anything within the realm of France.

In this season, while the King of England lay at siege before Cambrai with forty thousand men of arms, and greatly constrained them by assaults, King Philip made his summons at Péronne in Vermandois. And the King of England counselled with Sir Robert d'Artois, in whom he had great affiance, demanding of him whether it were better for him to enter into the realm of France and to encounter his adversary, or else to abide still before Cambrai till he had won it by force. The lords of England and such other of his council saw well how the city was strong and well-furnished of men of war and victuals and artillery, and that it should be long to abide there till they had won the city, whereof they were in no certainty. And also they saw well how that winter approached near, and as yet had done no manner of enterprise, but lay at great expense. Then they counselled the king to set forward into the realm, whereas they might find more plenty of forage. This counsel was taken, and all the lords ordained to dislodge, and trussed tents and pavilions and all manner of harness, and so departed and rode toward Mount Saint-Martin, the which was at the entry of France. Thus they rode in good order, every lord among his own men. Marshals of the English host were the Earl of Northampton, and Gloucester and the Earl of Suffolk; and Constable of England was the Earl of Warwick. And so they passed there the river Scheldt at their ease.

And when the Earl of Hainault had accompanied the king unto the departing out of the Empire, and that he should pass the river and enter into the realm of France, then he took leave of the king and said how he would ride no further with him at that time, for King Philip his uncle had sent for him, and he would not have his evil-will, but that he would go and serve him in France as he had served the King of England in the Empire. So thus the Earl of Hainault and the Earl of Namur and their companies rode back to Quesnoy. And the Earl of Hainault gave the most part of his company leave to depart, desiring them to be ready when he sent for them, for he said that shortly after he would go to King Philip his uncle.

How King Edward made Sir Henry of Flanders knight (1339). [Ch. 39]

AS soon as King Edward had passed the river Scheldt and was entered into the realm of France, he called to him Sir Henry of Flanders, who was as then a young squire, and there he made him knight and gave him yearly two hundred pounds sterling, sufficiently assigned him in England. Then the king went and lodged in the abbey of Mount Saint-Martin, and there tarried two days, and his people abroad in the country; and the Duke of Brabant was lodged in the abbey of Vaucelles.

When the French king at Compiègne heard these tidings, then he enforced his summons and sent the Earl of Eu and of Guines, his constable, to Saint-Quentin, to keep the town and frontiers there against his enemies, and sent the Lord of Ham to his; and sent many men of arms to Guise and Ribemont, to Bohain, and the fortresses joining to the entry of the realm; and so went himself toward Péronne.

In the mean season that King Edward lay at the abbey of Mount Saint-Martin, his men ran abroad in the country to Bapaume and near to Péronne and to Saint-Quentin. They found the country plentiful, for there had been no war for a long season. And so it fortuned that Sir Henry of Flanders, to advance his body and to increase his honour, went on a day with other knights, whereof Sir John of Hainault was chief, and with him the Lord of Fauquemont, the Lord of Berg, the Lord of Bautersem, the Lord of Cuyk and divers other to the number of five hundred. And they advised a town thereby, called Honnecourt, wherein much people were gathered on trust of the fortresses, and therein they had conveyed all their goods; and there had been Sir Arnold of Baquehem and Sir William of Duvenvoorde and their company, but they attained nothing there.

There was at this Honnecourt an abbot of great wisdom and hardiness; and he caused to be made without the town a barrier overthwart the street, like a grate, not past half a foot wide every grate, and he made great provisions of stones and quicklime, and men ready to defend the place. And these lords, when they came thither, they lighted afoot and entered to the barrier with their glaives in their hands and there began a sore assault, and they within valiantly defended themselves. There was the abbot himself, who received and gave many great strokes. There was a fierce assault: they within cast down stones, pieces of timber, pots full of chalk,* and did much hurt to the assailers. And Sir Henry of Flanders, who held his glaive in his hands and gave therewith great strokes; at the last the abbot took the glaive in his hands and drew it so to him, that at last he set hands on Sir Henry's arm, and drew it so sore that he pulled out his arm at the barrier to the shoulder and held him at a great advantage, for an the barrier had been wide enough, he had drawn him through; but Sir Henry would not let his weapon go for saving of his honour. Then the other knights struck at the abbot to rescue their fellow: so this wrestling endured a long space, but finally the knight was rescued, but his glaive abode with the abbot. And on a day, when I wrote this book, as I passed by I was shewed the glaive by the monks there, that kept it for a treasure.

So this said day Honnecourt was sore assailed, the which endured till it was night, and divers were slain and sore hurt. Sir John of Hainault lost there a knight of Holland called Sir Herman. When the Flemings, Hainaulters, Englishmen and Germans saw the fierce wills of them within, and saw how they could get nothing there, [they] withdrew themselves against night. And the next day on the morning the king departed from Mount Saint-Martin, commanding that no person should do any hurt to the abbey, the which commandment was kept. And so then they entered into Vermandois, and took that day their lodging betimes on the Mount Saint-Quentin in good order of battle; and they of Saint-Quentin might well see them, howbeit they had no desire to issue out of their town. The foreriders came running to the barriers skirmishing, and the host tarried still on the Mount till the next day. Then the lords took counsel what way they should draw, and by the advice of the Duke of Brabant they took the way to Thiérache, for that way their provision came daily to them; and were determined that if King Philip did follow them, as they supposed he would do, that then they would abide him in the plain field and give him battle. Then they went forth in three great battles: the marshals and the Germans had the first, the King of England in the middleward, and the Duke of Brabant in the rearward. Thus they rode forth, burning and pilling the country, a three or four leagues a day, and ever took their lodging betimes.

* Quicklime.

And a company of Englishmen and Germans passed the river of Somme by the abbey of Vermand, and wasted the country all about. Another company, whereof Sir John of Hainault, the Lord of Fauquemont and Sir Arnold of Baquehem were chief, rode to Origny-Saint-Benoiste, a good town, but it was but easily closed: incontinent it was taken by assault and robbed, and an abbey of ladies violated, and the town burnt. Then they departed and rode toward Guise and Ribemont, and the King of England lodged at Boheries, and there tarried a day, and his men ran abroad and destroyed the country. Then the king took the way to La Flamengerie, to come to l'Eschelle in Thiérache; and the marshals and the Bishop of Lincoln with a five hundred spears passed the river of Oise and entered into Laonnois, toward the land of the Lord of Coucy, and burnt Saint-Gobain and the town of Marle, and on a night lodged in the valley beside Laon. And the next day they drew again to their host, for they knew by some of their prisoners that the French king was come to Saint-Quentin with a hundred thousand men, and there to pass the river of Somme. So these lords in their returning burnt a good town called Crécy and divers other towns and hamlets thereabout.

Now let us speak of Sir John of Hainault and his company, who were a five hundred spears. He came to Guise and burnt all the town and beat down the mills. And within the fortresses was the Lady Jane, his own daughter, wife to the Earl of Blois called Louis; she desired her father to spare the heritage of the earl his son-in-law, but for all that Sir John of Hainault would not spare his enterprise. And so then he returned again to the king, who was lodged in the abbey of Fervaques, and ever his people ran over the country.

And the Lord of Fauquemont with a hundred spears came to Nouvion in Thiérache, a great town; and the men of the town were fled into a great wood and had all their goods with them, and had fortified the wood with felling of timber about them. The Germans rode thither and there met with them Sir Arnold of Baquehem and his company; and so there they assailed them in the wood, who defended them as well as they might. But finally they were conquered and put to flight; and there were slain and sore hurt more than forty, and lost all that they had. Thus the country was over-ridden, for they did what they list.

How the King of England and the French king took day of journey to fight together (1339). [Ch. 40]

THE King of England departed from Fervaques and went to Montreuil, and there lodged a night; and the next day he went to La Flamengerie and made all his men to lodge near about him, whereof he had more than forty thousand. And there he was counselled to abide King Philip and to fight with him.

The French king departed from Saint-Quentin, and daily men came to him from all parts, and so came to Buironfosse. There the king tarried, and said how he would not go thence till he had fought with the King of England and with his allies, seeing they were within two leagues together. And when the Earl of Hainault, who was at Quesnoy ready purveyed of men of war, knew that the French king was at Buironfosse, thinking there to give battle to the Englishmen, he rode forth till he came to the French host with five hundred spears, and presented himself to the king his uncle, who made him but small cheer because he had been with his adversary before Cambrai. Howbeit the earl excused himself so sagely that the king and his counsel were well content. And it was ordained by the marshals, that is to say by the Marshal Bertrand and by the Marshal of Trie, that the earl should be lodged next the English host.

Thus these two kings were lodged between Buironfosse and La Flamengerie, in the plain fields without any advantage. I think there was never seen before so goodly an assembly of noblemen together as was there. When the King of England, being in the Chapel of Thiérache,* knew how the King Philip was within two leagues, then he called the lords of his host together and demanded of them what he should do, his honour saved, for he said that his intention was to give battle. Then the lords beheld each other, and they desired the Duke of Brabant to show first his intent. The duke said that he was of the accord that they should give battle, for otherwise, he said, they could not depart saving their honours: wherefore he counselled that they should send heralds to the French king to demand a day of battle. Then a herald of the Duke of Gueldres, who could well the language of French, was informed what he should say, and so he rode till he came into the French host. And then he drew him to King Philip and to his council and said, 'Sir, the King of England is in the field and desireth to have battle, power against power.' The which King Philip granted, and took the day, the Friday next after; and as then it was Wednesday. And so the herald returned, well rewarded with good furred gowns given him by the French king and other lords because of the tidings he had brought. So thus the journey was agreed and knowledge was made thereof to all the lords of both the hosts, and so every man made him ready to the matter.

The Thursday in the morning there were two knights of the Earl of Hainault's, the Lord Fagnolle and the Lord of Tupigny. They mounted on their horses and they two all only departed from the French host and rode to aview the English host: so they rode coasting the host. And it fortuned that the Lord of Fagnolle's horse took the bridle in the teeth in such wise that his master could not rule him; and so, whether he would or not, the horse brought him into the English host, and there he fell into the hands of the Germans, who perceived well that he was none of their company and set on him and took his horse. And so he was prisoner to a five or six gentlemen of Germany, and anon they set him to his ransom. And

* This is in fact the village, la Capelle-en-Thiérache.

when they understood that he was a Hainaulter, they demanded of him if he knew
Sir John of Hainault, and he answered, 'Yes,' and desired them for the love of
God to bring him to his presence, for he knew well that he would quit him his
ransom.   Thereof were the Germans joyous, and so brought him to the Lord
Beaumont, who incontinent did pledge him out from his master's hands; and the
Lord of Fagnolle returned again to the Earl of Hainault, and he had his horse
again, delivered him at the request of the Lord Beaumont.   Thus passed that day,
and none other thing done that ought to be remembered.

How these kings ordained their battles at Buironfosse (1339). [Ch. 41]

WHEN the Friday came, in the morning both hosts apparelled themselves ready,
and every lord heard mass among their own companies and divers were shriven.
   First we will speak of the order of the Englishmen, who drew them forward into
the field and made three battles afoot, and did all their horses and baggages into
a little wood behind them, and fortified it. . . . . It was a great beauty to behold
the banners and standards waving in the wind, and horses barded, and knights
and squires richly armed.   The Frenchmen ordained three great battles, in each
of them fifteen thousand men of arms and twenty thousand men afoot.

How these two kings departed from Buironfosse without battle (1339). [Ch. 42]

IT might well be marvelled how so goodly a sight of men of war so near together
should depart without battle.   But the Frenchmen were not all of one accord:
they were of divers opinions.   Some said it were a great shame an they fought not,
seeing their enemies so near them in their own country, ranged in the field, and
also had promised to fight with them; and some other said it should be a great
folly to fight, for it was hard to know every man's mind, and jeopardy of treason:
for, they said, if fortune were contrary to their king, as to lose the field, he then
should put all his whole realm in a jeopardy to be lost; and though he did discomfit
his enemies, yet for all that he should be never the nearer of the realm of England,
nor of such lands pertaining to any of those lords that be with him allied.
   Thus in striving of divers opinions the day passed till it was past noon; and
then suddenly there started an hare among the Frenchmen, and such as saw her
cried and made great bruit, whereby such as were behind thought they before
had been fighting, and so put on their helmets and took their spears in their hands.
And so there were made divers new knights, and specially the Earl of Hainault
made fourteen, who were ever after called Knights of the Hare.   Thus that battle
stood still all that Friday.   And beside this strife between the councillors of France,

there was brought in letters to the host, of recommendation to the French king and to his council from King Robert of Sicily, the which king, as it was said, was a great astronomer and full of great science. He had oftentimes sought his books on the estate of the Kings of England and of France, and he found by his astrology and by the influence of the heavens, that if the French king ever fought with King Edward of England, he should be discomfited: wherefore he, like a king of great wisdom and as he that doubted the peril of the French king his cousin, sent oftentimes letters to King Philip and to his council, that in no wise he should make any battle against the Englishmen, whereas King Edward was personally present. So that, what for doubt and for such writing from the King of Sicily, divers of the great lords of France were sore abashed; and also King Philip was informed thereof. Howbeit, yet he had great will to give battle, but he was so counselled to the contrary, that the day passed without battle, and every man withdrew to their lodgings.

And when the Earl of Hainault saw that they should not fight, he departed with all his whole company and went back the same night to Quesnoy. And the King of England, the Duke of Brabant and all the other lords returned and trussed all their baggages, and went the same night to Avesnes in Hainault. And the next day they took leave each of other; and the Germans and Brabances departed, and the king went into Brabant with the duke his cousin.

The same Friday that the battle should have been, the French king, when he came to his lodging, he was sore displeased because he departed without battle. But they of his council said how right nobly he had borne himself, for he had valiantly pursued his enemies and had done so much that he had put them out of his realm, and how that the King of England should make many such voyages or he conquered the realm of France. The next day King Philip gave licence to all manner of men to depart, and he thanked right courteously the great lords of their aid and succour. Thus ended this great journey, and every man went to their own. The French king went to Saint-Omer, and sent men of war to his garrisons, and specially to Tournai, to Lille, and to Douai, and to the other towns marching on the Empire. He sent to Tournai Sir Godemar du Fay and made him captain there and regent of that country thereabout, and he sent Sir Edward of Beaujeu to Mortagne. And when he had ordered part of his business, then he drew toward Paris.

How King Edward took on him to bear the arms of France and the name, to be called king thereof.
(1339).   [Ch. 43]

WHEN that King Edward was departed from La Flamengerie and came into Brabant and went straight to Brussels, the Duke of Gueldres, the Marquis of

Juliers, the Marquis of Brandenburg, the Earl of Mons, Sir John of Hainault, the Lord of Fauquemont, and all the lords of the Empire such as had been at that journey, brought him thither to take advice and counsel what should be done more in the matter that they had begun. And to have expedition in the cause, they ordained a parliament to be holden at the town of Brussels, and thither to come was desired James van Artevelde of Ghent, who came thither with a great company, and all the councils of the good towns of Flanders. There the King of England was sore desired of all his allies of the Empire that he should require them of Flanders to aid and to maintain his war, and to defy the French king, and to go with him whereas he would have them; and in their so doing, he to promise them to recover Lille, Douai and Béthune.

This request was well heard of the Flemings, and thereupon they desired to take counsel among themselves. And so they took counsel at good leisure, and then they said to the king, 'Sir, or this time ye have made to us request in this behalf: sir, if we might well do this, saving your honour and to save ourselves, we would gladly do this; but, sir, we be bound by faith and oath and on the sum of two millions of florins in the Pope's chamber, that we may make nor move no war against the King of France, whosoever it be, on pain to lose the said sum and beside that to run in the sentence of cursing. But, sir, if ye will take on you the arms of France and quarter them with the arms of England and call yourself King of France, as ye ought to be of right, then we will take you for rightful King of France and demand of you quittance of our bonds, and so ye to give us pardon thereof as King of France. By this means we shall be assured and dispensed withal, and so then we will go with you whithersoever ye will have us.' Then the king took counsel, for he thought it was a sore matter to take on him the arms of France and the name, and as then had conquered nothing thereof, nor could not tell what should fall thereof, nor whether he should conquer it or not. And on the other side, loth he was to refuse the comfort and aid of the Flemings, who might do him more aid than any other. So the king took counsel of the lords of the Empire and of the Lord Robert d'Artois and with other of his special friends; so that finally the good and the evil weighed. He answered to the Flemings that if they would swear and seal to this accord, and to promise to maintain his war, how he would do all this with a good will, and promised to get them again Lille, Douai and Béthune: and all they answered how they were content. Then there was a day assigned to meet at Ghent, at which day the king was there, and the most part of the said lords, and all the councils generally in Flanders. And so then all these said matters were rehearsed, sworn and sealed; and the king quartered the arms of France with England, and from thenceforth took on him the name of the King of France, and so continued till he left it again by composition, as ye shall hear after in this book. And so at this council they determined that the next summer after they would make great war into France, promising to

D

besiege the city of Tournai; whereof the Flemings were joyful, for they thought to be strong enough to get it, and that once gotten, they believed shortly after to win again Lille, Douai and Béthune, with the appurtenances pertaining or holden of the Earl of Flanders.

Thus every man departed and went home: the King of England went to Antwerp, and the queen abode still at Ghent and was oftentimes visited by James van Artevelde and by other lords, ladies and damosels of Ghent. The king left in Flanders the Earl of Salisbury and the Earl of Suffolk:* they went to Ypres and there kept a great garrison and made sore war against them of Lille and thereabout. And when the king's ships were ready, he took the sea and so sailed into England and came to London about the feast of Saint Andrew, where he was honourably received. And there he had complaints made him of the destruction of Southampton: and he said that he trusted or a year longer that it should be well revenged.

How the Frenchmen burnt in the lands of Sir John of Hainault (1339). [Ch. 44]

NOW let us speak of King Philip, who greatly fortified his navy that he had on the sea, whereof Sir Quieret, Behuchet and Barbavara were captains; and they had under them a great retinue of Genoese, Normans, Bretons and Picards. They did that winter great damage to the realm of England: sometime they came to Dover, Sandwich, Winchelsea, Hastings and Rye, and did much sorrow to the Englishmen, for they were a great number as a forty thousand men. There was none that could issue out of England, but they were robbed, taken or slain. So they won great pillage, and specially they won a great ship called the *Christofer*, laden with wools, as she was going into Flanders, the which ship had cost the King of England much money, and all they that were taken within the ship were slain and drowned; of the which conquest the Frenchmen were right joyous.

The French king then sent and wrote to the Lord of Bosmont, the Lord of Vervins, to the Vidame of Chalons, the Lord John de la Bove, the Lord John and Gerard of Lor, that they should make an army and to ride into the lands of Sir John of Hainault, and to burn and destroy there as much as they might......

Of the battle on the sea before Sluys in Flanders between the King of England and the Frenchmen (1340). [Ch. 50]

NOW let us leave somewhat to speak of the Earl of Hainault and of the Duke of Normandy, and speak of the King of England, who was on the sea to the intent to arrive in Flanders, and so into Hainault, to make war against the Frenchmen.

* It was the Earl of Suffolk's eldest son who was left, not the Earl.

This was on Midsummer Eve, in the year of our Lord MCCCXL, all the English fleet was departed out of the river of Thames and took the ways to Sluys. And the same time, between Blankenberge and Sluys on the sea, was Sir Hugh Quieret, Sir Nicholas Behuchet and Barbavara, and more than sixscore great vessels, beside other. And they were of Normans, *bidaus*,* Genoese and Picards about the number of forty thousand: there they were laid by the French king to defend the King of England's passage.

The King of England and his came sailing till he came before Sluys, and when he saw so great a number of ships that their masts seemed to be like a great wood, he demanded of the master of his ship what people he thought they were. He answered and said, 'Sir, I think they be Normans laid here by the French king, and hath done great displeasure in England, burnt your town of Southampton and taken your great ship the *Christofer*.' 'Ah,' quoth the king, 'I have long desired to fight with the Frenchmen and now shall I fight with some of them, by the grace of God and Saint George; for truly they have done me so many dis-pleasures that I shall be revenged, and I may.' Then the king set all his ships in order, the greatest before, well-furnished with archers; and ever between two ships of archers he had one ship with men of arms. And then he made another battle to lie aloof with archers, to comfort ever them that were most weary, if need were. And there were a great number of countesses, ladies, knights' wives and other damosels, that were going to see the Queen at Ghent: these ladies the king caused to be well kept with three hundred men of arms and five hundred archers.

When the king and his marshalls had ordered his battles, he drew up the sails and came with a quarter wind to have the vantage of the sun; and so at last they turned a little to get the wind at will. And when the Normans saw them recule back, they had to marvel why they did so, and some said, 'They think themself not meet to meddle with us, wherefore they will go back.' They saw well how the King of England was there personally, by reason of his banners. Then they did apparel their fleet in order, for they were sage and good men of war on the sea, and did set the *Christofer*, the which they had won the year before, to be foremost, with many trumpets and instruments, and so set on their enemies.

There began a sore battle on both parts. Archers and crossbows began to shoot and men of arms approached and fought hand to hand; and the better to come together, they had great hooks and grappers of iron to cast out of one ship into another, and so tied they fast together. There were many deeds of arms done, taking and rescuing again. And at last the great *Christofer* was first won by the Englishmen and all that were within it taken or slain. Then there was great noise and cry, and the Englishmen approached the *Christofer* with archers, and made him to pass on before to fight with the Genoese. This battle was right fierce and terrible,

* Light armed soldiers.

for the battles on the sea are more dangerous and fiercer than the battles by land: for on the sea there is no reculing nor fleeing, there is no remedy but to fight and to abide fortune, and every man to show his prowess. Of a truth Sir Hugh Quieret and Sir Behuchet and Barbavara were right good and expert men of war.

This battle endured from the morning till it was noon, and the Englishmen endured much pain, for their enemies were four against one, and all good men on the sea. There the King of England was a noble knight of his own hand, he was in the flower of his youth; in likewise so was the Earl of Derby, Pembroke, Hereford, Huntingdon, Northampton and Gloucester, Sir Raynold Cobham, Sir Richard Stafford, the Lord Percy, Sir Walter of Manny, Sir Henry of Flanders, Sir John Beauchamp, the Lord Felton, the Lord Bradestan, Sir [John] Chandos, the Lord Delaware, the Lord of Multon, Sir Robert d'Artois called Earl of Richmond, and divers other lords and knights, who bore themselves so valiantly with some succours that they had of Bruges and of the country thereabout, that they obtained the victory. So that the Frenchmen, Normans and other were discomfited, slain and drowned: there was not one that escaped, but all were slain.

When this victory was achieved, the king all that night abode in his ship before Sluys, with great noise of trumpets and other instruments. Thither came to see the king divers of Flanders, such as had heard of the king's coming. And then the king demanded of the burgesses of Bruges how James van Artevelde did: they answered that he was gone to the Earl of Hainault against the Duke of Normandy with sixty thousand Flemings. And on the next day, the which was Midsummer Day, the king and all his took land, and the king on foot went a pilgrimage to our Lady of Ardembourg, and there heard mass and dined, and then took his horse and rode to Ghent, where the queen received him with great joy; and all his carriage came after, little and little. Then the king wrote to the Earl of Hainault and to them within the castle of Thun, certifying them of his arrival. And when the earl knew thereof, and that he had discomfited the army on the sea, he dislodged and gave leave to all the soldiers to depart, and took with him to Valenciennes all the great lords, and there feasted them honourably, and specially the Duke of Brabant and James van Artevelde. And there James van Artevelde openly in the market-place, in the presence of all the lords and of all such as would hear him, declared what right the King of England had to the crown of France, and also what puissance the three countries were of, Flanders, Hainault and Brabant, surely joined in one alliance. And he did so by his great wisdom and pleasant words, that all people that heard him praised him much, and said how he had nobly spoken and by great experience. And thus he was greatly praised and it was said that he was well worthy to govern the county of Flanders.

Then the lords departed and promised to meet again within eight days at Ghent, to see the King of England: and so they did. And the king feasted them honourably, and so did the queen, who was as then newly purified of a son called John, who was after Duke of Lancaster by his wife, daughter to Duke Henry of Lancaster. Then there was a council set to be at Vilvorde, and a day limited.

How King Robert of Sicily did all that he might to pacify the Kings of France and England (1340). [Ch. 51]

WHEN the French king heard how his army on the sea was discomfited, he dislodged and drew to Arras, and gave leave to his men to depart till he heard other tidings; and sent Sir Godemar du Fay to Tournai to see that there lacked nothing. He feared more the Flemings than any other, and sent the Lord of Beaujeu to Mortagne to keep the frontiers against Hainault; and he sent many men of war to Saint-Omer, to Aire and to Saint-Venant, and purveyed sufficiently for all the fortresses fronting on Flanders.

In this season there reigned a king in Sicily called Robert, who was reputed to be a great astronomer, and always he warned the French king and his council that in no wise he should fight against the King of England; for he said it was given the King of England to be right fortunate in all his deeds. This King Robert would gladly have seen these two kings at a good accord, for he loved so much the crown of France, that he was right sorry to see the desolation thereof. This King of Sicily was at Avignon with Pope Clement and with the college there, and declared to them the perils that were likely to fall in the realm of France by the war between the said two kings, desiring them that they would help to find some means to appease them; whereunto the Pope and the Cardinals answered how they would gladly intend thereto, so that the two kings would hear them.

How the King of England besieged the city of Tournai with great puissance (1340).   [Ch. 53]

. . . . . NOW let us return to the King of England. When the time approached that he and his allies should meet before Tournai, and that the corn began to ripe, he departed from Ghent with seven earls of his country, eight prelates, twenty-eight bannerets, two hundred knights, four thousand men of arms, and nine thousand archers, beside footmen. All his host passed through the town of Oudenarde, and so passed the river Scheldt and lodged before Tournai at the gate called Saint-Martin, the way toward Lille and Douai. Then anon after came the Duke of Brabant with more than twenty thousand men, knights, squires and commons; and he lodged at the bridge of Rieux by the river Scheldt between the abbey of Saint Nicholas and the Valenciennes gate. Next to him came the Earl

of Hainault with a goodly company of his country, with many of Holland and
Zealand; and he was lodged between the king and the Duke of Brabant. Then
came James van Artevelde with more than sixty thousand Flemings, beside them
of Ypres, Poperinge, Cassel, Bruges, and they were set on the other side, as ye
shall hear after. James van Artevelde lodged at the gate Sainte-Fontaine. The
Duke of Gueldres, the Earl of Juliers, the Marquis of Brandenburg, the Marquis
of Meissen, the Earl of Mons, the Earl of Salm, the Lord of Fauquemont, Sir Arnold
of Baquehem and all the Germans were lodged on the other side, toward Hainault.
Thus the city of Tournai was environed round about, and every host might resort
each to other, so that none could issue out without spying.

How the Scots won again great part of Scotland while the siege was before Tournai (1340).
[Ch. 55]

NOW it is to be remembered how Sir William Douglas, son of James Douglas'
brother who died in Spain, and the Earl Patrick, the Earl of Sutherland, Sir Robert
of Erskine, Sir Simon Fraser and Alexander Ramsey, they were captains in such
part of Scotland as was left unwon by the Englishmen. And they had continued
in the forest of Jedburgh the space of seven year, winter and summer, and as they
might they made war against the Englishmen being there in garrison. Sometime
they had good adventure and some time evil. And while the King of England
was at siege before Tournai, the French king sent men of war into Scotland, and
they arrived at Perth. And they desired the Scots in the French king's name, that
they would set on and make such war in the realm of England, that the king might
be fain to return home to rescue his own realm, and to leave up the siege at Tournai:
and the French king promised them men and money to aid them so to do. And
so the Scots departed out of the forest of Jedburgh and passed through Scotland,
and won again divers fortresses; and so passed the town of Berwick and the river
of Tyne, and entered into the country of Northumberland, the which sometime
was a realm. There they found great plenty of beasts and wasted and burnt all
the country to Durham: then they returned by another way, destroying the
country. In this voyage they destroyed more than three days' journey into the
realm of England, and then returned into Scotland and conquered again all the
fortresses that were holden by the Englishmen, except the city of Berwick and
three other castles, the which did them great trouble. They were so strong that
it would have been hard to have found any such in any country: the one was
Stirling, another Roxburgh, and the third the chief of all Scotland, Edinburgh,
the which castle standeth on a high rock, that a man must rest once or twice or
he come to the highest of the hill; and captain there was Sir Walter Limousin,

who had before so valiantly kept the castle of Thun against the Frenchmen.

So it was that Sir William Douglas devised a feat and discovered his intention to his companions, to the Earl Patrick, to Sir Simon Fraser and to Alexander Ramsey; and all they agreed together. Then they took a two hundred of the wild Scots and entered into the sea, and made provision of oats, meal, coals and wood; and so peaceably they arrived at a port near to the castle of Edinburgh. And in the night they armed them and took a ten or twelve of their company, such as they did trust best, and did disguise them in poor torn coats and hats, like poor men of the country, and charged a twelve small horses with sacks, some with oats, some with wheatmeal and some with coals. And they did set all their company in a bushment in an old destroyed abbey thereby, near to the foot of the hill. And when the day began to appear, covertly armed as they were, they went up the hill with their merchandise. And when they were in the mid-way, Sir William Douglas and Sir Simon Fraser, disguised as they were, went a little before and came to the porter and said, 'Sir, in great fear we have brought hither oats and wheatmeal, and if ye have any need thereof, we will sell it to you good cheap.' 'Marry,' said the porter, 'and we have need thereof; but it is so early that I dare not awake the captain nor his steward. But let them come in and I shall open the outer gate.' And so they all entered into the gate of the bails: Sir William Douglas saw well how the porter had keys in his hands of the great gate of the castle. Then when the first gate was opened, as ye have heard, their horses with carriages entered in; and the two that came last, laden with coals, they made them to fall down on the ground-sill of the gate, to the intent that the gate should not be closed again. And then they took the porter and slew him so peaceably that he never spake word. Then they took the great keys and opened the castle gate. Then Sir William Douglas blew a horn and did cast their torn coats and laid all the other sacks overthwart the gate, to the intent that it should not be shut again. And when they of the bushment heard the horn, in all haste they mounted the hill. Then the watchman of the castle with noise of the horn awoke, and saw how the people were coming all armed to the castle-ward. Then he blew his horn and cried, 'Treason! Treason! Sirs, arise and arm you shortly, for yonder be men of arms approaching to your fortress.' Then every man arose and armed them and came to the gate. But Sir William Douglas and his twelve companions defended so the gate that they could not close it: and so by great valiantness they kept the entry open till their bushment came. They within defended the castle as well as they might, and hurt divers of them without; but Sir William and the Scots did so much that they conquered the fortress, and all the Englishmen within slain, except the captain and six other squires. So the Scots tarried there all that day, and made a knight of the country captain there, called Simon Wisby, and with him divers others of the country. These tidings came to the King of England before Tournai.

Of the great host that the French king assembled
to raise the siege before Tournai (1340). [Ch. 57]

YE have heard before how the King of England had besieged the city of Tournai with more than sixscore thousand men of arms, with the Flemings. And because the victuals within the city began to minish, the French lords within caused to avoid out of the town all manner of poor people, such as were not furnished to abide the adventure of the siege. They were put out in the open day, and they passed through the Duke of Brabant's host, who showed them grace, for he caused them to be safely brought to the French host at Arras, whereas the king lay; and there he [King Philip] made a great assembly of men of his own country and part out of the Empire. Thither came to him the King of Bohemia, the Duke of Lorraine, the Earl of Bar, the Bishop of Metz and of Verdun, the Earl of Montbeliard, Sir John of Châlons, the Earl of Geneva, the Earl of Savoy and the Lord Louis of Savoy his brother. All these lords came to serve the French king with all their powers. Also thither came the Duke of Brittany, the Duke of Burgundy, the Duke of Bourbon, the Earl of Alençon, the Earl of Flanders, the Earl Forez, the Earl Armagnac, the Earl of Blois, Sir Charles of Blois, the Earl of Harcourt, the Earl Dammartin, the Lord Coucy, and divers other lords and knights. And after came the King of Navarre with a goodly number of men of war out of the country in France that he held of the French king, and thereby he came to serve him. Also there was the King of Scots with a certain number appointed to him.

How the siege before Tournai was broken up
by reason of a truce (1340).   [Ch. 63]

THIS siege endured a long season: the space of eleven weeks, three days less. And at that season the Lady Jane of Valois, sister to the French king and mother to the Earl of Hainault, travailed greatly, what on the one part and on the other, to have a respite and a peace between the parties, so that they might depart without battle. And divers times she kneeled at the feet of the French king in that behalf, and also made great labour to the lords of the Empire, and specially to the Duke of Brabant and to the Duke of Juliers, who had her daughter in marriage, and also to Sir John of Hainault. So much the good lady procured with the aid and counsel of Louis d'Agimont, who was well-beloved with both parties, that it was granted that each party should send four sufficient persons to treat on some good way to accord the parties, and a truce for three days; these appointers should meet in a little chapel standing in the fields called Esplechin. At the day appointed the persons met, and the good lady with them; of the French party there was Charles King of Bohemia, Charles Earl of Alençon, brother to the French king, and the Bishop of Liége, the Earl of Flanders and the Earl of

Armagnac. Of the English party there was the Duke of Brabant, the Bishop of Lincoln, the Duke of Gueldres, the Duke of Juliers and Sir John of Hainault. And when they were all met, they made each to other great salutations and good cheer, and then entered into their treaty. And all that day they communed on divers ways of accord, and always the good lady of Valois was among them, desiring affectuously all the parties that they would do their labour to make a peace. Howbeit the first day passed without anything doing, and so they returned and promised to meet again the next day: the which day they came together again in the same place and so fell again into their treaty, and so fell into certain points agreeable, but it was as then so late that they could not put it in writing as that day. And to make an end and to make perfect the matter if they might, the third day they met again, and so finally accorded on a truce to endure for a year between all parties and all their men, and also between them that were in Scotland, and all such as made war in Gascony, Poitou and in Saintonge. And this truce to begin the fortieth day next ensuing, and within that space every party to give knowledge to his men without malengine; and if such companies will not keep the peace, let them be at their choice: but as for France, Picardy, Burgundy, Brittany and Normandy, to be bound to this peace without any exception; and this peace to begin incontinent and between the hosts of the two kings. Also it was determined that both parties in each of their names should send four or five personages as their ambassadors and to meet at Arras; and the Pope in like wise to send thither four, and there to make a full confirmation without any mean. Also by this truce every party to enjoy and possess all and everything that they were as then in possession of.

This truce incontinent was cried in both hosts, whereof the Brabances were right glad, for they were sore weary with so long lying at the siege. So that the next day, as soon as it was daylight, ye should have seen tents taken down, chariots charged and people remove so thick that a man would have thought to have seen a new world. Thus the good town of Tournai was safe without any great damage. Howbeit they within endured great pain; their victuals began to fail, for, as it was said, they had as then scant to serve them a three or four days at the most. The Brabances departed quickly, for they had great desire thereto. The King of England departed sore against his mind, if he might have done otherwise, but in manner he was fain to follow the wills of the other lords and to believe their counsels. And the French king could abide no longer thereas he lay, for the evil air and the weather hot. So the Frenchmen had the honour of that journey, because they had rescued Tournai and caused their enemies to depart. The King of England and the lords on his party said how they had the honour, by reason that they had tarried so long within the realm, and besieged one of the good towns thereof, and also had wasted and burnt in the French country; and that the French king had not rescued it in time and hour, as he ought to have done, by giving of battle, and finally agreed to a truce, their enemies being still at the siege and burning his country.

Thus these lords departed from the siege of Tournai and every man drew to his own. The King of England came to Ghent to the queen his wife, and shortly after passed the sea, and all his, except such as should be at the parliament at Arras. The Earl of Hainault returned to his country and held a noble feast at Mons in Hainault, and a great joust, in the which Gerard of Werchin, Seneschal of Hainault, did joust, and was so sore hurt that he died of the stroke. He had a son called John, who was after a good knight and a hardy, but he was but a while in good health. The French king gave leave to every man to depart, and went himself to Lille, and thither came they of Tournai, and the king received them joyously and did show them great grace: he gave them freely their franchise, the which they had lost long before, wherewith they were joyous. For Sir Godemar du Fay and divers other knights and been long governors there; then they made new provost and jurates according to their ancient usages. Then the king departed from Lille to go to Paris.

Now then came the season that the council should be at Arras. And for Pope Clement thither came in legation the Cardinal of Naples and the Cardinal of Clermont, who came to Paris, whereas the king made them much honour, and so came to Arras. For the French king there was the Earl of Alençon, the Duke of Bourbon, the Earl of Flanders, the Earl of Blois, the Archbishop of Sens, the Bishop of Beauvais and the Bishop of Auxerre; and for the King of England there was the Bishop of Lincoln, the Bishop of Durham, the Earl of Warwick, Sir Robert d'Artois, Sir John of Hainault, and Sir Henry of Flanders. At the which treaty there were many matters put forth, and so continued a fifteen days and agreed of no point of effect. For the Englishmen demanded and the Frenchmen would nothing give, but all only to render the county of Ponthieu, the which was given with Queen Isabel in marriage with the King of England. So this parliament brake up and nothing done, but the truce to be relonged two years longer: that was all the cardinals could get. Then every man departed, and the two cardinals went through Hainault at the desire of the earl, who feasted them nobly.

Now speaketh the history of the wars of Brittany, and how the duke died without heir, whereby the dissension fell (1341).   [Ch. 64]

WHEN that this said truce was agreed and sealed before the city of Tournai, every lord and all manner of people dislodged, and every man drew into his own country. The Duke of Brittany, who had been there with the French king, as well-furnished as any other prince that was there, departed homeward. And in his way a sickness took him, so that he died; at which time he had no child, nor had never none by the duchess, nor had no trust to have. He had a brother by the father's side called Earl of Montfort, who was as then living, and he had to his wife, sister to the Earl Louis of Flanders. This said had another brother, both by father and mother, who was as then dead; and he had a daughter alive, and the duke her uncle had married her to the Lord Charles of Blois, eldest son of the Earl Guy of Blois, that the same earl had by the sister of King Philip of France who as then reigned, and had promised with her in marriage the Duchy of Brittany after his decease. For he doubted that the Earl Montfort would claim the inheritance as next of blood, and yet he was not his proper brother-german, and the duke thought that the daughter of his brother-german ought by reason to be more near to the inheritance after his decease than the Earl Montfort his brother. And because he feared that after his decease the Earl of Montfort would take away the right from his young niece, therefore he married her with the said Sir Charles of Blois, to the intent that King Philip, uncle to her husband, should aid to keep her right against the Earl Montfort, if he meddle anything in the matter.

As soon as the Earl Montfort knew that the duke his brother was dead, he went incontinent to Nantes, the sovereign city of all Brittany. And he did so much to the burgesses and to the people of the country thereabout, that he was received as their chief lord, as most next of blood to his brother deceased, and so did to him homage and fealty. Then he and his wife, who had both the hearts of a lion, determined with their council to call a court and to keep a solemn feast at Nantes at a day limited, against the which day they sent for all the nobles and councils of the good towns of Brittany, to be there to do their homage and fealty to him as to their sovereign lord.

In the mean season, or this feast began, the Earl Montfort with a great number of men of war departed from Nantes and went to Limoges, for he was informed that the treasure that his father had gathered many a day before was there kept secret. When he came there he entered into the city with great triumph, and did him much honour, and was nobly received of the burgesses, of the clergy and of the commons, and they all did him fealty as to their sovereign lord; and by such means as he found, that great treasure was delivered to him. And when he had tarried there at his pleasure, he departed with all his treasure and came to Nantes to the countess his wife. And so there he tarried in great joy till the day come of the feast, and made great provisions against the same. And when the day came and no man appeared for no commandment, except one knight called Sir Hervé de Leon, a noble and puissant man, so they kept the feast for three days as well as they might with such as were there. Then it was determined to retain soldiers a-horseback and afoot, and so to dispense his great treasure to attain to his purpose of the duchy, and to constrain all rebels to come to mercy. So soldiers were retained on all sides and largely paid, so that they had a great number afoot and a-horseback, nobles and other of divers countries.

How the Earl Montfort did homage to the King of England for the Duchy of Brittany (1341).
[Ch. 68]

THUS the Earl Montfort conquered the country and made himself to be called Duke of Brittany. Then he went to a port on the seaside called Roscoff; then he sent his people abroad to the towns and fortresses that he had won. Then he took the sea, with a certain with him, and so arrived in Cornwall in England at a port called Chepse. Then he inquired where the king was and it was showed him how that he was at Windsor: then he rode thitherward and came to Windsor, where he was received with great joy and feast both of the king and of the queen, and of all the lords. Then he showed the king and his council how he was in possession of the Duchy of Brittany, fallen to him by succession by the death of his brother, last Duke of Brittany; but he feared lest that Sir Charles of Blois and the French king would put him out thereof by puissance, whereof he said he had come thither to relieve and to hold the duchy of the King of England, by fealty and homage, for ever; so that he would defend him against the French king and all other that should put him to any trouble for the matter. The King of England imagined that his war against the French king should be well fortified by that means, and how that he could not have no more profitable way for him to enter into France than by Brittany, remembering how the Germans and Brabances had done little or nothing for him but cause him to spend much money: wherefore joyously he condescended to the Earl Montfort's desire, and there took homage by the hands of the earl, calling himself Duke of Brittany. And there the King of England, in the presence of such lords as were there, both of Brittany and of England, promised that he would aid, defend, and keep him as his liege man, against every man, French king and other. This homage and promises were written and sealed and every party had his part delivered. Beside that, the king and the queen gave to the earl and to his company many great gifts, in such wise that they reputed him for a noble king and worthy to reign in great prosperity. Then the earl took his leave and departed and took again the sea, and arrived again at the foresaid port of Roscoff in base Brittany; and so came to Nantes to his wife, who said how he had wrought by good and discreet counsel.

How the Earl Montfort was summoned to be at the Parliament of Paris at the request of the Lord Charles of Blois (1341).   [Ch. 69]

WHEN Sir Charles of Blois, who held himself rightful inheritor to Brittany by reason of his wife, heard how the Earl of Montfort conquered before the country, the which by reason ought to be his, then he came to Paris to complain to King

Philip his uncle: whereupon the king counselled with the nobles of the realm what he might do in that matter. And it was counselled him that the Earl Montfort should be by sufficient messengers summoned to appear at Paris, and there to hear what answer he would make. So these messengers were sent forth and they found the earl at Nantes, making good cheer, and he made them great feast. And finally he answered how he would obey the king's commandment, and then made him ready and departed from Nantes, and so came to Paris with a four hundred horse with him. And the next day he and all his mounted on their horses and rode to the king's palace; there the king and his twelve peers with other great lords of France tarried his coming, and the Lord Charles of Blois with them. Then the earl entered into the king's chamber: he was well regarded and saluted of every person. Then he inclined himself to the king and said, 'Sir, I am come hither at your commandment and pleasure.' Then the king said, 'Earl of Montfort, for your so doing I can you good thank. Howbeit, I have marvel how that ye durst undertake on you the Duchy of Brittany, wherein you have no right; for there is another nearer than ye be, and ye would disinherit him. And to maintain your quarrel ye have been with mine adversary the King of England, and, as it is showed me, ye have done him homage for the same.' Then the earl said, 'Sir, believe it not, for surely ye are but evil informed in that behalf. But sir, as for the right that ye speak of, saving your displeasure, ye do me therein wrong; for sir, I know none so near to my brother that is departed as I. If it were judged, or plainly declared by right, that there were another nearer than I, I would not be rebel nor ashamed to leave it.' 'Well, sir,' quoth the king, 'Ye say well. But I command you in all that ye hold of me that ye depart not out of this city of Paris this fifteen days, by the which time the twelve peers and lords of my realm shall judge this matter, and then ye shall know what right ye have. And if ye do otherwise, ye shall displease me.' Then the earl said, 'Sir, all shall be at your pleasure.'

Then he went from the court to his lodging to dinner. When he came to his lodging he entered into his chamber, and there sat and imagined many doubts. And finally, with a small company he mounted on his horse and returned again into Brittany, or the king or any other wist where he was become. Some thought he had been but a little sick in his lodging. And when he came to Nantes, he showed the countess what he had done, and then by her counsel he rode to all the towns and fortresses that he had won, and established in them good captains and soldiers a-horseback and foot, and did give them good wages.

How the Duchy of Brittany was judged to Sir Charles of Blois (1341).   [Ch. 70]

IT is to be thought that the French king was sore displeased when he knew that the Earl of Montfort was so departed. Howbeit he tarried till the fifteenth day, that the lords should give their judgement on the Duchy of Brittany. When the day came they judged it clearly to Sir Charles of Blois' wife, who was daughter to the brother-german of the duke last dead, by the father side, whom they judged to have more right than the Earl of Montfort, who came by another father who was never Duke of Brittany. Another reason there was: they said, though that the Earl of Montfort had any right, he had forfeited it two ways: the one because he had relieved the duchy of another lord than of the French king of whom he ought to hold it; the other reason was because he had broken the king's command-ment and disobeyed his arrest and prison, as in going away without leave.

When this judgement was given in plain audience by all the lords, then the king called to him the Lord Charles of Blois his nephew, and said, 'Fair nephew, ye have judged to you a fair heritage and a great. Therefore haste you, and go and conquer it against him that keepeth it wrongfully, and desire all your friends to aid you. And I shall not fail you for my part; I shall lend you gold and silver enough, and shall command my son, the Duke of Normandy, to go with you.' Then Sir Charles of Blois inclined him to his uncle, thanking him right humbly. Then he desired the Duke of Normandy his cousin, the Earl of Alençon his uncle, the Duke of Burgundy, the Earl of Blois his brother, the Duke of Bourbon, the Lord Louis of Spain, the Lord James of Bourbon, the Earl of Eu, Constable of France, the Earl of Guyenne his son, the Viscount of Rohan, and all the other lords that were there. And all they said how they would gladly go with him and with their lord the Duke of Normandy. Then these lords departed to make them ready, and to make provision against that journey.

The lords of France that entered into Brittany with Sir Charles of Blois (1341).   [Ch. 71]

WHEN all these lords of Normandy, the Duke of Alençon, the Duke of Burgundy, and all other such as should go with Sir Charles of Blois to aid him to conquer the Duchy of Brittany, were ready, they departed, some from Paris and some from other places. And they assembled together at the city of Angers and from thence they went to Ancenis, the which is the end of the realm on that side, and there tarried a three days. Then they went forth into the country of Brittany. And when they were in the fields they numbered their company to a five thousand men of arms, beside the Genoese, the which were a three thousand; and three knights of Genoa did lead them, the one called Sir Othes Doria, and the other Sir Charles Grimaldi. And beside all they had many crossbows, of whom Sir Galoys de la Baulme was captain. Then all these went to a strong castle standing on a high mountain, called Champtoceaux: there was the entry of Brittany. It was furnished with men of war, and captains there were two knights of Lorraine called Sir Giles and Sir Valerain. The lords of France took counsel to besiege this castle for they thought if they should leave such a fortress behind them it should do them great damage. So they besieged it round about and made many assaults; specially the Genoese did what they might to attain praise at the beginning. But they lost oftentimes of their company, for they within defended themselves so sagely that it was long or they took any damage. But finally the assailants brought thither so much timber, wood, and faggots, that they filled therewith the dykes so that they might go just to the walls. They within cast out stones, chalk, and burning fire; howbeit they without came to the foot of the walls and had instruments whereby they might, under covert, mine the walls. Then they within yielded up the castle, their lives and goods saved. Then the Duke of Normandy, who was chief there, delivered the castle to Sir Charles of Blois as his own, who incontinent set there a good garrison to keep the entry and to conduct such as came after them.

Then they went towards Nantes, whereas they heard how the Earl of Montfort their enemy was. The marshals and currours of their host found by the way as they went a good town, closed with dykes, the which they fiercely assailed. And in the town there were but few people and evil-armed, so that anon the town was won, robbed, and the one half burnt and all the people put to the sword. This town was called Carquefou, within a four or five leagues to Nantes; the lords lay thereabout all that night. The next morning they drew towards Nantes and laid siege round about it, and pight up their tents and pavilions.

Then the men of war within the town and the burgesses armed them and went to their defences as they were appointed. Some of the host went to the barriers to skirmish, and some of the soldiers within and young burgesses issued out against them, so that there were divers slain and hurt on both parties. There were divers such skirmishes. On a morning, some of the soldiers within the city issued out at adventure and they found a fifteen carts with victuals coming to the host-ward and a sixty persons to convey it. And they of the city were a two hundred; they set on them and anon discomfited them and slew divers. And some flew away and escaped and showed in the host how it was. Then some went to rescue the prey and overtook them near to the barriers. There began a great skirmish: there came so many from the host that they within had much ado. Howbeit they took the horses out of the carts and did drive them in at the gate, to the intent that they without should not drive lightly away the carriages. Then other soldiers of the city issued out to help their companions, and also of the burgesses to aid their parents. So the fray multiplied and divers were slain and sore hurt on both parties, for always people increased from the host and some new ever issued out of the city. Then at last Sir Hervé the captain saw that it was time to retreat, for by his abiding he saw he might rather lose than win. Then he caused them of the city to draw aback, as well as he might, yet they were pursued so near that many were slain and taken, more than two hundred of the burgesses of the town; whereof the Earl of Montfort blamed sore Sir Hervé de Leon that he caused the retreat so soon. Wherewith Sir Hervé was sore displeased in his mind, and after that he would no more come to the earl's council so often as he did before: many had marvel why he did so.

How the Earl Montfort was taken at Nantes, and how he died (1341).   [Ch. 72]

AS I heard reported, there were certain burgesses of the city saw how their goods went to waste, both without and within, and had of their children and friends in prison, and doubted that worse should come to them after. Then they advised and spoke together secretly, so that finally they concluded to treat with the lords of France, so that they might come to have peace and to have their children and friends clearly delivered out of prison. They made this treaty so secretly that at last it was agreed that they should have all the prisoners delivered, and they to set open one of the gates that the French lords might enter to take the Earl Montfort in the castle, without doing of any manner of hurt to the city or to the inhabitants or goods therein. Some said this was purchased by the means and agreement of Sir Hervé de Leon, who had been before one of the earl's chief councillors. Thus as it was devised, so it was done. In a morning the French lords entered and went straight to the castle and brake open the gates, and there took the Earl Montfort prisoner, and led him clean out of the city into their field without doing of any more hurt in the city. This was the year of our Lord God MCCCXLI, about the feast of All Saints.

Then the lords of France entered into the city with great joy; and all the burgesses and other did fealty and homage to the Lord Charles of Blois as to their right sovereign lord, and there they tarried a three days in great feast. Then Sir Charles of Blois was counselled to abide there about the city of Nantes till the next summer: and so he did, and set captains in such garrisons as he had won. Then the other lords went to Paris to the king and delivered him the Earl of Montfort as prisoner. The king set him in the castle of Louvre, whereas he was long, and at last, as I heard reported, there he died.

Now let us speak of the countess his wife, who had the courage of a man and the heart of a lion. She was in the city of Rennes when her lord was taken, and howbeit that she had great sorrow at her heart, yet she valiantly recomforted her friends and soldiers, and showed them a little son that she had, called John, and said, 'Ah, sirs, be not too sore abashed of the earl my lord, whom we have lost: he was but a man. See here my little child who shall be, by the grace of God, his restorer, and he shall do for you all. And I have riches enough, ye shall not lack; and I trust I shall purchase for such a captain that ye shall be all recomforted.' When she had thus comforted her friends and soldiers in Rennes, then she went to all her other fortresses and good towns, and led ever with her John, her young son, and did to them as she did at Rennes. And fortified all her garrisons of everything that they wanted, and paid largely and gave freely, whereas she thought it well-employed. Then she went to Hennebont, and there she and her son tarried all that winter. Oftentimes she sent to visit her garrisons, and paid every man full well and truly their wages.

How the King of England the third time made war on the Scots (1341).   [Ch. 73]

YE have heard here before that the siege being before Tournai, how the lords of Scotland had taken again divers towns and fortresses from the Englishmen, such as they held in Scotland. There were no more remaining in the Englishmen's hands but only the castle of Stirling, the city of Berwick, and Roxburgh. And the Scots lay still at siege, with certain Frenchmen with them such as King Philip had sent thither to help them before Stirling; and they within were so sore constrained that they saw well they could not long endure.

And when the King of England was returned from the siege of Tournai and came into his own realm, he was counselled to ride toward Scotland: and so he did. He rode thitherward between Michaelmas and All Saints, commanding every man to follow him to Berwick. Then every man began to stir and to draw thither as they were commanded. The king at last came to York and there tarried for his people. The lords of Scotland were informed of the coming of the King of England, wherefore they made sorer assaults to the castle of Stirling and constrained so them within with engines and cannons, that they were fain to yield up the castle, saving their lives and members but nothing they should carry away.

These tidings came to the King of England whereas he was. Then he departed and drew toward Stirling, and came to Newcastle-upon-Tyne and there lodged and tarried more than a month abiding provision for his host; the which was put on the sea between Saint Andrews-tide and All Saints; but divers of their ships were perished for they had such tempest on the sea that small provision came thither. Some were driven into Holland and into Friesland, whereby the English host had great default of victuals, and everything was dear and winter was at hand, so that they wist not where to have forage. And in Scotland the Scots had put all their goods into fortresses. And the King of England had there more than six thousand horsemen and forty thousand footmen.

The lords of Scotland, after their winning of Stirling, they drew into the forests of Jedburgh; and they understood well how the King of England lay at Newcastle with a great number, to burn and to exile the realm of Scotland. Then they took counsel what they should do. They thought themself too small a company to maintain the war, seeing how they had continued the wars more than seven year without head or captain, and yet as then they could perceive no succour from

E

their own king. Then they determined to send to the King of England a bishop and an abbot to desire a truce, the which messengers departed from Scotland and came to Newcastle where they found the king. These messengers showed to the king and to his council the cause of their coming. So then it was agreed a truce to endure four months, on the condition that they of Scotland should send sufficient ambassadors into France to King David, that without he would come within the month of May next following, so puissantly as to resist and defend his realm, else they clearly to yield themself English and never to take him more for their king. So then these two prelates returned again into Scotland, and incontinent they ordained to send into France Sir Robert Erskine and Sir Simon Fraser and two other knights, to show to the king their appointment. The King of England agreed the sooner to this truce because his host lacked victual. So he came back again and sent every man home. The Scottish messengers went toward France and took shipping at Dover. . . .

How King David of Scotland came with a great host to Newcastle-upon-Tyne.   [Ch. 74]

WHEN that young King David of Scotland was come into his country, his men came about him with great joy and solemnity and brought him to the town of Perth. Thither came people from all parties to see him, and then every man showed him the damages and the destruction that King Edward and the Englishmen had done in Scotland. Then he said, 'Well, I shall be well revenged, or else lose all my realm and my life in the pain.' Then he sent messengers to all parts far and near, desiring every man to help him in his business. At his sending, thither came the Earl of Orkney, a great prince and a puissant; he had married the king's sister. He brought a great number of men of war with him and divers other lords and knights of Sweden, of Norway, and of Denmark: some for love and some for wages. So that when they were all together they were a sixty thousand men afoot, and on hackneys a three thousand armed after their manner. When they were all ready, they removed to go into England to do there as much hurt as they might, for the truce was as then expired, or else to fight with the King of England who had caused them to suffer much disease.

The Scots departed from Perth and went to Dunfermline, and the next day, there they passed a little arm of the sea. Then they went with great diligence and passed by Edinburgh, and after by Roxburgh, the which was as then English, but they made none assault there because they would have none of their company hurt, nor to waste none of their artillery: they thought to do a greater deed or they returned into Scotland. And so after they passed not far off from Berwick and went by without any assault giving, and so entered into the country of Northumberland and came to the river of Tyne, burning all the country round about them, and at last came to Newcastle-upon-Tyne. And there he lay and all his people about the town that night. And in the morning a certain number of gentlemen that were in the town issued out, to the number of two hundred spears, to make a skrye in the Scottish host right on the Earl of Moray's tents; who bare in his armour silver, three oreillers gules. There they took him in his bed and slew many or the host was moved and won great pillage. Then they returned into the town boldly with great joy and delivered the Earl of Moray as prisoner to the captain of the castle, the Lord John Nevill. When the Scots were up, they armed them and ran like madmen to the barriers of the town, and made a great assault, the which endured long: but little it availed them, and they lost there many men. For there were many good men of war within, who defended themself so wisely that the Scots were fain at last to withdraw aback to their loss.

How King David of Scotland destroyed the city of Durham.   [Ch. 75]

WHEN that King David and his council saw that his tarrying about Newcastle was dangerous, and that he could not win thereby neither profit nor honour, then he departed and entered into the country of the Bishopric of Durham and there burnt and wasted all before them. And so came to the city of Durham and laid siege round about it, and made many great assaults like madmen because they had lost the Earl of Moray. And they knew well that there was much richness in the city, for all the country thereabout had fled thither. The Scots made engines and instruments to come to the walls to make the fiercer assault. And when the Scots were gone from Newcastle, then Sir John Nevill, captain there, mounted on a good horse and took a way far off from the Scots; and did so much that within five days he came to Chertsey, whereas King Edward lay as then. There he showed the king tidings of the Scots. Then the king sent forth messengers into every part commanding every man between the age of sixty and fifteen, all excuses laid apart, to draw northward and to meet him in that country, to aid and defend his country that the Scots destroyed. Then lords, knights, squires, and all other drew toward the north. The king departed himself hastily and tarried for no man; and every man followed as well as they might.

In the mean season, the Scots assaulted the city of Durham with engines and other instruments so fiercely that they within could not defend themself, but that the city was won by force, and robbed and clean burnt, and all manner of people put to death without mercy, men, women and children, monks, priests and canons, so that there abode alive no manner a person, house nor church, but it was destroyed. The which was great pity so to destroy Christian blood, and the churches of God where-in that God was honoured and served.

How the King of England was in amours with the Countess of Salisbury (1341). [Ch. 77]

THE same day that the Scots departed from the said castle, King Edward came thither with all his host about noon, and came to the same place whereas the Scots had lodged, and was sore displeased that he found not the Scots there, for he came thither in such haste that his horse and men were sore travailed. Then he commanded to lodge there that night, and said how he would go see the castle and the noble lady therein, for he had not seen her since she was married before. Then every man took his lodging as he list. And as soon as the king was unarmed, he took a ten or twelve knights with him and went to the castle to salute the Countess of Salisbury and to see the manner of the assaults of the Scots and the defence that was made against them.

As soon as the lady knew of the king's coming, she set open the gates and came out so richly beseen, that every man marvelled of her beauty and could not cease to regard her nobleness with her great beauty, and the gracious words and counte-nance that she made. When she came to the king, she kneeled down to the earth, thanking him of his succours, and so led him into the castle to make him cheer and honour, as she that could right well do it. Every man regarded her marvel-lously: the king himself could not withhold his regarding of her, for he thought that he never saw before so noble nor so fair a lady. He was stricken therewith to the heart with a sparkle of fine love that endured long after: he thought no lady in the world so worthy to be beloved as she. Thus they entered into the castle hand in hand. The lady led him first into the hall and after into the chamber, nobly apparelled. The king regarded so the lady that he was abashed. At last he went to a window to rest him and so fell in a great study. The lady went about to make cheer to the lords and knights that were there, and commanded to dress the hall for dinner. When she had all devised and commanded, then she came to the king with a merry cheer, who was in a great study, and she said, 'Dear sir, why do ye study so? For, your grace not displeased, it appertaineth not to you so to do. Rather ye should make good cheer and be joyful, seeing ye have chased away your enemies, who durst not abide you. Let other men study for the remnant.' Then the king said, 'Ah dear lady, know for truth that since I entered into the castle, there is a study come to my mind so that I cannot choose but to muse, nor I cannot tell what shall fall thereof: put it out of my heart I cannot.' 'Ah sir,' quoth the lady, 'ye ought always to make good cheer to comfort therewith your people. God hath aided you so in your business and hath given you so great graces, that ye be the most doubted and honoured prince in all Christendom. And if the King of Scots have done you any despite or damage, ye may well amend it when it shall please you, as ye have done divers times or this. Sir, leave your musing and come into the hall, if it please you; your dinner is all ready.' 'Ah fair lady,' quoth the king, 'other things lieth at my heart that ye know not of. But surely the sweet behaving, the perfect wisdom, the good grace, nobleness, and excellent beauty that I see in you hath so sore surprised my heart that I cannot but love you, and without your love I am but dead.' Then the lady said, 'Ah, right noble prince, for God's sake mock nor tempt me not. I cannot believe that it is true that ye say, nor that so noble a prince as ye be would think to dishonour me and my lord my husband, who is so valiant a knight and hath done your grace so good service, and as yet lieth in prison for your quarrel. Certainly, sir, ye should in this case have but a small praise and nothing the better thereby. I had never as yet such a thought in my heart, nor I trust in God never shall have, for no man living. If I had any such intention, your grace ought not all only to blame me, but also to punish my body, yea and by true justice to be dismembered.'

Therewith the lady departed from the king and went into the hall to haste the dinner. Then she returned again to the king and brought some of his knights with her, and said, 'Sir, if it please you to come into the hall, your knights abideth for you to wash. Ye have been too long fasting.' Then the king went into the hall and washed, and sat down among his lords, and the lady also. The king ate but little; he sat still musing and, as he durst, he cast his eyes upon the lady. Of his sadness his knights had marvel, for he was not accustomed so to be. Some thought it was because the Scots were escaped from him.

All that day the king tarried there and wist not what to do. Sometime he imagined that honour and troth defended him to set his heart in such a case, to dishonour such a lady and so true a knight as her husband was, who had always well and truly served him. On the other part, love so constrained him that the power thereof surmounted honour and troth. Thus the king debated in himself all that day and all that night. In the morning he arose and dislodged all his host, and drew after the Scots to chase them out of his realm. Then he took leave of the lady, saying, 'My dear lady, to God I commend you till I return again, requiring you to advise you otherwise than ye have said to me.' 'Noble prince,' quoth the lady, 'God the Father Glorious be your conduct, and put you out of all villain thoughts. Sir, I am and ever shall be ready to do your grace service to your honour and to mine.' Therewith the king departed all abashed; and so followed the Scots till he came to the city of Berwick, and went and lodged within four leagues of the forest of Jedburgh, whereas King David and all his company were entered, in trust of the great wilderness. The King of England tarried there a three days to see if the Scots would issue out to fight with him. In these three days there were divers skirmishes on both parties, and divers slain, taken, and sore hurt among the Scots. Sir William Douglas was he that did most trouble to the Englishmen: he bare azure, a comble silver, three stars gules.

How Sir Charles de Blois besieged the Countess of Montfort in Hennebont (1342).   [Ch. 80]

WHEN the city of Rennes was given up, the burgesses made their homage and fealty to the Lord Charles of Blois. Then he was counselled to go and lay siege to Hennebont, whereas the countess was, saying that the earl being in prison, if they might get the countess and her son, it should make an end of all the war. Then they went all to Hennebont and laid siege thereto, and to the castle also, as far as they might by land. With the countess in Hennebont there was the Bishop of Leon in Brittany; also there was Sir Ives of Tresiguidy, the Lord of Landernau, Sir William of Cadoudal, and the Chatelain of Guingamp, the two brethren of Quirich, Sir Henry and Sir Oliver of Spinefort, and divers other. When the countess and her company understood that the Frenchmen were coming to lay siege to the town of Hennebont, then it was commanded to sound the watch-bell alarm, and every man to be armed and draw to their defence.

When Sir Charles and the Frenchmen came near to the town, they commanded to lodge there that night. Some of the young lusty companions came skirmishing to the barriers, and some of them within issued out to them, so that there was a great affray. But the Genoese and Frenchmen lost more than they won. When night came on, every man drew to their lodging. The next day the lords took counsel to assail the barriers, to see the manner of them within; and so the third day they made a great assault to the barriers from morning till it was noon. Then the assailants drew aback sore beaten and divers slain. When the lords of France saw their men draw aback, they were sore displeased and caused the assault to begin again, more fiercer than it was before, and they within defended themselves valiantly. The countess herself wore harness on her body and rode on a great courser from street to street, desiring her people to make good defence; and she caused damosels and other women to cut short their kirtles and to carry stones and pots full of chalk to the walls, to be cast down to their enemies. This lady did there an hardy enterprise. She mounted up to the height of a tower to see how the Frenchmen were ordered without: she saw how that all the lords and all the other people of the host were all gone out of their field to the assault; then she took again her courser, armed as she was, and caused three hundred men a-horseback to be ready, and she went with them to another gate where there was none assault. She issued out and her company, and dashed into the French lodgings and cut down tents and set fire in their lodgings: she found no defence there, but a certain of varlets and boys, who ran away. When the lords of France looked behind them and saw their lodgings afire and heard the cry and noise there, they returned to the field crying, 'Treason! Treason!' so that all the assault was left. When the countess saw that, she drew together her company, and when she saw she could not enter again into the town without great damage, she took another way and went to the castle of Brest, the which was not far thence. When Sir Louis of Spain, who was marshal of the host, was come to the field and saw their lodgings burning and saw the countess and her company going away, he followed after her with a great number. He chased her so near that he slew and hurt divers of them that were behind, evil-horsed, but the countess and the most part of her company rode so well that they came to Brest, and there they were received with great joy.

The next day the lords of France, who had lost their tents and their provisions, then took counsel to lodge in bowers of trees more nearer to the town; and they had great marvel when they knew that the countess herself had done that enterprise. They of the town wist not where the countess was become, whereof they were in great trouble, for it was five days or they heard any tidings. The countess did so much at Brest that she got together a five hundred spears, and then about midnight she departed from Brest, and by the same rising she came along by the one side of the host; and came to one of the gates of Hennebont, the which was opened for her, and therein she entered and all her company, with great noise of trumpets and canayrs, whereof the French host had great marvel and armed them and ran to the town to assault it, and they within ready to defend. There began a fierce assault and endured till noon, but the Frenchmen lost more than they within. At noon the assault ceased: then they took counsel that Sir Charles de Blois should go from that siege and give assault to the castle of Auray, the which King Arthur made, and with him should go the Duke of Bourbon, the Earl of Blois, the Marshal of France, Sir Robert Bertrand; and that Sir Hervé de Leon and part of the Genoese, and the Lord Louis of Spain and the Viscount of Rohan, with all the Spaniards, should abide still before Hennebont. For they saw well they could have no profit to assail Hennebont any more, but they sent for twelve great engines to Rennes, to the intent to cast into the town and castle day and night. So they divided their host, the one still before Hennebont, the other with Sir Charles of Blois before Auray. They within Auray were well fortified and were a two hundred companions able for to maintain the war; and Sir Henry of Spine-fort and Sir Oliver his brother were chief captains there.

A four leagues from that castle was the good town of Vannes, pertaining to the countess, and captain there was Sir Geoffrey of Malestroit. Not far thence also was the good town of Dinan; the Chatelain of Guingamp was captain there: he was at Hennebont with the countess and had left in the town of Dinan his wife and his children, and had left there captain in his stead Raynold his son. Between these two towns stood a strong castle pertaining to Sir Charles de Blois, and was well kept with soldiers, Burgundians; captain there was Sir Gerard of Malain, and with him another knight called Peter Porteboeuf. They wasted all the country about them and constrained sore the said two towns, for there could neither merchandise nor provision enter into any of them but in great danger. On a day they would ride toward Vannes and another day toward Dinan; and on a day Sir Raynold of Guingamp laid a bushment, and the same day Sir Gerard of Malain rode forth and had taken a fifteen merchants and all their goods, and was driving them towards their castle, called Roche-Piriou, and so fell in the bushment. And there Sir Raynold of Guingamp took Sir Gerard prisoner, and a twenty-five of his company, and rescued the merchants and led forth their prisoners to Dinan; whereof Sir Raynold was much praised and well worthy.

Now let us speak of the Countess of Montfort, who was besieged in Hennebont by Sir Louis of Spain, who kept the siege there; and he had so broken and bruised the walls of the town with his engines, so that they within began to be abashed. And on a day the Bishop of Leon spake with Sir Hervé of Leon his nephew, by whom, as it was said, that the Earl Montfort was taken. So long they spake together that they agreed that the bishop should do what he could to cause the company within to agree to yield up the town and castle to Sir Charles de Blois, and Sir Hervé de Leon on the other side should purchase peace for them all of Sir Charles de Blois, and to lose nothing of their goods. Thus the bishop entered again into the town: the countess incontinent doubted of some evil purchase. Then she desired the lords and knights that were there, that for the love of God they should be in no doubt; for she said she was in surety that they should have succours within three days. Howbeit the bishop spake so much and showed so many reasons to the lords, that they were in a great trouble all that night. The next morning they drew to counsel again, so that they were near of accord to have given up the town, and Sir Hervé was come near to the town to have taken possession thereof. Then the countess looked down along the sea, out at a window in the castle, and began to smile for great joy that she had to see the succours coming, the which she had so long desired. Then she cried out aloud and said twice, 'I see the succours of England coming'. Then they of the town ran to the walls and saw a great number of ships, great and small, freshly decked, coming toward Hennebont. They thought well it was the succours of England, who had been on the sea sixty days by reason of contrary winds.

How Sir Walter of Manny brought the English-
men into Brittany (1342).   [Ch. 81]

WHEN the Seneschal of Guingamp, Sir Ives of Tresiguidy, Sir Galeran of Landernau and the other knights saw these succours coming, then they said to the bishop, 'Sir, ye may well leave your treaty,' for they said they were not content as then to follow his counsel. Then the bishop said, 'Sirs, then our company shall depart, for I will go to him that hath most right as me seemeth.' Then he departed from Hennebont, and defied the countess and all her aiders, and so went to Sir Hervé de Leon and showed him how the matter went. Then Sir Hervé was sore displeased and caused incontinent to rear up the greatest engines that they had near to the castle, and commanded that they should not cease to cast day and night. Then he departed thence and brought the bishop to Sir Louis of Spain, who received him with great joy, and so did Sir Charles of Blois.

Then the countess dressed up halls and chambers to lodge the lords of England that were coming, and did send against them right nobly. And when they were aland, she came to them with great reverence and feasted them the best she might, and thanked them right humbly, and caused all the knights and other to lodge at their ease in the castle and in the town; and the next day she made them a great feast at dinner. All night and the next day also, the engines never ceased to cast. And after dinner Sir Walter of Manny, who was chief of that company, demanded of the state of the town and of the host without, and said, 'I have a great desire to issue out and to break down this great engine that standeth so near us, if any will follow me.' Then Sir Ives of Tresiguidy said how he would not fail him at this his first beginning, and so said the Lord of Landernau. Then they armed them, and so they issued out privily at a certain gate, and with them a three hundred archers, who shot so wholly together that they that kept the engine fled away. And the men of arms came after the archers and slew divers of them that fled, and beat down the great engine and brake it all to pieces. Then they ran in among the tents and lodgings and set fire in divers places, and slew and hurt divers till the host began to stir; then they withdrew fair and easily, and they of the host ran after them like madmen. Then Sir Walter said, 'Let me never be beloved with my lady, without I have a course with one of these followers.' And therewith turned his spear in the rest, and in likewise so did the two brethren of Levedale and the Hase of Brabant, Sir Ives of Tresiguidy, Sir Galeran of Landernau and divers other companions. They ran at the first comers: there might well a been legs seen turned upward. There began a sore meddling, for they of the host always increased, wherefore it behoved the Englishmen to withdraw toward their fortress. There might well a been seen on both parties many noble deeds, taking and rescuing. The Englishmen drew sagely to the dykes and there made a stall, till all their men were in safeguard; and all the residue of the town issued out to rescue their company and caused them of the host to recule back. So when they of the host saw how they could do no good, they drew to their lodgings, and they of the fortress in likewise to their lodgings. Then the countess descended down from the castle with a glad cheer, and came and kissed Sir Walter of Manny and his companions one after another, two or three times, like a valiant lady.

How the King of England sent Sir Robert d'Artois into Brittany (1342).   [Ch. 90]

AMONG all other things the King of England would succour the Countess of Montfort, who was with the queen. Then the king desired his cousin, Sir Robert d'Artois, to take a certain number of men of war and archers and to go with the countess into Brittany: and so he did, and they departed and took shipping at Southampton, and were on the sea a great season because of contrary winds. They departed about Easter.

At this great council at London, the king was advised to send to Scotland for the performance of a truce to endure for two or three years, considering that the king had so much business in other places. The King of England was loath thereto for he would have made such war into Scotland that they should have been fain to have desired peace: howbeit his council showed him such reasons that he agreed thereto. Among other things his council said that it was great wisdom when a prince hath war in divers places at one time, to agree with one by truce, another to pacify with fair words, and on the third to make war. Then was there a bishop [of Lincoln] sent on that legation; and so he went forth and in process returned again, and brought relation how that the King of Scots would agree to no truce without the agreement of the French king. Then the King of England said openly that he would never rest till he had so arrayed the realm of Scotland that it should never be recovered. Then he commanded that every man should be with him at Berwick by Easter, except such as were appointed to go into Brittany.

The feast of Easter came and the king held a great court at Berwick, for the chief of the lords and knights of England were there and there tarried the space of three weeks. In the mean season certain good men laboured between the parties to have a truce, and so there a truce was agreed to endure for two year, and confirmed by the French king. Then every man departed and the king went to Windsor. Then he sent the Lord Thomas Holland and the Lord John Hardeshulle to Bayon with two hundred men of arms and four hundred archers, to keep the frontiers there.

Now let us speak of Sir Robert d'Artois. That year fell so high that it was near to the entering of May, in the mid of the which month the truce between the Lord Charles of Blois and the Countess of Montfort should expire. Sir Charles of Blois was well-certified of the purchase that the Countess of Montfort had made in England, and of the comfort that the king had promised her; for the which intent the Lord Louis of Spain, Sir Charles Grimaldi, and Sir Othes Doria were laid on the sea about Guernsey with a three thousand Genoese and a thousand men of arms and a thirty-two great ships.

Of the battle of Guernsey between Sir Robert d'Artois and Sir Louis of Spain on the sea (1342).
[Ch. 91]

SIR Robert d'Artois, Earl of Richmond, and with him the Earl of Pembroke, the Earl of Salisbury, the Earl of Suffolk, the Earl of Oxford, the Baron of Stafford, the Lord Spenser, the Lord Bouchier, and divers other knights of England and their companies were with the Countess of Montfort on the sea, and at last came before the isle of Guernsey. Then they perceived the great fleet of the Genoese, whereof Sir Louis of Spain was chief captain. Then their mariners said, 'Sirs, arm you quickly, for yonder be Genoese and Spaniards that will set on you.' Then the Englishmen sounded their trumpets and reared up their banners and standards with their arms and devices, with the banner of Saint George, and set their ships in order with their archers before: and as the wind served them they sailed forth. They were a forty-six vessels, great and small, but Sir Louis of Spain had nine greater than any of the other and three galleys. And in the three galleys were the three chief captains, as Sir Louis of Spain, Sir Charles Grimaldi, and Sir Othes Doria. And when they approached near together, the Genoese began to shoot with their crossbows, and the archers of England against them. There was sore shooting between them and many hurt on both parties. And when the lords, knights, and squires came near together, there was a sore battle. The countess that day was worth a man; she had the heart of a lion and had in her hand a sharp glaive, wherewith she fought fiercely.

The Spaniards and Genoese that were in the great vessels, they cast down great bars of iron and pieces of timber, the which troubled sore the English archers. This battle began about the time of evensong and the night departed them, for it was very dark so that one could scant know another. Then they withdrew each from other and cast anchors and abode still in their harness, for they thought to fight again in the morning. But about midnight there rose such a tempest so horrible as though all the world should have ended. There was none so hardy but would gladly have been aland. The ships dashed so together that they weened all would have riven in pieces. The lords of England demanded counsel of their mariners what was best to do. They answered, to take land as soon as they might, for the tempest was so great that if they took the sea they were in danger of drowning. Then they drew up their anchors and bare but a quarter sail, and drew from that place. The Genoese on the other side drew up their anchors and took the deep of the sea, for their vessels were greater than the English ships, they might better abide the brunt of the sea: for if the great vessels had come near the land, they were likely to have been broken. And as they departed they took four English ships laded with victual, and tailed them to their ships. The storm was so hideous that in less than a day they were driven a hundred leagues from the place where they were before. And the English ships took a little haven not far from the city of Vannes, whereof they were right glad.

How Sir Robert d'Artois took the city of Vannes in Brittany (1342).   [Ch. 92]

THUS, by this torment of the sea, brake and departed the battle on the sea between Sir Robert d'Artois and Sir Louis of Spain. No man could tell to whom to give the honour for they departed against both their wills. The Englishmen took land not far off from Vannes; and brought all their horse and harness aland. Then they devised to send their navy to Hennebont and to go themself and lay siege to Vannes; therein were captains Sir Hervé of Leon and Sir Oliver of Clisson, and with them the Lord of Tournemine and the Lord of Loheac. When they saw the Englishmen come to besiege them they took good heed to their defences, both to the castle and to the walls and gates. And at every gate they set a knight with ten men of arms and twenty crossbows.

Now let us speak of Sir Louis of Spain and his company. They were sore tormented on the sea and in great danger all that night and the next day till noon, and lost two of their ships, men and all. Then the third day about prime, the sea appeased. Then they demanded of the mariners what part of land was next: they answered, the realm of Navarre, and that the wind had driven them out of Brittany more than sixscore leagues. Then there they cast anchor and abode the flood, and when the tide came they had good wind to return to Rochelle. So they coasted Bayonne but they would not come near it, and they met four ships of Bayonne coming from Flanders. They set on them and took them shortly, and slew all that were in them. Then they sailed towards Rochelle and in a few days they arrived at Guérande: there they took land and heard there how Sir Robert d'Artois lay at siege before Vannes. Then they sent to the Lord Charles of Blois to know his pleasure what they should do.

Sir Robert d'Artois lay at siege with a thousand men of arms and three thousand archers, and wasted all the country about and burnt to Dinan and to Coët, so that none durst abide in the plain country. There were many assaults and skirmishes at the barriers of Vannes. The Countess of Montfort was still with Sir Robert d'Artois at the siege. Also Sir Walter of Manny, who was in Hennebont, delivered the keeping of the town to Sir William Cadoudal and to Sir Gerard of Rochfort, and took with him Sir Ives of Tresiguidy and a hundred men of arms and two hundred archers, and departed from Hennebont and went to the siege before Vannes. Then incontinent there was made a great assault in three places all at once. The archers shot so thick that they within scant durst appear at their defence. This assault endured a whole day, and many hurt on both parties. Against night the Englishmen withdrew to their lodgings, and they within, in likewise sore weary of travail, and they disarmed them. But they of the host without did not so, for they kept on still their harness except their head-pieces, and so drank and refreshed them. And then, by the advice of Sir Robert d'Artois, they ordained again three battles, and two of them to assault at the gates and the third battle to keep themself privy till the other two battles had assailed along, so that all the strength of the town should be there by all likelihood to defend. Then it was ordained that this third battle should set on the most feeblest place of all the town with ladders, ropes, and hooks of iron to cast on the walls. And as they devised, so it was done. Sir Robert d'Artois with the first battle came and made assault in the night at one of the gates, and the Earl of Salisbury with the second battle at another gate. And because it was dark, to the intent to make them within the more abashed, they made great fires so that the brightness thereof gave light into the city, whereby they within had weened that their houses had been afire, and cried, 'Treason!' Many were abed to rest them of their travail the day before, and so rose suddenly and ran towards the light without order or good array and without counsel of their captains; every man within armed them. Thus while they were in this trouble, the Earl of Oxford and Sir Walter of Manny with the third battle came to the walls, whereas there was no defence made, and with their ladders mounted up and entered into the town. The Frenchmen took no heed of them, they were so occupied in other places, till they saw their enemies in the streets. Then every man fled away to save themself. The captains had no leisure to go into the castle but were fain to take their horses and issued out at a postern: happy was he that might get out to save himself. All that ever were seen by the Englishmen were taken or slain and the town overrun and robbed. And the countess and Sir Robert d'Artois entered into the town with great joy.

How Sir Robert d'Artois died and where he was buried (1342).   [Ch. 93]

THUS, as I have showed you, the city of Vannes was taken; and a five days after the Countess of Montfort, Sir Walter of Manny, Sir Ives of Tresiguidy, and divers other knights of England and of Brittany returned to Hennebont. And the Earl of Salisbury, the Earl of Pembroke, the Earl of Suffolk, the Earl of Cornwall, departed from Vannes, from Sir Robert d'Artois, with three thousand men of arms and three thousand archers, and went and laid siege to the city of Rennes. And Sir Charles de Blois was departed thence but four days before and was gone to Nantes, but he had left in the city many lords, knights and squires. And still Sir Louis of Spain was on the sea and kept so the frontiers against England, that none could go between England and Brittany without great danger. They had done that year to England great damage.

For the taking thus of Vannes by the Englishmen the country was sore abashed, for they thought that there had been such captains that had been able to have defended it against all the world. They knew well the town was strong and well provided of men of war and artillery. For this misadventure Sir Hervé of Leon and the Lord Clisson were sore abashed, for their enemies spake shame against them. These two knights were so sore displeased with the matter that they got together a company of knights and soldiers, so that a day appointed they met before the city of Vannes, more than twelve thousand of one and other. Thither came the Lord Robert of Beaumanoir, Marshal of Brittany. They laid siege to the city on all sides and then assailed it fiercely. When Sir Robert d'Artois saw how he was besieged in the city he was not negligent to keep his defence, and they without were fierce because they would not that they that lay at siege at Rennes should not* trouble them. They made so fierce assault and gave them within so much ado that they won the barriers, and after the gates, and so entered into the city by force. The Englishmen were put to the chase and divers hurt and slain, and specially Sir Robert d'Artois was sore hurt, and escaped hardly untaken: he departed at a postern and the Lord Stafford with him. The Lord Spencer was taken by Sir Hervé of Leon but he was so sore hurt that he died the third day after.

Thus the Frenchmen won again the city of Vannes. And Sir Robert d'Artois tarried a season in Hennebont sore hurt, and at last he was counselled to go into England to seek help for his hurts. But he was so sore handled on the sea that his sores rankled; and at last landed and was brought to London, and within a short space after he died of the same hurts and was buried in London in the church of Saint Paul. The king did as nobly his obsequy as though it had been for his own proper cousin-german, the Earl of Derby. His death was greatly bemoaned in England and the King of England swore that he would never rest till he had revenged his death, and said how he would go himself into Brittany and bring the country in such case, that it should not be recovered again in forty year after. Incontinent he sent out letters throughout his realm, that every nobleman and other should come to him within a month after; and prepared a great navy of ships. And at the end of the month he took the sea, and took landing in Brittany not far from Vannes, thereas Sir Robert d'Artois arrived. He was three days alanding of all his provision; the fourth day he went toward Vannes. And all this season the Earl of Salisbury and the Earl of Pembroke were lying at siege before Rennes.

How the King of England came into Brittany to make war there (1342).   [Ch. 94]

AFTER the King of England had been aland a certain space he went and laid siege to Vannes. And within the town there was Sir Oliver of Clisson, and Sir Hervé of Leon, the Lord of Tournemine, Sir Geoffrey of Malestroit, and Sir Guy

* To make this passage intelligible, the last 'not' should be ignored.

of Loheac; they supposed well before that the King of England would come into Brittany, wherefore they had provided the town and castle with all things necessary. The king made a great assault that endured half a day, but little good they did, the city was so well-defended. When the Countess of Montfort knew that the King of England was come, she departed from Hennebont, accompanied with Sir Walter of Manny and divers other knights and squires, and came before Vannes to see the king and the lords of the host; and a four days after she returned again to Hennebont with all her own company.

Now let us speak of Sir Charles of Blois, who was in Nantes. And as soon as he knew that the King of England was arrived in Brittany, he sent word thereof to the French king his uncle desiring him of succour. When the King of England saw this city so strong and heard reported how the country thereabout was so poor and so sore wasted, that they wist not where to get any forage neither for man nor beast, then he ordained to divide his number: first the Earl of Arundel, the Lord Stafford, Sir Walter of Manny, Sir Ives of Tresiguidy, and Sir Richard of Rochfort, with a six hundred men of arms and six thousand archers, to keep still the siege before Vannes and to ride and destroy the country all about. And the king went to Rennes where he was joyfully received with them that lay at siege there before, and had done a long season. And when the king had been there a five days, he understood that Sir Charles de Blois was at Nantes and made there a great assembly of men of war. Then the king departed from Rennes and left them still there that were there before to continue their siege. Then the king came before Nantes and besieged it as far as he might, but he could not lay round about, the city was so great. The marshal of the host rode abroad and destroyed great part of the country. The king ordained his battle on a little mountain without the town and there tarried from the morning till it was noon, weening that Sir Charles of Blois would have issued out to have given him battle. And when they saw it would not be, they drew to their lodgings; the fore-riders ran to the barriers and skirmished and burnt the suburbs. Thus the king lay before Nantes and Sir Charles within, who wrote to the French king the state of the Englishmen.

The French king had commanded his son, the Duke of Normandy, to give aid to Sir Charles of Blois, the which duke was as then come to Angers and there made his assembly of men of war. The King of England made divers assaults to Nantes, but ever he lost of his men and won nothing. And when he saw that by assaults he could do nothing and that Sir Charles would not issue out into the field to fight with him, then he ordained the Earl of Oxford, Sir Henry Viscount of Beaumont, the Lord Percy, the Lord Ros, the Lord Mowbray, the Lord Delaware, the Lord Raynold Cobham, and the Lord John Lisle, with six hundred men of arms and two hundred archers, to keep still the siege there and to ride and destroy the country all about. And then the king went and laid siege to the town of Dinan, whereof Sir Peter Portebeouf was captain. The king made there fierce assaults and they within defended themself valiantly. Thus the King of England all at one season had sieges lying to three cities and a good town in Brittany.

How Sir Hervé of Leon and the Lord Clisson were taken prisoners before Vannes (1342).
[Ch. 95]

WHILE the King of England was thus in Brittany wasting and destroying the country, such as he had lying at siege before Vannes gave divers assaults, and specially at one of the gates. And on a day there was a great assault and many feats of arms done on both parties. They within set open the gate and came to the barriers, because they saw the Earl of Warwick's banner, and the Earl of Arundel's, the Lord Stafford's, and Sir Walter of Manny's adventuring themself jeopardously, as they thought: wherefore the Lord Clisson, Sir Hervé of Leon, and other adventured themself courageously. There was a sore skirmish; finally the Englishmen were put back. Then the knights of Brittany opened the barriers and adventured themself and left six knights with a good number to keep the town, and they issued out after the Englishmen. And the Englishmen reculed wisely, and ever fought as they saw their advantage. The Englishmen multiplied in such wise that at last the Frenchmen and Bretons were fain to recule back again to their town, not in so good order as they came forth. Then the Englishmen followed them again and many were slain and hurt. They of the town saw their men recule again and chased: then they closed their barriers in so evil a time that the Lord Clisson and Sir Hervé of Leon were closed without, and there they were both taken prisoners. And on the other side the Lord Stafford was gone in so far that he was closed in between the gate and the barriers, and there he was taken prisoner and divers that were with him taken and slain. Thus the Englishmen drew to their lodgings and the Bretons into the city of Vannes.

How the King of England and the Duke of Normandy were host against host lodged before Vannes (1342).
[Ch. 98]

WHILE the Duke of Normandy was at Nantes, the lords of England that lay at siege before Rennes on a day made a great and fierce assault, for they had made many instruments to assault withal. This assault endured a whole day, but they won nothing but lost divers of their men . . . . . Howbeit the Englishmen lay there still and overran and wasted the country all about. Then the Duke of Normandy departed with all his host and drew toward Vannes the sooner to find his enemies, for he was informed how they of Vannes were in most jeopardy and in peril of losing. Then the two marshals went forth and Sir Geoffrey of Charney and the Earl of Guines, Constable of France, made the rearguard.

So thus the Frenchmen came to Vannes on the other side against thereas the King of England lay. They lay along by a fair meadow-side and made a great dyke about their host. The marshals and foreriders oftentimes skirmished together on both parties. Then the King of England sent for the Earl of Salisbury, the Earl of Pembroke, and the other that lay at siege at Rennes, to come to him: and so they did. The Englishmen and the Bretons of that party were well to the number of two thousand and five hundred men of arms and six thousand archers and four thousand of other men afoot. The Frenchmen were four times as many, well apparelled. The King of England had so fortified his host that the Frenchmen could take no advantage of him, and he made no more assaults to the town because of sparing of his men and artillery. Thus these two hosts lay one against another a long season, till it was well onward into winter. Then Pope Clement the Sixth sent the Cardinal of Preneste and the Cardinal of Clermont to entreat for a peace; and they rode oftentimes between the parties, but they could bring them to no peace.

In the mean season there were many skirmishes and many men taken, slain, and overthrown on both parties. The Englishmen durst not go a-foraging but in great companies, for they were ever in danger by reason of the bushments that were laid for them. Also Sir Louis of Spain kept so the sea coast, that with much danger anything came to the English host. The Frenchmen thought to keep the king there in manner as besieged. Also the Frenchmen endured much pain with wet and cold, for day and night it rained on them, whereby they lost many of their horses and were fain to dislodge and lie in the plain fields, they had so much water in their lodgings.

At last these cardinals did so much that there was a truce agreed for three year. The King of England and the Duke of Normandy swore to uphold the same without breaking, as the custom is in suchlike cases.

How the French king caused the heads to be stricken off of the Lord Clisson and divers other lords of Brittany and of Normandy (1343).
[Ch. 99]

THUS this great assembly broke up and the siege raised at Vannes. The Duke of Normandy went to Nantes and had with him the two cardinals. And the King of England went to Hennebont, to the Countess of Montfort. There was an exchange made between the Baron of Stafford and the Lord Clisson. When the king had tarried at Hennebont as long as it pleased him, then he left there the

F

Earl of Pembroke, Sir William Cadoudal and other, and then returned into England about Christmas. And the Duke of Normandy returned into France, and gave leave to every man to depart.

And anon after the Lord Clisson was taken upon suspicions of treason and was put into the Châtelet of Paris, whereof many had great marvel: lords and knights spake each to other thereof and said, 'What matter is that is laid against the Lord Clisson?' There was none could tell, but some imagined that it was false envy because the King of England bore more favour to deliver him in exchange rather than Sir Hervé of Leon who was still in prison. Because the king showed him that advantage, his enemies suspected in him peradventure that was not true; upon the which suspect he was beheaded at Paris, without mercy or excuse. He was greatly bemoaned. Anon after there were divers knights were accused in semblable case, as the Lord of Malestroit and his son, the Lord of Avaugour, Sir Thibaut of Morilon, and divers other lords of Brittany to the number of ten knights and squires; and they lost all their heads at Paris . . . . .

Of the Order of Saint George that King Edward stablished in the castle of Windsor (1343).
[Ch. 100]

IN this season the King of England took pleasure to new re-edify the castle of Windsor, the which was begun by King Arthur; and there first began the Table Round, whereby sprang the fame of so many noble knights throughout all the world. Then King Edward determined to make an order and a brotherhood of a certain number of knights, and to be called Knights of the Blue Garter, and a feast to be kept yearly at Windsor on Saint George's Day. And to begin this order the king assembled together earls, lords and knights of his realm, and showed them his intention; and they all joyously agreed to his pleasure, because they saw it was a thing much honourable and whereby great amity and love should grow and increase. Then was there chosen out a certain number of the most valiantest men of the realm, and they swore and sealed to maintain the ordinances such as were devised. And the king made a chapel in the castle of Windsor, of Saint George, and stablished certain canons there to serve God, and endowed them with fair rent. Then the king sent to publish this feast by his heralds into France, Scotland, Burgundy, Hainault, Flanders, Brabant, and into the Empire of Germany, giving to every knight and squire that would come to the said feast fifteen days of safe-conduct before the feast and after: the which feast to begin at Windsor on Saint George Day next after in the year of our Lord MCCCXLIV, and the queen to be there accompanied with three hundred ladies and damosels, all of noble lineage and apparelled accordingly.

How the Earl of Derby conquered Bergerac
(1345).   [Ch. 103]

WHEN the Earl of Derby had been at Bordeaux a fifteen days, he understood how these lords and knights of Gascony were at Bergerac. In a morning he drew thitherward, and he caused Sir Walter of Manny and Sir Franque de Hall to go before, who were marshals of his host. That morning they rode three leagues to a castle that was English called Montcroullier, but a little league from Bergerac; there they tarried all that day and that night. The next morning their currours ran to the barriers of Bergerac, and at their return they reported to Sir Walter of Manny how they had seen part of the demeanour of the Frenchmen, the which they thought to be but simple. That morning the Englishmen dined betimes, and as they sat at dinner Sir Walter of Manny beheld the Earl of Derby and said, 'Sir, if we were good men of arms we should drink this evening with the French lords being in Bergerac.' Quoth the earl, 'And for me it shall not be let.' When every man heard that they said, 'Let us go arm us, for we shall ride incontinent to Bergerac.' There was no more to-do, but shortly every man was armed and a-horseback. When the Earl of Derby saw his company so well-willed, he was right joyous, and said, 'Let us ride to our enemies, in the name of God and Saint George.' So they rode forth with their banners displayed in all the heat of the day, till they came to the bails of Bergerac, the which were not easy to win for part of the river of Dordogne went about it.

When the Frenchmen saw the Englishmen come to assail them, they said among themself how they should soon be driven back. They issued out in good order; they had many of the villeins of the country ill-armed. The Englishmen approached and the archers began to shoot fiercely. And when those footmen felt the arrows light among them and saw the banners and standards wave with the wind, the which they had not been accustomed to see before, then they reculed back among their own men of arms. Then the English men of arms approached and dashed in among their enemies and slew and beat down on every part, for the French men of arms could neither approach forward nor backward for their own footmen, who reculed without order and did stop them their way. There were many slain and sore hurt. The English archers were on both sides the way and shot so wholly together that none durst approach nor issue through them. So the Frenchmen were put aback into the suburbs of Bergerac, but it was to such a mischief for them, that the first bridge and bails were won by clean force, for the Englishmen entered with them and there on the pavement many knights were slain and sore hurt, and divers prisoners taken of them that adventured themself to defend the passage. And the Lord of Mirepoix was slain under Sir Walter of Manny's banner, who was the first that entered.

When the Earl of Lisle saw that the Englishmen had won the suburbs and slain his men without mercy, he then reculed back into the town and passed the bridge with great trouble and danger. Before that bridge there was a sore skirmish, the lords and knights fought hand to hand. The Lord of Manny advanced himself so far among his enemies that he was in great danger. The Englishmen took there the Viscount of Bousquetyne, the Lord of Castelnau, the Lord of Chastellon, the Lord de Lescu; all other of the Frenchmen entered into the town and closed their gates and let down their portcullises, and then went to the walls to their defences. This assault and skirmish endured till the evening. Then the Englishmen withdrew, right sore weary, and entered into the suburbs, the which they had won, where they found wine and victual sufficient for their whole host for two months.

The next morning the Earl of Derby caused his trumpets to be sounded and set his people in order of battle, and approached the town and made a sore assault, the which endured till noon. Little did the Englishmen at that assault for they within defended themself valiantly. At noon the Englishmen withdrew, for they saw well they did but lose their pain. Then the lords went to counsel and determined to assault the town by water, for it was closed but with pales. Then the Earl of Derby sent to the navy at Bordeaux for ships and there was brought from Bordeaux to Bergerac sixty ships and barks. The next day in the evening they ordered their battles, and in the next morning, by the sun-rising, the navy was ready to assault by water; the Baron of Stafford was captain. The Englishmen and archers adventured themself valiantly and came to a great barrier before the pales, the which anon was cast down to the earth. Then they of the town came to the Earl de Lisle and to the other lords and knights that were there, and said, 'Sirs, take heed what ye will do: we be in a great jeopardy to be all lost. If this town be lost we lose all that we have, and our lives also. Yet it were better that ye yielded ourself to the Earl of Derby than to have more damage.' The Earl of Lisle said, 'Go we to the place whereas needeth most defence, for we will not as yet yield up the town.' So they went to defend the pales.

The archers that were in the barks shot so wholly together that none durst appear at their defence without they were slain or sore hurt. There were within a two hundred Genoese crossbows and near were pavised against the shot; they held the English archers well a-work all the day and many hurt on both parties. Finally, the Englishmen did so much that they broke down a great pane of the pales. Then they within reculed back and desired a treaty and a truce, the which was granted to endure all that day and the next night, so that they should not fortify in the mean season. So either party drew to their lodgings. This night the lords within the town were in great council and finally, about midnight, they trussed bag and baggage and departed out of the town of Bergerac and took the way to the town of La Réole, the which was not far from thence.

The next morning the Englishmen again entered into their barks and came to the same place where they had broken the pales, and there they found certain of the town who desired them that they would pray the Earl of Derby to take them to mercy, saving their lives and goods, and from thenceforth they would be obeisant to the King of England. The Earl of Oxford and the Earl of Pembroke said they would speak gladly for them, and so they came to the Earl of Derby and showed him the intent of them of the town. The Earl of Derby said, 'He that mercy desireth, mercy ought to have. Bid them open their gates and show them they shall be assured of me and all mine.' These two lords went again to them of the town and showed them the Earl of Derby's intent. Then they assembled all the people together and sounded their bells and opened their gates, and issued out men and women in procession and humbly met the Earl of Derby; and so brought him into the chief church and there swore faith and homage to the earl in the name of the King of England, by virtue of a procuration that the earl had.

How the Earl of Lisle laid siege before Auberoche (1345).   [Ch. 106]

AT the returning of the Earl of Derby to Bordeaux, he was joyfully received and met with procession and offered him everything in the town at his pleasure. There he tarried and sported him with the burgesses, ladies and damosels of the town.

Now let us speak of the Earl of Lisle, who was at La Réole. When he understood that the Earl of Derby was at Bordeaux and lay still, and no likelihood that he would stir any further that season, then he wrote to the Earl of Périgord, of Caraman, of Comminges, and of Bruniquel, and to all the other lords of Gascony of the French party, that they should assemble their men and come and meet him before Auberoche, for his mind was to lay siege thereto. They all obeyed him for he was as king in those parts of Gascony. The lords and knights within Auberoche was not ware of any siege till it was laid round about them so that none could issue out nor enter without perceiving. The Frenchmen brought with them four great engines from Toulouse, the which did cast day and night: they made no other assault. So within six days they had broken the roofs of the towers and chambers, that they within durst not abide but within low vaults. The intent of them of the host was to slay them all within, or else to have them yield simply.

The Earl of Derby had knowledge how the siege lay before Auberoche, but he knew not that his company were so sore oppressed as they were. When Sir Franque de Hall, Sir Aleyne de Fyneforde and Sir John of Lyndall, who were thus besieged within Auberoche, saw themself thus hardly bestood, they demanded among their varlets if there were any, for a good reward, would bear a letter to the Earl of Derby to Bordeaux. One varlet stepped forth and said he would gladly bear it, not for the advantage of his reward, but rather to help to deliver them out of danger. In the night, the varlet took the letter, sealed with their seals, and then went down the dykes and so past through the host: there was none other remedy. He was met with the first watch and passed by them, for he spoke good Gascon and named a lord of the host and said he pertained to him, but then again he was taken among the tents and so brought into the heart of the host. He was searched and the letter found on him, and so he was kept safe till the morning that the lords were assembled together. Then the letter was brought to the Earl of Lisle. They had great joy when they perceived that they within were so sore constrained that they could not long endure. Then they took the varlet and hanged the letter about his neck, and did put him into an engine and did cast him into the town, the varlet fell down dead, wherewith they within were sore troubled.

The same season, the Earl of Périgord and his uncle, Sir Charles of Poitiers, and the Viscount of Caraman and the Lord of Duras, were a-horseback and passed by the walls of the town as near as they might and cried to them within, and said in mockery, 'Sirs, demand of your messenger where he found the Earl of Derby, since he went out but this night and is returned again so shortly.' Then Sir Franque de Hall said, 'Sirs, though we be here enclosed, we shall issue out when it shall please God and the Earl of Derby: as would to God he knew in what case we be in, for and he knew it, there is none of you that durst keep the field; and if ye would send him word thereof, one of us shall yield himself prisoner to you to be ransomed as a gentleman ought to be.' The Frenchmen answered, 'Nay, nay, sirs, the matter shall not go so. The Earl of Derby shall know it well enough when with our engines we have beaten down the castle to the earth, and that ye have yielded up simply for saving of your lives.' 'Certainly,' quoth Sir Franque, 'we shall not yield ourself so. We would rather die here within.' So the Frenchmen returned again to their host and the three English knights were sore abashed, for the stones that fell in the town gave so sore strokes that it seemed like thunder falled from heaven.

How the Earl of Derby took before Auberoche the Earl of Lisle and divers other earls and viscounts to the number of nine (1345).

[Ch. 107]

ALL the matter of taking of this messenger with the letter and necessity of them within Auberoche, was showed to the Earl of Derby by a spy that had been in the French host. Then the Earl of Derby sent to the Earl of Pembroke, being at Bergerac, to meet with him at a certain place; also he sent for the Lord Stafford and to Sir Stephen Tombey, being at Libourne. And the earl himself with Sir Walter of Manny and his company rode towards Auberoche, and rode so secretly with such guides as knew the country, that the earl came to Libourne and there tarried a day, abiding the Earl of Pembroke. And when he saw that he came not, he went forth for the great desire that he had to aid them in Auberoche. Thus the Earl of Derby, the Earl of Oxford, Sir Walter of Manny, Sir Richard Hastings, Sir Stephen Tombey, the Lord Ferrers and the other issued out at Libourne and rode all the night, and in the morning they were within two little leagues of Auberoche. They entered into a wood and lighted from their horses and tied their horses to pasture, abiding for the Earl of Pembroke, and there tarried till it was noon. They wist not well then what to do, because they were but three hundred spears and six hundred archers, and the Frenchmen before Auberoche were a ten or twelve thousand men; yet they thought it a great shame to lose their companions in Auberoche. Finally Sir Walter of Manny said, 'Sirs, let us leap on our horses and let us coast under the covert of this wood, till we be on the same side that joineth to their host, and when we be near, put the spurs to the horses and cry our cries. We shall enter while they be at supper and unware of us: we shall see them be so discomfited, that they shall keep none array.'

All the lords and knights agreed to his saying. Then every man took his horse and ordained all their pages and baggage to abide still thereas they were. So they rode still along by the wood and came to a little river in a vale near to the French host. Then they displayed their banners and pennons and dashed their spurs to their horses, and came in a front into the French host among the Gascons, who were nothing ware of that bushment. They were going to supper, and some ready set at their meat. The Englishmen cried, 'A Derby! A Derby!' and over-threw tents and pavilions, and slew and hurt many. The Frenchmen wist not what to do, they were so hasted. When they came into the field and assembled together, they found the English archers there ready to receive them, who shot so fiercely that they slew man and horse and hurt many. The Earl of Lisle was taken prisoner in his own tent and sore hurt, and the Earl of Périgord and Sir Roger his uncle in their tents. And there was slain the Lord of Duras [and] Sir Aymar of Poitiers, and the Earl of Valentinois his brother was taken. Every man fled that might best, but the Earl of Comminges, the Viscount of Caraman and of Villemur and of Bruniquel, and the Lord de la Bard and of Terride, and other that were lodged on the other side of the castle, drew back and went into the field with their banners. The Englishmen, who had overcome all the other, dashed in fiercely among them. There was many a proper feat of arms done, many taken and rescued again. When they within the castle heard that noise without and saw the English banners and pennons, incontinent they armed them and issued out and rushed into the thickest of the press: they greatly refreshed the Englishmen that had fought there before. Whereto should I make long process? All those of the Earl of Lisle's party were nigh all taken or slain: if the night had not come on, there had but few escaped. There were taken that day, what earls and viscounts to the number of nine, and of lords, knights, and squires taken so that there was no Englishman of arms but that had two or three prisoners. This battle was on Saint Lawrence night, the year of our Lord MCCCXLV. The Englishmen dealt like good companions with the prisoners and suffered many to depart on their oath and promise to return again at a certain day to Bergerac or to Bordeaux.

Then the Englishmen entered into Auberoche, and there the Earl of Derby gave a supper to the most part of the earls and viscounts prisoners, and to many of the knights and squires. The Englishmen gave laud to God, in that a thousand of them had overcome ten thousand of their enemies and had rescued the town of Auberoche, and saved their companions that were within, who by all likelihood should have been taken within two days after.

The next day anon upon sun-rising thither came the Earl of Pembroke with his company, a three hundred spears and a four thousand archers. Then he said to the Earl of Derby, 'Certainly, cousin, ye have done me great uncourtesy to fight our enemies without me. Seeing that ye sent for me, ye might have been sure I would not fail to come.' 'Fair cousin,' quoth the Earl of Derby, 'we desired greatly to have had you with us. We tarried all day till it was far past noon, and when we saw that ye came not, we durst not abide no longer: for if our enemies had known of our coming, they had been in a great advantage over us, and now we have the advantage over them. I pray you, be content, and help to guide us to Bordeaux.' So they tarried all that day and the next night in Auberoche. And the next day betimes they departed, and left captain in Auberoche a knight of Gascony called Alexander of Chaumont. Thus they rode to Bordeaux and led with them the most part of their prisoners.

How the Earl of Derby laid siege to La Réole, and how that the town was yielded to him (1345). [Ch. 109]

THUS the Earl of Derby came before La Réole and laid siege thereto on all sides, and made bastides in the fields and on the ways, so that no provision could enter into the town and nigh every day there was assault. The siege endured a long space. And when the month was expired that they of Montségur should give up their town, the earl sent thither, and they of the town gave up and became under the obeisance of the King of England. The captain, Sir Hugh Badefol, became servant to the earl, with other that were within, upon certain wages that they had.

The Englishmen, that had lain long before La Réole, more than nine weeks, had made in the mean space two belfries of great timber with three stages, every belfry on four great wheels, and the sides towards the town were covered with cure boly* to defend them from fire and from shot, and into every stage there were pointed an hundred archers. By strength of men these two belfries were brought to the walls of the town, for they had so filled the dykes that they might well be

* *Cuir bouilli* or boiled hide.

brought just to the walls. The archers in these stages shot so wholly together, that none durst appear at their defence without they were well pavised. And between these two belfries there were a two hundred men with pick-axes to mine the walls, and so they brake through the walls. Then the burgesses of the town came to one of the gates to speak with some lord of the host. When the Earl of Derby knew thereof, he sent to them Sir Walter of Manny and the Baron of Stafford; and when they came there, they found that they of the town would yield them, their lives and goods saved.

[When] Sir Agot des Baux, who was captain within, knew that the people of the town would yield up, he went into the castle with his company of soldiers, and while they of the town were entreating, he conveyed out of the town great quantity of wine and other provision, and then closed the castle gates and said how he would not yield up so soon. The foresaid two lords returned to the Earl of Derby showing him how they of the town would yield themselves and the town, their lives and goods saved. Then the earl sent to know how the captain would do with the castle, and it was brought word again to him how he would not yield. Then the earl studied a little and said, 'Well, go take them of the town to mercy, for by the town we shall have the castle.' Then these lords went again to them of the town and received them to mercy, so that they should go out into the field and deliver the Earl of Derby the keys of the town, saying, 'Sir, from henceforth we knowledge ourselves subjects and obeisant to the King of England': and so they did and sware that they should give no comfort to them of the castle, but to grieve them to the best of their powers. Then the earl commanded that no man should do any hurt to the town of La Réole nor to none of them within.

Then the earl entered into the town and laid siege round about the castle, as near as he might, and reared up all his engines, the which cast night and day against the walls, but they did little hurt, the walls were so strong of hard stone: it was said that of old time it had been wrought by the hands of the Saracens, who made their works so strongly that there is none such nowadays.

When the earl saw that he could do no good with his engines, he caused them to cease. Then he called to him his miners, to the intent that they should make a mine under all the walls, the which was not soon made.

How Sir Walter of Manny found in the town of La Réole the sepulchre of his father (1345).
[Ch. 110]

WHILE this siege endured and that the miners were a-work, the Lord Walter of Manny remembered how that his father was slain going a pilgrimage to Saint James, and how he heard in his youth how he should be buried in La Réole or thereabout. Then he made it to be inquired in the town, if there were any man could show him his father's tomb, he should have a hundred crowns for his labour: and there was an aged man came to Sir Walter and said, 'Sir, I think I can bring you near to the place where your father was buried.' Then the Lord of Manny said, 'If your words be true, I shall keep covenant and more.'

Now ye shall hear the manner how the Lord Walter's father was slain. It was true that sometime there was a bishop in Cambrésis, a Gascon born of the house of Mirepoix; and so it fortuned that in his days there was at a time a great tourneying before Cambrai, whereas there were five hundred knights on both parties. And there was a knight Gascon tourneyed with the Lord of Manny, father to Sir Walter, and this knight of Gascony was so sore hurt and beaten, that he had never health after, but died. This knight was of kin to the said bishop; wherefore the Lord of Manny was in his indignation and of all his lineage.

A two or three year after, certain good men laboured to make peace between them, and so they did; and for amends the Lord of Manny was bound to go a pilgrimage to Saint James. And so he went thitherward. And as he came forby the town of La Réole, the same season the Earl Charles of Valois, brother to King Philip, lay at siege before La Réole, the which as then was English, and divers other towns and cities then pertaining to the King of England, father to the king that laid siege to Tournai: so that the Lord of Manny, after the returning of his pilgrimage, he came to see the Earl of Valois, who was there as king. And as the Lord of Manny went at night to his lodging, he was watched by the way by certain of them of the lineage of him that the Lord of Manny had made his pilgrimage for, and so without the earl's lodging he was slain and murdered, and no man knew who did it. Howbeit they of that lineage were held suspect in the matter, but they were so strong and made such excuses, that the matter passed, for there was none that would pursue the Lord of Manny's quarrel. Then the Earl of Valois caused him to be buried in a little chapel in the field, the which as then was without the town of La Réole. And when the Earl of Valois had won the town, then the walls were made more larger, so that the chapel was within the town.

Thus was Sir Walter of Manny's father slain; and this old man remembered all this matter, for he was present when he was buried. Then Sir Walter of Manny went with this good aged man to the place whereas his father was buried, and there they found a little tomb of marble over him, the which his servants laid on him after he was buried. Then the old man said, 'Sir, surely under this tomb lieth your father.' Then the Lord of Manny read the scripture on the tomb, the which was in Latin, and there he found that the old man had said truth, and gave him his reward. And within two days after he made the tomb to be raised and the bones of his father to be taken up and put in a coffer, and after did send them to Valenciennes in the county of Hainault, and in the Friars there made them to be buried again honourably, and did there his obsequy right goodly, the which is yet kept yearly.

How the Earl of Derby won the castle of La Réole (1345).   [Ch. III]

NOW let us return to the siege about the castle of La Réole, the which had endured eleven weeks. So long wrought the miners that at last they came under the base court, but under the donjon they could not get, for it stood on a hard rock. Then Sir Agot des Baux, their captain, said to his company, 'Sirs, we be undermined, so that we are in great danger.' Then they were all sore afraid and said, 'Sir, ye are in great danger, and we also, without ye find some remedy; ye are our chief and we will obey you truly. We have kept this house right honourably a long season, and though we now make a composition, we cannot be blamed. Assay if ye can get grant of the Earl of Derby to let us depart, our lives and goods saved, and we to deliver to him this castle.'

Then Sir Agot descended down from the high tower and did put out his head at a little window and made a token to speak with some of the host. Then he was demanded what he would have: he said he would fain speak with the Earl of Derby or with the Lord of Manny. When the earl knew thereof, he said to the Lord of Manny and the Lord Stafford, 'Let us go to the fortress and know what the captain will say.' Then they rode together, and when Sir Agot saw them, he took off his cap and saluted them, each after other, and said, 'Lords, it is of truth that the French king sent me to this town to defend and to keep it and the castle to my power. And ye know right well how I have acquit myself in that behalf, and yet would if I might: but always a man may not abide in one place. Sir, if it will please you, I and all my company would depart, our lives and goods saved, and we shall yield unto you the fortress.'

Then the Earl of Derby said, 'Sir Agot, ye shall not go so away; we know right well we have so sore oppressed you that we may have you when we list, for your fortress standeth but upon stays. Yield you simply, and we will receive you.' Sir Agot said: 'Sir, if we did so, I think in you so much honour and gentleness, that ye would deal but courteously with us, as ye would the French king should deal with any of your knights. For God's sake, sir, blemish not your nobleness for a poor sort of soldiers that be here within, who hath won with much pain and peril their poor living, whom I have brought hither out of Provence, of Savoy, and out of Dauphiné. Sir, know for truth that if the least of us should not come to mercy, as well as the best, we will rather sell our lives in such wise that all the world should speak of us. Sir, we desire you to bear us some company of arms, and we shall pray for you.'

Then the earl and the other two lords went apart and spake together. They spake long together of divers things; finally they regarded the truth of Sir Agot, and considered how he was a stranger, and also they saw that they could not undermine the donjon, [and so] they agreed to receive them to mercy. Then the earl said to Sir Agot, 'Sir, we would gladly to all strangers bear good company of arms. I am content that ye and all your company depart with your lives saved, so that you bear away nothing but your armour.' 'So be it,' quoth Sir Agot. Then he went to his company and showed them how he had sped. Then they did on their harness and took their horses, whereof they had no more but six. Some bought horses of the Englishmen, the which they paid for truly. Thus Sir Agot des Baux departed from La Réole and yielded up the castle to the Englishmen, and Sir Agot and his company went to Toulouse.

How Sir Godfrey Harcourt was banished out of France (1345). [Ch. 114]

IN this season Sir Godfrey of Harcourt fell in the indignation of the French king, who was a great baron in Normandy and brother to the Earl of Harcourt, lord of Saint-Sauveur-le-Vicomte and divers other towns in Normandy. And it was said all was but for envy, for a little before he was as great with the king and with the Duke of Normandy as he would desire; but he was as then openly banished the realm of France, and if the king could have got him in his ire, he would have served him as he did Sir Oliver of Clisson, who was beheaded the year before at Paris. This Sir Godfrey had some friends, who gave him warning secretly how the king was displeased with him. Then he avoided the realm as soon as he might, and went into Brabant to the duke there, who was his cousin, who received him joyfully. And there he tarried a long space and lived of such revenues as he had in Brabant, for out of France he could get nothing: the king had seized all his lands there of Cotentin, and took the profit thereof himself. The Duke of Brabant could in no wise get again this knight into the king's favour, for nothing that he could do. This displeasure cost greatly the realm of France after, and specially the country of Normandy, for the tokens thereof remained a hundred year after, as ye shall hear in this history.

Of the death of James van Artevelde of Ghent (1345). [Ch. 115]

IN this season reigned in Flanders in great prosperity and puissance James van Artevelde of Ghent, who was as great with the King of England as he would desire; and he had promised the king to make him lord and heritor of Flanders, and to endow his son the Prince of Wales therewith, and to make the county of Flanders a dukedom. For the which cause about the feast of Saint John Baptist, the year of our Lord God MCCCXLV, the King of England was come to Sluys with many lords and knights, and had brought thither with him the young prince his son, on the trust of the promise of James van Artevelde. The king with all his navy lay in the haven of Sluys, and there he kept his house, and thither came to visit him his friends of Flanders.

There were great councils between the king and James van Artevelde on the one party and the councils of the good towns of Flanders on the other party: so that they of the country were not of the agreement with the king nor with James van Artevelde who preached to them that they should disherit the Earl Louis their own natural lord, and also his young son Louis, and to enherit the son of the King of England; the which thing they said surely they would never agree unto. And so the last day of their council, the which was kept in the haven of Sluys in the king's great ship called the *Katherine*, there they gave a final answer by common accord, and said, 'Sir, ye have desired us to a thing that is great and weighty, the which hereafter may sore touch the country of Flanders and our heirs. Truly we know not at this day no person in the world that we love the preferment of so much as we do yours; but, sir, this thing we cannot do alone, without that all the commonalty of Flanders accord to the same. Sir, we shall go home, and every man speak with his company generally in every town, and as the most part agree, we shall be content. And within a month we shall be here with you again and then give you a full answer, so that ye shall be content.' The king nor James van Artevelde could as then have none other answer: they would fain have had a short day, but it would not be. So thus departed that council, and every man went home to their own towns.

James van Artevelde tarried a little season with the king, and still he promised the king to bring them to his intent. But he was deceived, for as soon as he came to Ghent, he went no more out again, for such of Ghent as had been at Sluys at the council there, when they were returned to Ghent, or James van Artevelde was come into the town, great and small they assembled in the market-place, and there it was openly shown what request the King of England had made to them by the setting on of James van Artevelde. Then every man began to murmur against James, for that request pleased them nothing, and said that by the grace of God there should no such untruth be found in them, as willingly to disherit their natural lord and his issue to enherit a stranger. And so they all departed from the market-place, not content with James van Artevelde.

Now behold and see what fortune fell. If he had been as welcome to Ghent as he was to Bruges and Ypres, they would [have] agreed to his opinion as they did, but he trusted so much in his prosperity and greatness, that he thought soon to reduce them to his pleasure.

When he returned, he came into Ghent about noon. They of the town knew of his coming, and many were assembled together in the street whereas he should pass, and when they saw him they began to murmur and began to run together, three heads in one hood, and said, 'Behold yonder great master, who will order all Flanders after his pleasure, the which is not to be suffered.' Also there were words sown through all the town, how James van Artevelde had nine year assembled all the revenues of Flanders without any count given, and thereby hath kept his estate, and also sent great riches out of the country into England secretly. These words set them of Ghent on fire, and as he rode through the street, he perceived that there was some new matter against him, for he saw such as were wont to make reverence to him as he came by, he saw them turn their backs toward him and enter into their houses. Then he began to doubt, and as soon as he was alighted in his lodging, he closed fast his gates, doors and windows: this was scant done but all the street was full of men, and specially of them of the small crafts. There they assailed his house both behind and before and the house broken up. He and his within the house defended themselves a long space, and slew and hurt many without, but finally he could not endure, for three parts of the men of the town were at that assault.

When James saw that he was so sore oppressed, he came to a window with great humility bare-headed, and said with fair language, 'Good people what aileth you? Why be you so sore troubled against me? In what manner have I displeased you? Show me and I shall make you amends at your pleasures.' Then such as heard him answered all with one voice, 'We will have account made of the great treasure of Flanders, that ye have sent out of the way without any title of reason.' Then James answered meekly and said, 'Certainly sirs, of the treasure of Flanders I never took nothing. Withdraw yourselves patiently into your houses and come again tomorrow in the morning, and I shall make you so good account, that of reason ye shall be content.' Then all they answered and said, 'Nay, we will have account made incontinent; ye shall not escape us so. We know for truth that ye have sent great riches into England without our knowledge, wherefore ye shall die.' When he heard that word he joined his hands together, and sore weeping said, 'Sirs, such as I am ye have made me, and ye have sworn to me or this to defend me against all persons, and now ye would slay me without reason. Ye may do it an ye will, for I am but one among you all. For God's sake take better advice, and remember the time past, and consider the great graces and courtesies that I have done to you; ye would now render to me a small reward for the great goodness that I have done to you, and to your town in time past. Ye know right well merchandise was nigh lost in all this country, and by my means it is recovered. Also I have governed you in great peace and rest, for in the time of my governing ye have had all things as ye would wish, corn, riches and all other merchandise.' Then they all cried with one voice, 'Come down to us and preach not so high, and give us account of the great treasure of Flanders, that ye have governed so long without any account making, the which pertaineth not to an officer to do, as to receive the goods of his lord or of a country without account.'

When James saw that he could not appease them, he drew in his head and closed his window, and so thought to steal out on the back-side into a church that joined to his house. But his house was so broken that four hundred persons were entered into his house, and finally there he was taken and slain without mercy and one Thomas Denis gave him his death-stroke. Thus James van Artevelde ended his days, who had been a great master in Flanders. Poor men first mounteth up, and unhappy men slayeth them at the end.* These tidings anon spread abroad the country: some were sorry thereof and some were glad.

In this season the Earl Louis of Flanders was at Termonde, and he was right joyous when he heard of the death of James van Artevelde, his old enemy; howbeit yet he durst not trust them of Flanders, nor go to Ghent.

When the King of England, who lay all this season at Sluys abiding the answer of the Flemings, heard how they of Ghent had slain James van Artevelde, his great friend, he was sore displeased. Incontinent he departed from Sluys and entered into the sea, sore threatening the Flemings and the country of Flanders, and said how his death should be well revenged. Then the councils of the good towns of Flanders imagined well how the King of England would be sore displeased with this deed. Then they determined to go and excuse themselves, specially they of Bruges, Ypres, Courtrai, Oudenarde and of [the] Franc. They sent into England to the king for a safe-conduct, that they might come to their excuse. The king who was as then somewhat assuaged of his displeasure, granted their desire. Then there came into England men of estate out of the good towns of Flanders, except Ghent. This was about the feast of Saint Michael, and the king being at Westminster beside London. There they so meekly excused them of the death of James van Artevelde, and sware solemnly that they knew nothing thereof until it was done: if they had, he was the man they would have defended to the best of their powers, and said how they were right sorry of his death, for he had governed the country right wisely. And also they said that though they of Ghent had done that deed, they should make a sufficient amends, also saying to the king and his council, that though he be dead, yet the king was never the farther off from the love and favour of them of Flanders in all things except the inheritance of Flanders, the which in no wise they of Flanders will put away from the right heirs. Saying also to the king, 'Sir, ye have fair issue, both sons and daughters: as for the Prince of Wales your eldest son, he cannot fail but to be a great prince, without the inheritance of Flanders. Sir, ye have a young daughter and we have a young lord who is heritor of Flanders; we have him in our keeping. May it please you to make a marriage between them two, so ever after the county of Flanders shall be in the issue of your child.'

These words and such others appeased the king, and finally was content with the Flemings and they with him. And so little and little the death of James van Artevelde was forgotten.

* A mistranslation for 'Poor men first raised him up and bad men killed him at the last.'

How Sir John of Hainault became French (1345).
[Ch. 117]

ANON after, the French king entreated and caused the Earl of Blois to entreat this Lord John of Hainault to become French, promising to give him more revenues in France than he had in England, to be assigned where he would himself devise. To this request he did not lightly agree, for he had spent all the flower of his youth in the service of the King of England, and was ever well-beloved with the king.

When the Earl Louis of Blois, who had married his daughter and had by her three sons, Louis, John and Guy, saw that he could not win him by that means, he thought he would assay another way, as to win the Lord of Fagnolle, who was chief companion and greatest of counsel with the Lord John of Hainault. And so they between them devised to make him believe that they of England would not pay him his pension, wherewith Sir John of Hainault was sore displeased, so that he renounced his service and goodwill that he bare to the King of England. And when the French king knew thereof, incontinent he sent sufficient messengers to him, and so retained him of his council with certain wages, and recompensed him in France with as much or more than he had in England.

How John Norwich escaped from Angoulême when the town was yielded to the Frenchmen (1346). [Ch. 119]

THUS these lords of France held a great season siege before Angoulême, and they ran over all the country that the Englishmen had won before, and did much trouble, and took many prisoners and great preys, the which they brought to their host. The two brothers of Bourbon achieved great laud and praise for always they went forth with the foremost.

When John Norwich saw that the duke would not depart thence till he had the town at his pleasure, and perceived how their victuals began to waste and that the Earl of Derby made no manner to rescue them; and also he saw well how they of the town inclined greatly to the French party, for they would have turned French or that time if they had durst, therefore he doubted of treason, wherefore he thought to save himself and his company.

On the eve of the Purification of our Lady, all alone he went to the walls of the city, without showing to any man what he would do. He made a token with his hat to them of the host; they that saw the sign came thither and demanded what he would. He said he would gladly speak with the Duke of Normandy or with one of his marshals. Incontinent this was showed to the duke who went thither and certain knights with him.

As soon as the captain saw the duke, he took off his cap and saluted the duke, and the duke saluted him and said, 'John, how is it with you, will you yield yourself?' 'Sir,' quoth he, 'I am not so yet determined; but, sir, I would desire you in the honour of our Lady, whose day shall be tomorrow, that ye would grant a truce to endure all only but tomorrow, so that you nor we, none to grieve other, but to be in peace that day.' The duke said, 'I am content'. And so they departed.

The next day, which was Candlemas Day, John Norwich and his company armed them and trussed all that they had to bear away; then they opened their gate and issued out. Then they of the host began to stir. Then the captain rode on before to them, and said, 'Sirs, beware, do no hurt to none of us, for we will do none; we have truce for this day all only, agreed by the duke your captain. If ye know it not, go and demand of him, for by reason of this truce, we may ride this day whither we will.' The duke was demanded what was his pleasure in this matter. The duke answered and said, 'Let them depart whither they will, a God's name, for we cannot let them, for I will keep that I have promised.' Thus John Norwich departed and all his company, and passed the French host without any damage and went to Aiguillon; and when the knights there knew how he had saved himself and his company, they said he had beguiled his enemies by a good subtlety.

The next day after, they of the city of Angoulême went to council and determined to yield up the town to the duke. They sent to him into the host certain messengers, who at last sped so well, that the duke took them to mercy and pardoned them all his evil-will; and so entered into the city and into the castle, and took homage of the citizens, and made captain there Antony Villers, and set a hundred soldiers with him.

Then the duke went to the castle of Damassene, where he held siege fifteen days and every day assault. Finally it was won, and all that were within slain. The duke gave that castle and the lands thereto to a squire of Beausse, called Le Borgne de Milly. Then the duke came to Tonneins, on the river of Garonne, and there lay at siege a certain space. At last they within yielded up, their goods and lives saved, and to be safely conducted to Bordeaux. So the strangers departed, but they of the town came under the obeisance of the duke. The duke tarried about the river of Garonne, till it was past Easter. And then he went to Port-Sainte-Marie on the same river, and there were a two hundred Englishmen that kept the town and the passage and was well-fortified, but it was taken with assault and all they within. Then there were set new captains and men of war, and new repaired the town, and then the duke went to Aiguillon.

How the Duke of Normandy laid siege to Aiguillon with a hundred thousand men (1346). [Ch. 120]

THE Duke of Normandy and these lords of France did so much that they came to the castle of Aiguillon. There they laid their siege about the fair meadows,

G

along by the river able to bear ships, every lord among his own company and every constable by himself, as it was ordained by the marshals. This siege endured till the feast of Saint-Rémy. There were well a hundred thousand men of war,* a-horseback and afoot. They made lightly every day two or three assaults, and most commonly from the morning till it was near night without ceasing, for ever there came new assaulters that would not suffer them within to rest.

The lords of France saw well they could not come well to the fortress without they passed the river, the which was large and deep. Then the duke commanded that a bridge should be made, whatsoever it cost, to pass the river. There were set a-work more than three hundred workmen, who did work day and night.

When the knights within saw this bridge more than half-made over the river, they decked three ships and entered into them a certain, and so came on the workmen and chased them away, with their defenders; and there they brake all to pieces that had been long a-making. When the French lords saw that, then they apparelled other ships to resist against their ships. And then the workmen began again to work on the bridge, on trust of their defenders. And when they had worked half a day and more, Sir Walter of Manny and his company entered into a ship, and came on the workmen, and made them to leave work and to recule back, and brake again all that they had made. This business was nigh every day, but at last the Frenchmen kept so well their workmen, that the bridge was made perforce. And then the lords and all their army passed over in manner of battle, and they assaulted the castle a whole day together without ceasing, but nothing they won. And at night they returned to their lodgings, and they within amended all that was broken, for they had with them workmen enough.

The next day the Frenchmen divided their assaulters into four parts, the first to begin in the morning and to continue till nine, the second till noon, the third to evensong time, and the fourth till night. After that manner they assailed the castle six days together. Howbeit they within were not so sore travailed, but always they defended themselves so valiantly, that they without won nothing, but only the bridge without the castle. Then the Frenchmen took other counsel. They sent to Toulouse for eight great engines, and they made there four greater, and they made all twelve to cast day and night against the castle, but they within were so well pavised, that never a stone of their engines did them any hurt; it brake somewhat the covering of some houses. They within had also great engines, the which brake down all the engines without, for in a short space they brake all to pieces six of the greatest of them without.

During this siege oftentimes Sir Walter of Manny issued out with a hundred or sixscore companions, and went on that side the river a-foraging, and returned again with great preys in the sight of them without. On a day, the Lord Charles of Montmorency, marshal of the host, rode forth with a five hundred with him,

* More probably about 60,000.

and when he returned, he drove before him a great number of beasts that he had got together in the country to refresh the host with victuals; and by adventure he encountered with Sir Walter of Manny. There was between them a great fight and many overthrown, hurt, and slain; the Frenchmen were five against one.

Tidings thereof came into Aiguillon. Then every man that might issued out, the Earl of Pembroke first of all and his company; and when he came he found Sir Walter of Manny afoot enclosed with his enemies, and did marvels in arms. Incontinent he was rescued and remounted again, and in the mean season, some of the Frenchmen chased their beasts quickly into the host, or else they had lost them, for they that issued out of Aiguillon set so fiercely on the Frenchmen, that they put them to the flight, and delivered their company that were taken and took many Frenchmen prisoners, and Sir Charles of Montmorency had much work to escape. Then the Englishmen returned into Aiguillon. Thus every day almost there were such encounters, besides the assaults.

On a day all the whole host armed them, and the duke commanded that they of Toulouse, of Carcassone, of Beaucaire, should make assault from the morning till noon, and they of Rouergue, Cahors and Agenois from noon till night; and the duke promised whosoever could win the bridge of the gate should have in reward a hundred crowns. Also the duke, the better to maintain this assault, he caused to come on the river divers ships and barges. Some entered into them to pass the river, and some went by the bridge. At the last some of them took a little vessel and went under the bridge, and did cast great hooks of iron to the draw-bridge, and then drew it to them so sore that they brake the chains of iron that held the bridge, and so pulled down the bridge perforce. Then the Frenchmen leapt on the bridges so hastily, that one overthrew another, for every man desired to win the hundred crowns. They within cast down bars of iron, pieces of timber, pots of lime and hot water, so that many were overthrown from the bridge into the water and into the dykes, and many slain and sore hurt; howbeit the bridge was won perforce, but it cost more than it was worth, for they could not for all that win the gate. Then they drew aback to their lodgings for it was late. Then they within issued out, and new made again their drawbridge, stronger than ever it was before.

The next day there came to the duke two cunning men, masters in carpentry, and said, 'Sir, if ye will let us have timber and workmen, we shall make four scaffolds as high or higher than the walls.' The duke commanded that it should be done, and to get carpenters in the country and to give them good wages. So these four scaffolds were made in four ships, but it was long first, and cost much or they were finished. Then such as should assail the castle in them were appointed and entered. And when they were passed half the river, they within the castle let go four martinets that they had newly made, to resist against these scaffolds. These four martinets did cast out so great stones, and so often fell on the scaffolds, that in a short space they were all too broken, so that they that were within them could not be pavised by them, so that they were fain to draw back again: and or they were again at land one of the scaffolds drowned in the water, and the most part of them that were within it; the which was great damage, for therein were good knights, desiring their bodies to advance.

When the duke saw that he could not come to his intent by that means, he caused the other three scaffolds to rest. Then he could see no way how he might get the castle, and he had promised not to depart thence till he had it at his will, without the king his father did send for him. Then he sent the Constable of France and the Earl of Tancarville to Paris to the king, and there they showed him the state of the siege of Aiguillon. The king's mind was that the duke should lie there still, till he had won them by famine, since he could not have them by assault.

How the King of England came over the sea again to rescue them in Aiguillon (1346).
[Ch. 121]

THE King of England, who had heard how his men were sore constrained in the castle of Aiguillon, then he thought to go over the sea into Gascony with a great army. There he made his provision, and sent for men all about his realm and in other places, where he thought to speed for his money. In the same season the Lord Godfrey of Harcourt came into England, who was banished out of France. He was well-received with the king and retained to be about him, and had fair lands assigned him in England to maintain his degree.

Then the king caused a great navy of ships to be ready in the haven of Southampton, and caused all manner of men of war to draw thither. About the feast of Saint John Baptist, the year of our Lord God MCCCXLVI, the king departed from the queen and left her in the guiding of the Earl of Kent his cousin; and he stablished the Lord Percy and the Lord Neville to be wardens of his realm with the Archbishop of York, the Bishop of Lincoln, and the Bishop of Durham, for he never voided his realm but that he left ever enough at home to keep and defend the realm, if need were. Then the king rode to Southampton, and there tarried for wind. Then he entered into his ship and the Prince of Wales with him, and the Lord Godfrey of Harcourt, and all other lords, earls, barons, and knights, with all their companies. They were in number a four thousand men of arms, and ten thousand archers, beside Irishmen and Welshmen that followed the host afoot.

Now I shall name you certain of the lords that went over with King Edward in that journey. First, Edward, his eldest son, Prince of Wales, who as then was of the age of thirteen years* or thereabout; the Earls of Hereford, Northampton,

* This Prince of Wales, better known as the Black Prince, was in fact sixteen.

Arundel, Cornwall, Warwick, Huntingdon, Suffolk and Oxford; and of barons the Lord Mortimer, who was after Earl of March, the Lords John, Louis, and Roger of Beauchamp, and the Lord Raynold Cobham. Of lords, the Lord of Mowbray, Ros, Lucy, Felton, Bradestan, Multon, Delaware, Mohun, Basset, Berkeley and Willoughby, with divers other lords; and of bachelors there was John Chandos, Fitzwarren, Peter and James Audley, Roger of Bartholomew of Burghersh, and Richard of Pembridge, with divers other that I cannot name. Few there were of strangers: there was [of the county] of Hainault, Sir Wulfart of Ghistelles, and five or six other knights of Germany, and many other that I cannot name. Thus they sailed forth that day in the name of God. They were well onward on their way towards Gascony, but on the third day there rose a contrary wind and drove them on the marches of Cornwall, and there they lay at anchor six days.

In that space the king had other counsel by the means of Sir Godfrey Harcourt. He counselled the king not to go into Gascony, but rather to set aland in Normandy, and said to the king, 'Sir, the country of Normandy is one of the plenteous countries of the world. Sir, on jeopardy on my head, if ye will land there, there is none that shall resist you. The people of Normandy have not been used to the war, and all the knights and squires of the country are now at the siege before Aiguillon with the duke; and sir, there ye shall find great towns that be not walled, whereby your men shall have such winning that they shall be the better thereby twenty year after; and sir, ye may follow with your army till ye come to Caen in Normandy. Sir, I require you believe me in this voyage.' The king, who was as then but in the flower of his youth, desiring nothing so much as to have deeds of arms, inclined greatly to the saying of the Lord Harcourt, whom he called cousin. Then he commanded the mariners to set their course to Normandy, and he took into his ship the token of the admiral the Earl of Warwick, and said how he would be admiral for that voyage, and so sailed on before as governor of that navy, and they had wind at will.

Then the king arrived in the isle of Cotentin, at a port called Saint-Vaast-la-Hougue. Tidings anon spread abroad how the Englishmen were aland. The towns of Cotentin sent word thereof to Paris, to King Philip: he had well heard before how the King of England was on the sea with a great army, but he wist not what way he would draw, either into Normandy, Brittany, or Gascony.

As soon as he knew that the King of England was aland in Normandy, he sent his constable, the Earl of Guines, and the Earl of Tancarville, who were but newly come to him from his son from the siege at Aiguillon, to the town of Caen, commanding them to keep that town against the Englishmen. They said they would do their best. They departed from Paris with a good number of men of war, and daily there came more to them by the way; and so came to the town of Caen where they were received with great joy of men of the town and of the country thereabout, that were drawn thither for surety. These lords took heed for the provision of the town, the which as then was not walled. The king thus was arrived at the port Saint-Vaast-la-Hougue near to Saint-Sauveur-le-Vicomte, the right heritage to the Lord Godfrey of Harcourt, who as then was there with the King of England.

How the King of England rode in three battles through Normandy (1346).   [Ch. 122]

WHEN the King of England arrived in the [port] Saint-Vaast-la-Hougue, the king issued out of his ship, and the first foot that he set on the ground, he fell so rudely, that the blood burst out of his nose. The knights that were about him took him up and said, 'Sir, for God's sake enter again into your ship, and come not aland this day, for this is but an evil sign for us.' Then the king answered quickly and said, 'Wherefore this is a good token for me, for the land desireth to have me.' Of the which answer all his men were right joyful. So that day and night the king lodged on the sands, and in the meantime discharged the ships of their horses and other baggages. There the king made two marshals of his host, the one the Lord Godfrey of Harcourt, and the other the Earl of Warwick, and the Earl of Arundel constable. And he ordained that the Earl of Huntingdon should keep the fleet of ships with a hundred men of arms and four hundred archers. And also he ordained three battles, one to go on his right-hand, closing to the sea-side, and the other on his left-hand, and the king himself in the midst, and every night to lodge all in one field.

Thus they set forth as they were ordained, and they that went by the sea took all the ships that they found in their ways. And so long they went forth, what by sea and what by land, that they came to a good port, and to a good town called Barfleur, the which incontinent was won, for they within gave up for fear of death. Howbeit, for all that, the town was robbed, and much gold and silver there found, and rich jewels: there was found so much riches, that the boys and villeins of the host set nothing by good furred gowns. They made all the men of the town issue out and to go into the ships, because they would not suffer them to be behind them, for fear of rebelling again.

After the town of Barfleur was thus taken and robbed without burning, then they spread abroad in the country and did what they list, for there was not to resist them. At last they came to a great and a rich town called Cherbourg; the town they won and robbed it, and burnt part thereof, but into the castle they could not come, it was so strong and well-furnished with men of war. Then they passed forth and came to Montebourg, and took it and robbed and burnt it clean. In this manner they burnt many other towns in that country, and won so much riches, that it was marvel to reckon it. Then they came to a great town well-closed, called Carentan, where there was also a strong castle, and many soldiers within to keep it; then the lords came out of their ships and fiercely made assault.

The burgesses of the town were in great fear of their lives, wives and children. They suffered the Englishmen to enter into the town against the will of all the soldiers that were there; they put all their goods to the Englishmen's pleasures. They thought that most advantage. When the soldiers within saw that, they went into the castle. The Englishmen went into the town, and two days together they made sore assaults, so that when they within saw no succour, they yielded up, their lives and goods saved, and so departed. The Englishmen had their pleasure of that good town and castle, and when they saw that they might not maintain to keep it, they set fire therein and burnt it, and made the burgesses of the town to enter into their ships, as they had done with them of Barfleur, Cherbourg and Montebourg, and of other towns that they had won on the sea-side. All this was done by the battle that went by the sea-side, and by them on the sea together.

Now let us speak of the king's battle. When he had sent his first battle along by the sea-side, as ye have heard, whereof one of his marshals the Earl of Warwick was captain and the Lord Cobham with him, then he made his other marshal to lead his host on his left hand, for he knew the issues and entries of Normandy better than any other did there. The Lord Godfrey as marshal rode forth with five hundred men of arms, and rode off from the king's battle as six or seven leagues, in burning and exiling the country, the which was plentiful of everything: the granges full of corn, the houses full of all riches, rich burgesses, carts and chariots, horse, swine, muttons, and other beasts. They took what them list and brought into the king's host, but the soldiers made no count to the king nor to none of his officers of the gold and silver that they did get: they kept that to themselves. Thus Sir Godfrey of Harcourt rode every day off from the king's host and for most part every night resorted to the king's field.

The king took his way to Saint-Lô, in Cotentin, but or he came there he lodged by a river, abiding for his men that rode along by the sea-side. And when they were come, they set forth their carriage, and the Earl of Warwick, the Earl of Suffolk, Sir Thomas Holland and Sir Raynold Cobham, and their company, rode out on the one side and wasted and exiled the country, as the Lord Harcourt had done; and the king ever rode between these battles, and every night they lodged together.

Of the great assembly that the French king made to resist the King of England (1346).
[Ch. 123]

THUS by the Englishmen was burnt, exiled, robbed, wasted and pilled, the good plentiful country of Normandy. Then the French king sent for the Lord

John of Hainault, who came to him with a great number. Also the king sent for other men of arms, dukes, earls, barons, knights and squires, and assembled together the greatest number of people that had been seen in France a hundred year before. He sent for men into so far countries that it was long or they came together, whereof the King of England did what him list in the mean season. The French king heard well what he did, and sware and said how they should never return again unfought withal, and that such hurts and damages as they had done should be dearly revenged; wherefore he had sent letters to his friends in the Empire, to such as were farthest off, and also to the gentle King of Bohemia, and to the Lord Charles his son, who from thenceforth was called King of Germany. He was made king by the aid of his father and the French king, and had taken on him the arms of the Empire. The French king desired them to come to him with all their powers, to the intent to fight with the King of England, who burnt and wasted his country.

These princes and lords made them ready with great number of men of arms, of Germans, Bohemians and Luxemburgers, and so came to the French king. Also King Philip sent to the Duke of Lorraine, who came to serve him with three hundred spears. Also there came the Earl [of] Salm in Saumois, the Earl of Sarrebruck, the Earl of Flanders, the Earl William of Namur, every man with a fair company.

Ye have heard here before of the order of the Englishmen, how they went to three battles, the marshals on the right-hand and on the left, the king and the Prince of Wales his son in the midst. They rode but small journeys, and every day took their lodgings between noon and three of the clock, and found the country so fruitful that they needed not to make no provision for their host, but all only for wine, and yet they found reasonably sufficient thereof. It was no marvel though they of the country were afraid, for before that time they had never seen men of war, nor they wist not what war or battle meant. They fled away as far as they might hear speaking of the Englishmen, and left their houses well stuffed, and granges full of corn, they wist not how to save and keep it.

The King of England and the prince had in their battle a three thousand men of arms and six thousand archers and a ten thousand men afoot, beside them that rode with the marshals. Thus as ye have heard, the king rode forth, wasting and burning the country, without breaking of his order. He left the city of Coutances, and went to a great town called Saint-Lô, a rich town of drapery and many rich burgesses. In that town there were dwelling an eight or nine-score burgesses, crafty men. When the king came there, he took his lodging without, for he would never lodge in the town for fear of fire, but he sent his men before, and anon the town was taken and clean robbed. It was hard to think the great riches that there was won, in cloths specially; cloth would there have been sold good cheap, if there had been any buyers.

Then the king went toward Caen, the which was a greater town and full of drapery and other merchandise, and rich burgesses, noble ladies and damosels, and fair churches, and specially two great and rich abbeys, one of the Trinity, another of Saint Stephen; and on the one side of the town, one of the fairest castles of all Normandy, and captain therein was Robert of Blangy, with three hundred Genoese. And in the town was the Earl of Eu and of Guines, Constable of France, and the Earl of Tancarville with a good number of men of war.

The King of England rode that day in good order, and lodged all his battles together that night, a two leagues from Caen in a town with a little haven called Ouistreham, and thither came all his navy of ships with the Earl of Huntingdon who was governor of them.

The constable and the other lords of France that night watched well the town of Caen, and in the morning armed them with all them of the town. Then the constable ordained that none should issue out, but keep their defences on the walls, gate, bridge and river, and left the suburbs void, because they were not closed; for they thought they should have enough to do to defend the town, because it was not closed but with the river. They of the town said how they would issue out, for they were strong enough to fight with the King of England. When the constable saw their goodwills, he said, 'In the name of God be it, ye shall not fight without me.' Then they issued out in good order, and made good face to fight and to defend them and to put their lives in adventure.

Of the battle of Caen, and how the Englishmen took the town (1346).   [Ch. 124]

THE same day the Englishmen rose early and apparelled them ready to go to Caen. The king heard mass before the sun-rising, and then took his horse and the prince his son, with Sir Godfrey of Harcourt marshal and leader of the host, whose counsel the king much followed. Then they drew toward Caen with their battles in good array, and so approached the good town of Caen.

When they of the town, who were ready in the field, saw these three battles coming in good order with their banners and standards waving in the wind, and the archers, the which they had not been accustomed to see, they were sore afraid, and fled away toward the town without any order or good array, for all that the constable could do: then the Englishmen pursued them eagerly. When the constable and the Earl Tancarville saw that, they took a gate at the entry and saved themselves and certain with them, for the Englishmen were entered into the town. Some of the knights and squires of France, such as knew the way to the castle, went thither, and the captain there received them all, for the castle was large. The Englishmen in the chase slew many, for they took none to mercy. Then the constable and the Earl of Tancarville, being in the little tower at the bridge foot, looked along the street and saw their men slain without mercy: they doubted to fall in their hands. At last they saw an English knight with one eye called Sir Thomas Holland, and a five or six other knights with him; they knew them, for they had seen them before in Prussia; in Granada, and in other viages. Then they called Sir Thomas, and said how they would yield themselves prisoners. Then Sir Thomas came thither with his company and mounted up into the gate, and there found the said lords with twenty-five knights with them, who yielded them to Sir Thomas; and he took them for his prisoners and left company to keep them, and then mounted again on his horse and rode into the streets, and saved many lives of ladies, damosels, and cloisterers from defiling, for the soldiers were without mercy.

It fell so well the same season for the Englishmen, that the river, which was able to bear ships, at that time was so low that men went in and out beside the bridge. They of the town were entered into their houses, and cast down into the street stones, timber, and iron, and slew and hurt more than five hundred Englishmen: wherewith the king was sore displeased. At night when he heard thereof, he commanded that the next day all should be put to the sword and the town burnt: but then Sir Godfrey of Harcourt said, 'Dear sir, for God's sake assuage somewhat your courage, and let it suffice you that ye have done. Ye have yet a great voyage to do, or ye come before Calais, whither ye purpose to go. And, sir, in this town there is much people who will defend their houses, and it will cost many of your men their lives, or ye have all at your will, whereby peradventure ye shall not keep your purpose to Calais, the which should redound to your rack. Sir, save your people, for ye shall have need of them or this month pass; for I think verily your adversary King Philip will meet with you to fight, and ye shall find many strait passages and encounters, wherefore your men, and ye had more, shall stand you in good stead; and sir, without any further slaying, ye shall be lord of this town; men and women will put all that they have to your pleasure.' Then the king said, 'Sir Godfrey, you are our marshal, ordain everything as ye will.'

Then Sir Godfrey with his banner rode from street to street, and commanded in the king's name none to be so hardy to put fire in any house, to slay any person, nor to violate any woman. When they of the town heard that cry, they received the Englishmen into their houses, and made them good cheer; and some opened their coffers, and bade them take what they list, so they might be assured of their lives. Howbeit there were done in the town many evil deeds, murders, and robberies.

Thus the Englishmen were lords of the town three days and won great riches, the which they sent by barques and barges to Saint-Sauveur, by the river of Ouistreham, a two leagues thence, whereas all their navy lay. Then the king sent the Earl of Huntingdon with two hundred men of arms and four hundred archers with his navy and prisoners and riches that they had got, back again to England.

And the king bought of Sir Thomas Holland the Constable of France and the Earl of Tancarville, and paid for them twenty thousand nobles.

How the French king followed the King of England in Beauvoisinois (1346).   [Ch. 126]

NOW let us speak of King Philip, who was at Saint-Denis, and his people about him and daily increased. Then on a day he departed, and rode so long that he came to Coppegueule, a three leagues from Amiens, and there he tarried. The King of England being at Airaines, wist not where for to pass the river of Somme, the which was large and deep, and all bridges were broken and the passages well kept. Then at the king's commandment his two marshals with a thousand men of arms and two thousand archers went along the river to find some passage, and passed by Longpré, and came to the bridge of Rémy, the which was well kept with a great number of knights and squires and men of the country. The Englishmen alighted afoot and assailed the Frenchmen from the morning till it was noon; but the bridge was so well fortified and defended, that the Englishmen departed without winning of anything.

Then they went to a great town called Fontaine on the river of Somme, the which was clean robbed and burnt, for it was not closed. Then they went to another town called Long-en-Ponthieu. They could not win the bridge, it was so well kept and defended. Then they departed and went to Picquigny, and found the town, the bridge and the castle so well fortified, that it was not likely to pass there; the French king had so well defended the passages, to the intent that the King of England should not pass the river of Somme to fight with him at his advantage, or else to famish him there.

When these two marshals had assayed in all places to find passage and could find none, they returned again to the king and showed how they could find no passage in no place. The same night the French king came to Amiens with more than a hundred thousand men. The King of England was right pensive, and the next morning heard mass before the sun-rising and then dislodged. And every man followed the marshals' banners, and so rode in the country of Vimeu, approaching to the good town of Abbeville, and found a town thereby, whereunto was come much people of the country in trust of a little defence that was there. But the Englishmen anon won it, and all they that were within slain, and many taken of the town and of the country. The king took his lodging in a great hospital that was there.

The same day the French king departed from Amiens, and came to Airaines about noon, and the Englishmen were departed thence in the morning. The Frenchmen found there great provision that the Englishmen had left behind them, because they departed in haste. There they found flesh ready on the broaches, bread and pasties in the ovens, wine in tuns and barrels, and the tables ready laid. There the French king lodged and tarried for his lords. That night the King of England was lodged at Oisemont.

At night when the two marshals were returned, who had that day overrun the country to the gates of Abbeville and to Saint-Valery, and made a great skirmish there, then the king assembled together his council and made to be brought before him certain prisoners of the country of Ponthieu and of Vimeu. The king right courteously demanded of them if there were any among them that knew any passage beneath Abbeville, that he and his host might pass over the river of Somme; if he would show him thereof, he should be quit of his ransom, and twenty of his company for his love. There was a varlet called Gobin Agace, who stepped forth and said to the king, 'Sir, I promise you on the jeopardy of my head, I shall bring you to such a place, whereas ye and all your host shall pass the river of Somme without peril. There be certain places in the passage that ye shall pass twelve men afront two times between day and night, ye shall not go in the water to the knees; but when the flood cometh, the river then waxeth so great, that no man can pass; but when the flood is gone, the which is two times between day and night, then the river is so low that it may be passed without danger, both a-horseback and afoot. The passage is hard in the bottom with white stones, so that all your carriage may go surely; therefore the passage is called Blanche-taque. An ye make ready to depart betimes, ye may be there by the sun-rising.' The king said, 'If this be true that ye say, I quit thee thy ransom and all thy company, and moreover shall give thee a hundred nobles.' Then the king commanded every man to be ready at the sound of the trumpet to depart.

Of the battle of Blanche-taque between the King of England and Sir Godemar du Fay. [Ch. 127]

THE King of England slept not much that night, for at midnight he arose and sounded his trumpet. Then incontinent they made ready carriages and all things, and at the breaking of the day they departed from the town of Oisemont, and rode after the guiding of Gobin Agace, so that they came by the sun-rising to Blanche-taque; but as then the flood was up so that they might not pass. So the king tarried there till it was prime: then the ebb came.

The French king had his currours in the country, who brought him word of the demeanour of the Englishmen. Then he thought to close the King of England between Abbeville and the river of Somme, and so to fight with him at his pleasure. And when he was at Amiens he had ordained a great baron of Normandy, called Sir Godemar du Fay, to go and keep the passage of Blanche-taque, where the Englishmen must pass, or else in none other place. He had with him a thousand men of arms and six thousand afoot, with the Genoese. So they went by Saint-Riquier in Ponthieu, and from thence to Crotoy, whereas the passage lay. And also he had with him a great number of men of the country, and also a great number of them of Montreuil, so that they were a twelve thousand men one and other.

When the English host was come thither, Sir Godemar du Fay arranged all his company to defend the passage. The King of England let not for all that, but when the flood was gone, he commanded his marshals to enter into the water in the name of God and Saint George. Then they that were hardy and courageous entered on both parties, and many a man reversed. There were some of the Frenchmen of Artois and Picardy that were as glad to joust in the water as on the dry land.

The Frenchmen defended so well the passage at the issuing out of the water that they had much to do. The Genoese did them great trouble with their crossbows. On the other side the archers of England shot so wholly together, that the Frenchmen were fain to give place to the Englishmen. There was a sore battle, and many a noble feat of arms done on both sides. Finally the Englishmen passed over and assembled together in the field; the king and the prince passed and all the lords. Then the Frenchmen kept none array, but departed he that might best. When Sir Godemar saw that discomfiture, he fled and saved himself. Some fled to Abbeville and some to Saint-Riquier. They that were there afoot could not flee, so that there were slain a great number of them of Abbeville, Montreuil, Arras, and of Saint-Riquier: the chase endured more than a great league. And as yet all the Englishmen were not past the river, and certain currours of the King of Bohemia and of Sir John Hainault came on them that were behind, and took certain horses and carriages and slew divers or they could take the passage.

The French king the same morning was departed from Airaines, trusting to have found the Englishmen between him and the river of Somme; but when he heard how that Sir Godemar du Fay and his company were discomfited, he tarried in the field and demanded of his marshals what was best to do. They said, 'Sir, ye cannot pass the river but at the bridge of Abbeville, for the flood is come in at Blanche-taque.' Then he returned and lodged at Abbeville.

The King of England when he was past the river, he thanked God, and so rode forth in like manner as he did before. Then he called Gobin Agace, and did quit him his ransom and all his company, and gave him a hundred nobles and a good horse. And so the king rode forth fair and easily and thought to have lodged in a great town called Noyelles; but when he knew that the town pertained to the Countess d'Aumale, sister to the Lord Robert of Artois, the king assured the town and country as much as pertained to her, and so went forth. And his marshals rode to Crotoy on the sea-side and burnt the town, and found in the haven many ships and barques charged with wines of Poitou, pertaining to the merchants of Saintonge and of Rochelle: they brought the best thereof to the king's host. Then one of the marshals rode to the gates of Abbeville, and from thence to Saint-Riquier, and after to the town of Rue-Saint-Esprit. This was on a Friday, and both battles of the marshals returned to the king's host about noon, and so lodged all together near to Crécy in Ponthieu.

The King of England was well informed how the French king followed after him to fight. Then he said to his company, 'Let us take here some plot of ground, for we will go no farther till we have seen our enemies. I have good cause here to abide them, for I am on the right heritage of the queen, my mother, the which land was given at her marriage. I will challenge it of mine adversary Philip of Valois.' And because that he had not the eighth part in number of men as the French king had, therefore he commanded his marshals to choose a plot of ground somewhat for his advantage. And so they did, and thither the king and his host went. Then he sent his curours to Abbeville, to see if the French king drew that day into the field or not. They went forth and returned again, and said how they could see none appearance of his coming. Then every man took their lodging for that day, and to be ready in the morning, at the sound of the trumpet, in the same place.

This Friday the French king tarried still in Abbeville abiding for his company, and sent his two marshals to ride out to see the dealing of the Englishmen; and at night they returned, and said how the Englishmen were lodged in the fields. That night the French king made a supper to all the chief lords that were there with him, and after supper the king desired them to be friends each to other. The king looked for the Earl of Savoy, who should come to him with a thousand spears, for he had received wages for a three months of them at Troyes in Champagne.

Of the order of the Englishmen at Crécy, and how they made three battles afoot. [Ch. 128]

ON the Friday, as I said before, the King of England lay in the fields, for the country was plentiful of wines and other victual, and if need had been, they had provision following in carts and other carriages. That night the king made a supper to all his chief lords of his host and made them good cheer. And when they were all departed to take their rest, then the king entered into his oratory and knelt down before the altar, praying God devoutly, that if he fought the next day, that he might achieve the journey to his honour. Then about midnight he laid him down to rest, and in the morning he rose betimes and heard mass, and the prince his son with him, and the most part of his company were confessed and houselled. And after the mass said, he commanded every man to be armed and to draw to the field to the same place before appointed. Then the king caused a park to be made by the wood-side behind his host, and there was set all carts and carriages, and in the park were all their horses, for every man was afoot; and into this park there was but one entry.

Then he ordained three battles. In the first was the young Prince of Wales, with him the Earl of Warwick, and Oxford, the Lord Godfrey of Harcourt, Sir Raynold Cobham, Sir Thomas Holland, the Lord Stafford, the Lord of Mohun, the Lord Delaware, Sir John Chandos, Sir Bartholomew de Burghersh, Sir Robert Nevill, the Lord Thomas Clifford, the Lord Bourchier, the Lord de Latimer, and divers other knights and squires that I cannot name; they were an eight hundred men of arms and two thousand archers, and a thousand of other with the Welshmen. Every lord drew to the field appointed under his own banner and pennon.

In the second battle was the Earl of Northampton, the Earl of Arundel, the Lord Ros, the Lord Lucy, the Lord Willoughby, the Lord Basset, the Lord of Saint-Aubin, Sir Louis Tufton, the Lord of Multon, the Lord Lascelles, and divers other, about an eight hundred men of arms and twelve hundred archers. The third battle had the king; he had seven hundred men of arms and two thousand archers. Then the king leapt on a hobby, with a white rod in his hand, one of his marshals on the one hand and the other on the other hand. He rode from rank to rank, desiring every man to take heed that day to his right and honour. He spake it so sweetly, and with so good countenance and merry cheer, that all such as were discomfited took courage in the seeing and hearing of him. And when he had thus visited all his battles, it was then nine of the day. Then he caused every man to eat and drink a little, and so they did at their leisure. And afterward they ordered again their battles: then every man lay down on the earth and by him his salet and bow, to be the more fresher when their enemies should come.

The order of the Frenchmen at Crécy, and how they beheld the demeanour of the Englishmen.
[Ch. 129]

THIS Saturday the French king rose betimes, and heard mass in Abbeville in his lodging in the Abbey of Saint Peter, and he departed after the sun-rising. When he was out of the town two leagues approaching toward his enemies, some of his lords said to him, 'Sir, it were good that ye ordered your battles, and let all your footmen pass somewhat on before, that they be not troubled with the horsemen.' Then the king sent four knights, the Moine [of] Bazeilles, the Lord of Noyers, the Lord of Beaujeu and the Lord d'Aubigny, to ride to aview the English host; and so they rode so near that they might well see part of their dealing. The Englishmen saw them well and knew well how they were come thither to aview them; they let them alone and made no countenance toward them, and let them return as they came.

And when the French king saw these four knights return again, he tarried till they came to him, and said, 'Sirs, what tidings?' These four knights each of them looked on other, for there was none would speak before his companion. Finally the king said to [the] Moine, who pertained to the King of Bohemia, and had done in his days so much that he was reputed for one of the valiantest knights of the world, 'Sir, speak you.' Then he said, 'Sir, I shall speak, sith it pleaseth you, under the correction of my fellows. Sir, we have ridden and seen the behaving of your enemies; know ye for truth they are rested in three battles abiding for you. Sir, I will counsel you as for my part, saving your displeasure, that you and all your company rest here and lodge for this night, for or they that be behind of your company be come hither, and or your battles be set in good order, it will be very late and your people be weary and out of array, and ye shall find your enemies fresh and ready to receive you. Early in the morning ye may order your battles at more leisure, and advise your enemies at more deliberation, and to regard well what way ye will assail them, for sir, surely they will abide you.'

Then the king commanded that it should be so done. Then his two marshals one rode before, another behind, saying to every banner, 'Tarry and abide here in the name of God and Saint Denis.' They that were foremost tarried, but they that were behind would not tarry, but rode forth, and said how they would in no wise abide till they were as far forward as the foremost: and when they before saw them come on behind, then they rode forward again, so that the king nor his marshals could not rule them. So they rode without order or good array, till they came in sight of their enemies. And as soon as the foremost saw them, they reculed them aback without good array; whereof they behind had marvel and were abashed, and thought that the foremost company had been fighting. Then they might have had leisure and room to have gone if they had list; some went forth and some abode still. The commons, of whom all the ways between Abbeville and Crécy were full, when they saw that they were near to their enemies, they took their swords and cried, 'Down with them, let us slay them all!' There was no man, though he were present at the journey, that could imagine or show the truth of the evil order that was among the French party, and yet they were a marvellous great number.

That I write in this book I learned specially of the Englishmen, who well beheld their dealing; and also certain knights of Sir John of Hainault's, who was always about King Philip, showed me as they knew.

Of the battle of Crécy between the King of England and the French king (1346). [Ch. 130]

THE Englishmen who were in three battles, lying on the ground to rest them, as soon as they saw the Frenchmen approach, they rose upon their feet fair and easily without any haste and arranged their battles. The first, which was the prince's battle, the archers there stood in manner of a herse* and the men of arms in the

* In triangle formation.

bottom of the battle. The Earl of Northampton and the Earl of Arundel with the second battle were on a wing in good order, ready to comfort the prince's battle, if need were.

The lords and knights of France came not to the assembly together in good order, for some came before and some came after, in such haste and evil order, that one of them did trouble another. When the French king saw the Englishmen, his blood changed, and said to his marshals, 'Make the Genoese go on before and begin the battle, in the name of God and Saint Denis'. There were of the Genoese crossbows about a fifteen thousand, but they were so weary of going afoot that day a six leagues armed with their crossbows, that they said to their constables, 'We be not well ordered to fight this day, for we be not in the case to do any great deed of arms; we have more need of rest.' These words came to the Earl of Alençon, who said, 'A man is well at ease to be charged with such a sort of rascals, to be faint and fail now at most need.' Also the same season there fell a great rain and an eclipse* with a terrible thunder, and before the rain there came flying over both battles a great number of crows, for fear of the tempest coming. Then anon the air began to wax clear and the sun to shine fair and bright, the which was right in the Frenchmen's eyes and on the Englishmen's backs.

When the Genoese were assembled together and began to approach, they made a great leap and cry to abash the Englishmen, but they stood still and stirred not for all that. Then the Genoese again the second time made another leap and a fell cry, and stepped forward a little, and the Englishmen removed not one foot. Thirdly, again they leapt and cried, and went forth till they came within shot: then they shot fiercely with their crossbows. Then the English archers stepped forth one pace, and let forth their arrows so wholly and so thick that it seemed snow. When the Genoese felt the arrows piercing through heads, arms and breasts, many of them cast down their crossbows and did cut their strings, and returned discomfited.

When the French king saw them fly away, he said, 'Slay these rascals, for they shall let and trouble us without reason.' Then ye should have seen the men of arms dash in among them and killed a great number of them; and ever still the Englishmen shot whereas they saw thickest press. The sharp arrows ran into the men of arms and into their horses, and many fell, horse and men, among the Genoese, and when they were down, they could not relieve again: the press was so thick that one overthrew another. And also among the Englishmen there were certain rascals that went afoot with great knives, and they went in among the men of arms and slew and murdered many as they lay on the ground, both earls, barons, knights and squires, whereof the King of England was after displeased, for he had rather they had been taken prisoners.

The valiant King of Bohemia, called Charles of Luxembourg, son to the noble

* Mistranslation of 'eclistre', flash of lightning.

H

Emperor, Henry of Luxembourg, for all that he was nigh blind, when he understood the order of the battle, he said to them about him, 'Where is the Lord Charles, my son?' His men said, 'Sir, we cannot tell, we think he be fighting.' Then he said, 'Sirs, ye are my men, my companions, and friends in this journey. I require you, bring me so far forward that I may strike one stroke with my sword.' They said they would do his commandment, and to the intent that they should not lose him in the press, they tied all their reins of their bridles each to other, and set the king before to accomplish his desire, and so they went on their enemies.

The Lord Charles of Bohemia, his son, who wrote himself King of Germany and bare the arms, he came in good order to the battle; but when he saw that the matter went awry on their party, he departed, I cannot tell you which way. The king his father was so far forward that he struck a stroke with his sword, yea and more than four, and fought valiantly and so did his company. And they adventured themselves so forward that they were there all slain, and the next day they were found in the place about the king, and all their horses tied each to other.

The Earl of Alençon came to the battle right ordinately and fought with the Englishmen, and the Earl of Flanders also on his part. These two lords with their companies coasted the English archers and came to the prince's battle, and there fought valiantly long. The French king would fain have come thither when he saw their banners, but there was a great hedge of archers before him. The same day the French king had given a great black courser to Sir John of Hainault, and he made the Lord Thierry of Senzeille to ride on him and to bear his banner. The same horse took the bridle in the teeth, and brought him through all the currours of the Englishmen. And as he would have returned again, he fell in a great dyke and was sore hurt, and had been there dead, an his page had not been, who followed him through all the battles and saw where his master lay in the dyke, and had none other let but for his horse, for the Englishmen would not issue out of their battle for taking of any prisoner. Then the page alighted and relieved his master; then he went not back again the same way that they came, there was too many in his way.

This battle between Broye and Crécy this Saturday was right cruel and fell, and many a feat of arms done that came not to my knowledge. In the night* divers knights and squires lost their masters, and sometime came on the Englishmen, who received them in such wise that they were ever nigh slain; for there was none taken to mercy nor to ransom, for so the Englishmen were determined.

In the morning the day of the battle, certain Frenchmen and Germans perforce opened the archers of the prince's battle and came and fought with the men of arms hand to hand. Then the second battle of the Englishmen came to succour the prince's battle, the which was time, for they had as then much ado; and they with the prince sent a messenger to the king, who was on a little windmill hill.

* Towards nightfall.

Then the knight said to the king, 'Sir, the Earl of Warwick, and the Earl of Oxford, Sir Raynold Cobham, and other such as be about the prince your son, are fiercely fought withal and are sore handled; wherefore they desire you that you and your battle will come and aid them, for if the Frenchmen increase, as they doubt they will, your son and they shall have much ado.' Then the king said, 'Is my son dead or hurt, or on the earth felled?' 'No, sir,' quoth the knight, 'but he is hardly matched, wherefore he hath need of your aid.' 'Well,' said the king, 'return to him, and to them that sent you hither, and say to them that they send no more to me for any adventure that falleth, as long as my son is alive. And also say to them that they suffer him this day to win his spurs; for if God be pleased, I will this journey be his and the honour thereof, and to them that be about him.' Then the knight returned again to them and showed the king's words, the which greatly encouraged them, and repined in that they had sent to the king as they did.

Sir Godfrey of Harcourt would gladly that the Earl of Harcourt, his brother, might have been saved, for he heard say by them that saw his banner how that he was there in the field on the French party. But Sir Godfrey could not come to him betimes, for he was slain or he could come at him, and so was also the Earl of Aumale, his nephew. In another place, the Earl of Alençon and the Earl of Flanders fought valiantly, every lord under his own banner; but finally they could not resist against the puissance of the Englishmen, and so there they were also slain, and divers other knights and squires. Also the Earl Louis of Blois, nephew to the French king, and the Duke of Lorraine fought under their banners, but at last they were closed in among a company of Englishmen and Welshmen, and they were slain for all their prowess. Also there was slain the Earl of Auxerre, the Earl of Saint-Pol and many other.

In the evening the French king, who had left about him no more than a three-score persons, one and other, whereof Sir John of Hainault was one, who had remounted once the king, for his horse was slain with an arrow, then he said to the king, 'Sir, depart hence, for it is time. Lose not yourself wilfully; if ye have loss at this time, ye shall recover it again another season.' And so he took the king's horse by the bridle, and led him away in a manner perforce.

Then the king rode till he came to the castle of Broye. The gate was closed, because it was by that time dark. Then the king called the captain, who came to the walls and said, 'Who is that calleth there this time of night?' Then the king said, 'Open your gate quickly, for this is the fortune of France.' The captain knew then it was the king, and opened the gate and let down the bridge. Then the king entered, and he had with him but five barons, Sir John of Hainault, Sir Charles of Montmorency, the Lord of Beaujeu, the Lord d'Aubigny, and the Lord of Montsault. The king would not tarry there, but drank and departed thence about midnight, and so rode by such guides as knew the country till he came in the morning to Amiens, and there he rested.

This Saturday the Englishmen never departed from their battles for chasing of any man, but kept still their field and ever defended themselves against all such as came to assail them. This battle ended about evensong time.

How the next day after the battle the Englishmen discomfited divers Frenchmen (1346).
[Ch. 131]

ON this Saturday, when the night was come and that the Englishmen heard no more noise of the Frenchmen, then they reputed themselves to have the victory, and the Frenchmen to be discomfited, slain and fled away. Then they made great fires and lighted up torches and candles, because it was very dark. Then the king avaled down from the little hill whereas he stood, and of all that day till then, his helm came never off on his head. Then he went with all his battle to his son the prince and embraced him in his arms and kissed him, and said, 'Fair son, God give you good perseverance. Ye are my good son, thus ye have acquitted you nobly: ye are worthy to keep a realm.' The prince inclined himself to the earth, honouring the king his father. This night they thanked God for their good adventure and made no boast thereof, for the king would that no man should be proud or make boast, but every man humbly to thank God.

On the Sunday in the morning, there was such a mist that a man might not see the breadth of an acre of land from him. Then there departed from the host, by the commandment of the king and marshals, five hundred spears and two thousand archers, to see if they might see any Frenchmen gathered again together in any place. The same morning out of Abbeville and Saint-Riquier in Ponthieu, the commons of Rouen and of Beauvais issued out of their towns, not knowing of the discomfiture the day before. They met with the Englishmen, weening they had been Frenchmen. And when the Englishmen saw them, they set on them freshly, and there was a sore battle; but at last the Frenchmen fled and kept none array. There were slain in the ways and in hedges and bushes more than seven thousand, and if the day had been clear there had never a one escaped. Anon after, another company of Frenchmen were met by the Englishmen: the Archbishop of Rouen, and the great Prior of France, who also knew nothing of the discomfiture the day before, for they heard that the French king should have fought the same Sunday, and they were going thitherward. When they met with the Englishmen, there was a great battle, for they were a great number, but they could not endure against the Englishmen, for they were nigh all slain, few escaped; the two lords were slain.

This morning the Englishmen met with divers Frenchmen that had lost their way on the Saturday and had lain all night in the fields, and wist not where the king was nor the captains. They were all slain, as many as were met with. And it was showed me that of the commons and men afoot of the cities and good towns of France, there was slain four times as many as were slain the Saturday in the great battle.

How the next day after the battle of Crécy they that were dead were numbered by the Englishmen.   [Ch. 132]

THE same Sunday, as the King of England came from mass, such as had been sent forth returned and showed the king what they had seen and done, and said, 'Sir, we think surely there is now no more appearance of any of our enemies.' Then the king sent to search how many were slain and what they were. Sir Raynold Cobham and Sir Richard Stafford with three heralds went to search the field and country; they visited all them that were slain and rode all day in the fields, and returned again to the host as the king was going to supper. They made just report of what they had seen, and said how there were eleven great princes dead, fourscore banners, twelve hundred knights, and more than thirty thousand other.*

The Englishmen kept still their field all that night. On the Monday in the morning the king prepared to depart. The king caused the dead bodies of the great lords to be taken up and conveyed to Montreuil, and there buried in holy ground, and made a cry in the country to grant truce for three days, to the intent that they of the country might search the field of Crécy to bury the dead bodies. Then the king went forth and came before the town of Montreuil-by-the-sea, and his marshals ran toward Hesdin and burnt Waben and Serain, but they did nothing to the castle, it was so strong and so well kept. They lodged that night on the river of Hesdin towards Blangy. The next day they rode toward Boulogne and came to the town of Wissant. There the king and the prince lodged, and tarried there a day to refresh his men. And on the Wednesday the king came before the strong town of Calais.

How the King of England laid siege to Calais, and how all the poor people were put out of the town (1346).   [Ch. 133]

IN the town of Calais there was captain a knight of Burgundy called Sir John de Vienne, and with him was Sir Arnold d'Audrehem, Sir John de Surie, Sir Baldwin de Bellebrune, Sir Geoffrey de la Motte, Sir Pepin de Wierre, and divers other knights and squires. When the King of England was come before Calais, he laid his siege and ordained bastides between the town and the river. He made carpenters to make houses and lodgings of great timber, and set the houses like

* Michael of Northburgh says there were 1,542 killed in the battle and about 2,000 the next day.

streets and covered them with reed and broom, so that it was like a little town. And there was everything to sell, and a market-place to be kept every Tuesday and Saturday for flesh and fish, mercery ware, houses for cloth, for bread, wine and all other things necessary, such as came out of England or out of Flanders; there they might buy what they list.

The Englishmen ran oftentimes into the country of Guines, and into Ternois, and to the gates of Saint-Omer, and sometime to Boulogne: they brought into their host great preys. The king would not assail the town of Calais, for he thought it but a lost labour; he spared his people and his artillery, and said how he would famish them in the town with long siege, without the French king come and raise his siege perforce.

When the captain of Calais saw the manner and the order of the Englishmen, then he constrained all poor and mean people to issue out of the town. And on a Wednesday there issued out of men, women, and children, more than seventeen hundred. And as they passed through the host they were demanded why they departed, and they answered and said, because they had nothing to live on. Then the king did them that grace, that he suffered them to pass through his host without danger, and gave them meat and drink to dinner, and every person two pence sterling in alms, for the which divers many of them prayed for the king's prosperity.

How the Duke of Normandy brake up his siege before Aiguillon (1346).   [Ch. 134]

THE Duke of Normandy being at siege before the strong castle of Aiguillon, so it was that about the midst of August, he made a great assault to the castle so that the most part of his host were at the assault. Thither was come newly the Lord Philip of Burgundy, Earl of Artois and of Boulogne, and cousin-german to the Duke of Normandy. He was as then a young lusty knight, and as soon as the skirmish was begun, he took his horse with the spurs and came on the skirmish-ward, and the horse took the bit in his teeth and bore away his master, and stumbled in a dyke and fell horse and man: the knight was so bruised with the fall that he had never health after, but died of the same hurt.

Then anon after the French king sent for his son the Duke of Normandy, commanding him in any wise to break up his siege before Aiguillon, and to return into France to defend his heritage from the Englishmen. And thereupon the duke took counsel of the lords that were there with him what was best to do, for he had promised not to depart thence till he had won the castle, but the lords counselled him, since the king his father had sent for him, to depart. Then the next day betimes the Frenchmen trussed bag and baggage in great haste and departed toward France. Then they that were within the fortress issued out with the pennon of the Lord Walter of Manny before them. They dashed in among the hinder company of the Frenchmen, and slew and took divers of them to the number of threescore, and brought them into their fortress; and by those prisoners they knew of the journey that the King of England had made that season into France, and how that he lay at siege before Calais.

Or the French king departed from Amiens to Paris-ward after the battle of Crécy, he was so sore displeased with Sir Godemar du Fay, because the king said he did not his duty truly in keeping of the passage of Blanche-taque whereas the Englishmen passed over the river of Somme, so that if the French king could have got him in that heat, it would have cost him his head; and divers of the king's council would that he should have died, and said he was a traitor, and causer of that great loss that the king had at Crécy. But Sir John of Hainault excused him and refrained the king's evil will, for he said how could it lie in his power to resist the whole puissance of the Englishmen, when all the flower of the realm of France together could not resist them.

Then anon after came to the king and to the queen the Duke of Normandy who was well received with them.

How Sir Walter of Manny rode through all France by safe-conduct to Calais (1346).

[Ch. 135]

IT was not long after but that Sir Walter of Manny fell in communication with a knight of Normandy, who was his prisoner, and demanded of him what money he would pay for his ransom. The knight answered and said he would gladly pay three thousand crowns. 'Well,' quoth the Lord Walter, 'I know well ye be kin to the Duke of Normandy and well-beloved with him, that I am sure; an if I would sore oppress you, I am sure ye would gladly pay ten thousand crowns; but I shall deal otherwise with you: I will trust you on your faith and promise. Ye shall go to the duke your lord, and by your means get a safe-conduct for me and twenty other of my company to ride through France to Calais, paying courteously for all our expenses. And if ye can get this of the duke or of the king, I shall clearly quit you your ransom with much thanks, for I greatly desire to see the king my master, nor I will lie but one night in a place till I come there. And if ye cannot do this, return again hither within a month, and yield yourself still as my prisoner.' The knight was content and so went to Paris to the duke his lord, and he obtained this passport for Sir Walter of Manny and twenty horse with him all only. This knight returned to Aiguillon and brought it to Sir Walter, and there he quitted the knight Norman of his ransom.

Then anon after, Sir Walter took his way and twenty horse with him, and so rode through Auvergne. And when he tarried in any place, he showed his letter and so was let pass: but when he came to Orleans, for all his letter he was arrested and brought to Paris, and there put in prison in the Châtelet. When the Duke of Normandy knew thereof, he went to the king his father and showed him how Sir Walter of Manny had his safe-conduct, wherefore he required the king as much as he might to deliver him, or else it should be said how he had betrayed him. The king answered and said how he should be put to death, for he reputed him for his great enemy. Then said the duke, 'Sir, if ye do so, surely I shall never bear armour against the King of England, nor all such as I may let.' And at his departing he said that he would never enter again into the king's host: thus the matter stood a certain time.

There was a knight of Hainault, called Sir Mansart d'Esne: he purchased all that he might to help Sir Walter of Manny, and went often in and out to the Duke of Normandy. Finally, the king was so counselled, that he was delivered out of prison and all his cost paid; and the king sent for him to his lodging of Nesle in Paris, and there he dined with the king, and the king presented him great gifts and jewels to the value of a thousand florins. Sir Walter of Manny received them on a condition, that when he came to Calais, that if the King of England his master were pleased that he should take them, then he was content to keep them, or else to send them again to the French king, who said he spake like a noble man.

Then he took his leave and departed, and rode so long by his journeys that he came into Hainault, and tarried at Valenciennes three days; and so from thence he went to Calais, and was welcome to the king. But when the king heard that Sir Walter of Manny had received gifts of the French king, he said to him, 'Sir Walter, ye have hitherto truly served us, and shall do, as we trust. Send again to King Philip the gifts that he gave you, ye have no cause to keep them: we thank God we have enough for us and for you: we be in good purpose to do much good for you, according to the good service that ye have done.'

Then Sir Walter took all those jewels and delivered them to a cousin of his called Mansart, and said, 'Ride into France to the king there and recommend me unto him, and say how I thank him a thousand times of the gift that he gave me; but show him how it is not the pleasure of his king my master that I should keep them, therefore I send them again to him.' This knight rode to Paris and showed all this to the king, who would not receive again the jewels, but did give them to the same knight, Sir Mansart, who thanked the king and was not in will to say nay.

How the King of Scotland during the siege before Calais came into England with a great host (1346).   [Ch. 137]

IT is long now since we spake of King David of Scotland; howbeit till now there was none occasion why, for the truce that was taken was well and truly kept, so that when the King of England had besieged Calais and lay there, then the Scots determined to make war into England and to be revenged of such hurts as they had taken before. For they said then how that the realm of England was void of men of war, for they were, as they said, with the King of England before Calais, and some in Brittany, Poitou and Gascony. The French king did what he could to stir the Scots to that war to the intent that the King of England should break up his siege and return to defend his own realm. The King of Scots made his summons to be at Perth on the river of Tay in Scotland. Thither came earls, barons and prelates of Scotland, and there agreed that in all haste possible they should enter into England. To come in that journey was desired John of the Out Isles, who governed the wild Scots, for to him they obeyed and to no man else. He came with a three thousand of the most outrageous people in all that country.

When all the Scots were assembled, they were of one and other a fifty thousand fighting men. They could not make their assembly so secret but that the Queen of England, who was as then in the marches of the North about York, knew all their dealing: then she sent all about for men and lay herself at York. Then all men of war and archers came to Newcastle with the queen. In the mean season the King of Scots departed from Perth and went to Dunfermline the first day. The next day they passed a little arm of the sea and so came to Stirling, and then to Edinburgh. Then they numbered their company, and they were a three thousand men of arms, knights and squires, and a thirty thousand of other, on hackneys. Then they came to Roxburgh, the first fortress English on that part; captain there was Sir William Montague. The Scots passed by without any assault making, and so went forth burning and destroying the country of Northumberland. And their currours ran to York and burnt as much as was without the walls, and returned again to their host within a day's journey of Newcastle-upon-Tyne.

Of the battle of Newcastle-upon-Tyne between the Queen of England and the King of Scots (1346). [Ch. 138]

THE Queen of England, who desired to defend her country, came to Newcastle-upon-Tyne and there tarried for her men, who came daily from all parts.

When the Scots knew that the Englishmen assembled at Newcastle, they drew thitherward and their currours came running before the town, and at their returning they burnt several small hamlets thereabout, so that the smoke thereof came into the town of Newcastle. Some of the Englishmen would have issued out to have fought with them that made the fires, but the captains would not suffer them to issue out.

The next day the King of Scots, with a forty thousand men, one and other, came and lodged within three little English mile of Newcastle in the land of the Lord Nevill, and the king sent to them within the town, that if they would issue out into the field, he would fight with them gladly. The lords and prelates of England said they were content to adventure their lives with the right and heritage of the King of England, their master. Then they all issued out of the town, and were in number a twelve hundred men of arms, three thousand archers, and seven thousand of other with the Welshmen.

Then the Scots came and lodged against them near together. Then every man was set in order of battle. Then the queen* came among her men and there was ordained four battles, one to aid another. The first had in governance the Bishop of Durham and the Lord Percy; the second the Archbishop of York and the Lord Nevill; the third the Bishop of Lincoln and the Lord Mowbray; the fourth the Lord Edward de Balliol, captain of Berwick, the Archbishop of Canterbury and the Lord Ros: every battle had like number, after their quantity. The queen went from battle to battle desiring them to do their devoir to defend the honour of her lord, the King of England, and in the name of God every man to be of good heart and courage, promising them that to her power she would remember them as well or better as though her lord the king were there personally. Then the queen departed from them, recommending them to God and Saint George.

Then anon after, the battles of the Scots began to set forward, and in likewise so did the Englishmen. Then the archers began to shoot on both parties, but the shot of the Scots endured but a short space, but the archers of England shot so fiercely, so that when the battles approached, there was a hard battle. They began at nine and endured till noon. The Scots had great axes, sharp and hard, and gave with them many great strokes. Howbeit finally the Englishmen obtained the place and victory, but they lost many of their men.

There were slain of the Scots the Earl of Fife, the Earl of Buchan, the Earl Patrick, the Earl of Sutherland, the Earl of Strathern, the Earl of Mar, the Earl John Douglas, and the Lord Alexander Ramsay, who bore the king's banner, and divers other knights and squires. And there the king was taken, who fought valiantly and was sore hurt. A squire of Northumberland took him, called John Copeland, and as soon as he had taken the king, he went with him out of the field with eight of his servants with him, and so rode all that day till he was a fifteen leagues from the place of the battle, and at night he came to a castle called Ogle; and then he said he would not deliver the King of Scots to no man nor woman living, but all only to the King of England, his lord.

The same day there was also taken in the field the Earl Moray, the Earl of March, the Lord William Douglas, the Lord Robert Erskine, the Bishop of Aberdeen, the Bishop of Saint Andrews, and divers other knights and barons. And there were slain of one and other a fifteen thousand, and the other saved themself as well as they might: this battle was beside Newcastle, the year of our Lord MCCCXLVI, the Saturday next after Saint Michael.

* She was in fact not present, being on her way to Calais.

How John Copeland had the King of Scots prisoner, and what profit he got thereby (1346).

[Ch. 139]

WHEN the Queen of England being at Newcastle understood how the journey was for her and her men, she then rode to the place where the battle had been. Then it was showed her how the King of Scots was taken by a squire called John Copeland, and he had carried away the king no man knew whither. Then the queen wrote to the squire commanding him to bring his prisoner the King of Scots, and how he had not well done to depart with him without leave. All that day the Englishmen tarried still in the same place and the queen with them, and the next day they returned to Newcastle.

When the queen's letter was brought to John Copeland, he answered and said, that as for the King of Scots his prisoner, he would not deliver him to no man nor woman living, but all only to the King of England his sovereign lord; as for the King of Scots, he said he should be safely kept, so that he would give account for him. Then the queen sent letters to the king to Calais, whereby the king was informed of the state of his realm. Then the king sent incontinent to John Copeland, that he should come over the sea to him to the siege before Calais. Then the same John did put his prisoner in safe-keeping in a strong castle, and so rode through England till he came to Dover and there took the sea and arrived before Calais.

When the King of England saw the squire he took him by the hand and said, 'Ah! welcome, my squire, that by your valiantness hath taken mine adversary, the King of Scots.' The squire knelt down and said, 'Sir, if God by his grace have suffered me to take the King of Scots by true conquest of arms, sir, I think no man ought to have any envy thereat, for as well God may send by His grace such a fortune to fall to a poor squire, as to a great lord; and, sir, I require your grace be not miscontent with me, though I did not deliver the King of Scots at the commandment of the queen. Sir, I hold of you, as mine oath is to you, and not to her but in all good manner.' The king said, 'John, the good service that ye have done and your valiantness is so much worth, that it must countervail your trespass and be taken for your excuse, and shame have they that bear you any evil will therefor. Ye shall return again home to your house, and then my pleasure is that you deliver your prisoner to the queen my wife; and in a reward I assign you near to your house, whereas ye think best yourself, five hundred pound sterling of yearly rent to you and to your heirs for ever, and here I make you squire for my body.' Then the third day he departed and returned again into England, and when he came home to his own house he assembled together his friends and kin, and so they took the King of Scots and rode with him to the city of York, and there from the king his lord he presented the King of Scots to the queen, and excused him so largely, that the queen and her council were content.

Then the queen made good provision for the city of York, the castle of Roxburgh, the city of Durham, the town of Newcastle-upon-Tyne, and in all other garrisons on the marches of Scotland, and left in those marches the Lord Percy and the Lord Nevill as governor there.

Then the queen departed from York towards London. Then she set the King of Scots in the strong Tower of London, and the Earl Moray and all other prisoners, and set good keeping over them. Then she went to Dover and took the sea, and had so good wind that in a short space she arrived before Calais, three days before the feast of All Saints; for whose coming the king made a great feast and dinner to all the lords and ladies that were there. The queen brought many ladies and damosels with her, as well to accompany her as to see their husbands, fathers, brethren and other friends that lay at siege there before Calais, and had done a long space.

How the French king assembled a great host to raise the King of England from the siege before Calais (1347). [Ch. 144]

KING Philip, who knew well how his men were sore constrained in Calais, commanded every man to be with him at the feast of Pentecost in the city of Amiens or thereabout: there was none durst say nay . . . When they were all at Amiens they took counsel. The French king would gladly that the passages of Flanders might have been opened to him, for then he thought he might send part of his men to Gravelines, and by that way to refresh the town of Calais, and on that side to fight easily with the Englishmen. He sent great messengers to Flanders to treat for that matter, but the King of England had there such friends that they would never accord to that courtesy. Then the French king said how he would go thither on the side toward Burgundy.

The King of England saw well how he could not get Calais but by famine. Then he made a strong castle and a high to close up the passage by the sea. And this castle was set between the town and the sea and was well fortified with springalles, bombards, bows, and other artillery; and in this castle were threescore men of arms and two hundred archers. They kept the haven in such wise that nothing could come in nor out: it was thought that thereby they within should the sooner be famished.

In that season the King of England so exhorted them of Flanders, that there issued out of Flanders a hundred thousand, and went and laid siege to the town of Aire and burnt the country all about . . . . The Flemings did the Frenchmen great trouble or they departed. And when the Flemings were returned, then the French king and his company departed from Arras and went to Hesdin; his host with the carriage held well in length a three leagues of that country, and there he tarried a day, and the next day to Blangy. There he rested to take advice what way to go forth. Then he was counselled to go through the country called la Belme, and that way he took with him a two hundred thousand one and other, and so passed by the county of Fauquembergues, and so came straight to the hill of Sangatte between Calais and Wissant. They came thither in goodly order with banners displayed, that it was great beauty to behold their puissant array. They of Calais, when they saw them lodge, it seemed to them a new siege.

How the King of England made the passages about Calais to be well kept, that the French king should not approach to raise his siege (1347).   [Ch. 145]

YE shall hear what the King of England did and caused to be done when he saw and knew that the French king came with so great an host to raise the siege, the which had cost him so much good and pain of his body, and lost many of his men, and knew well how he had so constrained the town that it could not long endure for default of victuals: it grieved him sore then to depart. Then he advised well how the Frenchmen could not approach neither to his host nor to the town but in two places, either by the downs by the sea-side or else above by the high way, and there was many dykes, rocks and marshes, and but one way to pass, over a bridge called Nieulet bridge. Then the king made all his navy to draw along by the coast of the downs, every ship well garnished with bombards, crossbows, archers, springalles and other artillery, whereby the French host might not pass that way. And the king caused the Earl of Derby to go and keep Nieulet bridge with a great number of men of arms and archers, so that the Frenchmen could not pass no way without they would have gone through the marshes, the which was impossible.

On the other side toward Calais, there was a high tower kept with thirty archers, and they kept the passage of the downs from the Frenchmen, the which was well fortified with great and double dykes. When the Frenchmen were thus lodged on the mount of Sangatte, the commons of Tournai who were a fifteen hundred came to that tower, and they within shot at them, but they passed the dykes and came to the foot of the wall with pikes and hooks. There was a sore assault, and many of them of Tournai sore hurt, but at last they won the tower and all that were within slain and the tower beaten down. The French king sent his marshals to advise what way he might approach to fight with the Englishmen. So they went forth, and when they had advised the passages and straits, they returned to the king and said how in no wise he could come to the Englishmen without he would lose his people. So the matter rested all that day and night after.

The next day after mass, the French king sent to the King of England the Lord Geoffrey of Charny, the Lord Eustace of Ribemont, Guy of Nesle, and the Lord of Beaujeu. And as they rode that strong way they saw well it was hard to pass that way; they praised much the order that the Earl of Derby kept there at the bridge of Nieulet by the which they passed. Then they rode till they came to the king, who was well accompanied with noblemen about him. Then they four alighted and came to the king and did their reverence to him.

Then the Lord Eustace of Ribemont said, 'Sir, the king my master sendeth you word by us that he is come to the mount of Sangatte to do battle with you, but he can find no way to come to you. Therefore, sir, he would that ye should appoint certain of your counsel, and in likewise of his, and they between them to advise a place for the battle.' The King of England was ready advised to answer and said, 'Sirs, I have well understand that ye desire me on the behalf of mine adversary, who keepeth wrongfully from me mine heritage, wherefore I am sorry: say unto him from me if ye list, that I am here and so have been nigh a whole year, and all this he knew right well. He might have come hither sooner if he had willed, but he hath suffered me to abide here so long, the which hath been greatly to my cost and charge. I now could do so much if I would, to be soon lord of Calais, wherefore I am not determined to follow his device and ease, nor to depart from that which I am at the point to win and that I have so sore desired and dearly bought. Wherefore if he nor his men can pass this way, let them seek some other passage if they think to come hither.' Then these lords departed and were conveyed till they were past Nieulet bridge. Then they showed the French king the King of England's answer.

In the mean season while the French king studied how to fight with the King of England, there came into his host two cardinals from Pope Clement in legation, who took great pain to ride between these hosts. And they procured so much that there was granted a certain treaty of accord and a respite between the two kings and their men, being there at siege and in the field all only. And so there were four lords appointed on either party to counsel together and to treat for a peace. For the French king there was the Duke of Burgundy and the Duke of Bourbon, Sir Louis of Savoy, and Sir John Hainault. And for the English party the Earl of Derby, the Earl of Northampton, the Lord Raynold Cobham and the Lord Walter of Manny. And the two cardinals were means between the parties. These lords met three days and many devices put forth, but none took effect. And in the mean season the King of England always fortified his host and field, and made dykes on the downs that the Frenchmen should not suddenly come on them.

These three days passed without any agreement. Then the two cardinals returned to Saint-Omer, and when the French king saw that he could do nothing, the next day he dislodged betimes and took his way to Amiens and gave every man leave to depart. When they within Calais saw their king depart they made great sorrow. Some of the Englishmen followed the tail of the Frenchmen and won somers, carts and carriages, horse, wine and other things, and took prisoners whom they brought into the host before Calais.

How the town of Calais was given up to the King of England (1347).   [Ch. 146]

AFTER that the French king was thus departed from Sangatte, they within Calais saw well how their succour failed them, for the which they were in great sorrow. Then they desired so much their captain, Sir John of Vienne, that he went to the walls of the town and made a sign to speak with some person of the host. When the king heard thereof, he sent thither Sir Walter of Manny and Sir Basset. Then Sir John of Vienne said to them, 'Sirs, ye be right valiant knights in deeds of arms, and ye know well how the king my master hath sent me and other to this town, and commanded us to keep it to his behoof in such wise that we take no blame nor to him no damage; and we have done all that lieth in our power. Now our succours have failed us and we be so sore strained that we have not to live withal, but that we must all die or else enrage for famine, without the noble and gentle king of yours will take mercy on us: the which to do we require you to desire him to have pity on us and to let us go and depart as we be, and let him take the town and castle and all the goods that be therein, the which is great abundance.' Then Sir Walter of Manny said, 'Sir, we know somewhat of the intention of the king our master, for he hath showed it unto us. Surely know for truth it is not his mind that ye nor they within the town should depart so, for it is his will that ye all should put yourselves into his pure will, to ransom all such as pleaseth him and to put to death such as he list. For they of Calais have done him such contraries and despites, and hath caused him to dispend so much good, and lost many of his men, that he is sore grieved against them.' Then the captain said, 'Sir, this is too hard a matter to us. We are here within a small sort of knights and squires, who hath truly served the king our master as well as ye serve yours in like case, and we have endured much pain and unease. But we shall yet endure as much pain as ever knights did rather than to consent that the worst lad in the town should have any more evil than the greatest of us all. Therefore, sir, we pray you that of your humility yet that ye will go and speak to the King of England and desire him to have pity of us, for we trust in him so much gentleness that by the grace of God his purpose shall change.'

Sir Walter of Manny and Sir Basset returned to the king and declared to him all that had been said. The king said he would none otherwise but that they should yield them up simply to his pleasure. Then Sir Walter said, 'Sir, saving your displeasure in this, ye may be in the wrong, for ye shall give by this an evil ensample: if ye send any of us your servants into any fortress, we will not be very glad to go if ye put any of them in the town to death after they be yielded, for in likewise they will deal with us if the case fell like.' The which words divers other lords that were there present sustained and maintained. Then the king said, 'Sirs, I will not be alone against you all; therefore, Sir Walter of Manny, ye shall go and say to the captain that all the grace that he shall find now in me is that they let six of the chief burgesses of the town come out bare-headed, bare-footed and bare-legged, and in their shirts, with halters about their necks, with the keys of the town and castle in their hands, and let them six yield themselves purely to my will, and the residue I will take to mercy.' Then Sir Walter returned and found Sir John of Vienne still on the wall, abiding for an answer. Then Sir Walter showed him all the grace that he could get of the king. 'Well' quoth Sir John, 'Sir, I require you tarry here a certain space till I go into the town and show this to the commons of the town who sent me hither.' Then Sir John went unto the market-place and sounded the common bell. Then incontinent men and women assembled there. Then the captain made report of all that he had done and said, 'Sirs, it will be none otherwise; therefore now take advice and make a short answer.' Then all the people began to weep and to make such sorrow that there was not so hard a heart if they had seen them but that would have had great pity of them; the captain himself wept piteously.

At last the most rich burgess of all the town, called Eustace of Saint-Pierre, rose up and said openly, 'Sirs, great and small, great mischief it should be to suffer to die such people as be in this town, either by famine or otherwise when there is a mean to save them: I think he or they should have great merit of our Lord God that might keep them from such mischief. As for my part, I have so good trust in our Lord God, that if I die in the quarrel to save the residue, that God would pardon me, wherefore to save them I will put my life in jeopardy.' When he had thus said, every man worshipped him, and divers knelt down at his feet with sore weeping and sore sighs. Then another honest burgess rose and said, 'I will keep company with my gossip Eustace.' He was called John d'Aire. Then rose up James of Wissant, who was rich in goods and heritage; he said also that he would hold company with his two cousins. In likewise so did Peter of Wissant his brother. And then rose two other: they said they would do the same. Then they went and apparelled them as the king desired. Then the captain went with them to the gate: there was great lamentation made of men, women and children at their departing. Then the gate was opened and he issued out with the six burgesses and closed the gate again, so that they were between the gate and the barriers.

Then he said to Sir Walter of Manny, 'Sir, I deliver here to you as captain of Calais, by the whole consent of all the people of the town, these six burgesses; and I swear to you truly that they be and were today most honourable, rich and most notable burgesses of all the town of Calais. Wherefore, gentle knight, I require you pray the king to have mercy on them, that they die not.' Quoth Sir Walter, 'I cannot say what the king will do, but I shall do for them the best I can.' Then the barriers were opened, the six burgesses went towards the king, and the captain entered again into the town.

When Sir Walter presented these burgesses to the king, they knelt down and held up their hands and said, 'Gentle king, behold here we six, who were burgesses of Calais and great merchants. We have brought to you the keys of the town and of the castle and we submit ourselves clearly into your will and pleasure, to save the residue of the people of Calais, who have suffered great pain. Sir, we beseech your grace to have mercy and pity on us through your high noblesse.' Then all the earls and barons and other that were there wept for pity. The king looked felly on them, for greatly he hated the people of Calais for the great damages and displeasures they had done him on the sea before. Then he commanded their heads to be stricken off. Then every man required the king for mercy, but he would hear no man in that behalf. Then Sir Walter of Manny said, 'Ah, noble king, for God's sake refrain your courage, ye have the name of sovereign noblesse, therefore now do not a thing that should blemish your renown, nor to give cause to some to speak of you villainy. Every man will say it is a great cruelty to put to death such honest persons, who by their own wills put themselves into your grace to save their company.' Then the king wryed away from him and commanded to send for the hangman, and said, 'They of Calais have caused many of my men to be slain, wherefore these shall die in likewise.' Then the queen, being great with child, knelt down and sore weeping said, 'Ah, gentle sir, since I passed the sea in great peril, I have desired nothing of you; therefore now I humbly require you, in the honour of the Son of the Virgin Mary and for the love of me that ye will take mercy of these six burgesses.' The king beheld the queen and stood still in a study a space, and then said, 'Ah, dame, I would ye had been as now in some other place, ye make such request to me that I cannot deny you; wherefore I give them to you, to do your pleasure with them.' Then the queen caused them to be brought into her chamber, and made the halters to be taken from their necks, and caused them to be new clothed, and gave them their dinner at their leisure; and then she gave each of them six nobles and made them to be brought out of the host in safeguard and set at their liberty.

How the King of England repeopled the town of Calais with Englishmen (1347).   [Ch. 147]

THUS the strong town of Calais was given up to King Edward of England, the year of our Lord God MCCCXLVII in the month of August. The King of England called to him Sir Walter of Manny and his two marshals, the Earl of Warwick and the Earl of Stafford, and said to them, 'Sirs, take here the keys of the town and castle of Calais. Go and take possession there and put in prison all the knights that be there, and all other soldiers that came thither simply to win their living. Cause them to avoid the town, and also all other men, women and children, for I would repeople again the town with pure Englishmen.'

So these three lords with a hundred with them went and took possession of

I

Calais, and did put in prison Sir John de Vienne, Sir John of Surie, Sir Baldwin of Bellebrune and other. Then they made all the soldiers to bring all their harness into a place appointed, and laid it all on a heap in the hall* of Calais. Then they made all manner of people to void and kept there no more persons but a priest and two other ancient personages, such as knew the customs, laws and ordinances of the town, and to sign out the heritages how they were divided. Then they prepared the castle to lodge the king and queen, and prepared other houses for the king's company. Then the king mounted on his horse and entered into the town with trumpets, tabours, nakers, and horns, and there the king lay till the queen was brought abed of a fair lady named Margaret.

The king gave to Sir Walter of Manny divers fair houses within the town, and to the Earl of Stafford, to the Lord of Cobham, to Sir Bartholomew of Burghersh, and to other lords, to repeople again the town. The king's mind was when he came into England to send out of London a thirty-six good burgesses to Calais to dwell there, and to do so much that the town might be peopled with pure Englishmen: the which intent the king fulfilled. Then the new town and bastide that was made without the town was pulled down, and the castle that stood on the haven rashed down, and the great timber and stones brought into the town. Then the king ordained men to keep the gates, walls and barriers, and amended all things within the town. And Sir John de Vienne and his company were sent into England and were half a year at London; then they were put to ransom.

Methink it was great pity of the burgesses and other men of the town of Calais, and women and children, when they were fain to forsake their houses, heritages and goods, and to bear away nothing, and they had no restorement of the French king, for whose sake they lost all. The most part of them went to Saint-Omer.

The Cardinal Guy de Boulogne, who was come into France in legation and was with the French king his cousin in the city of Amiens, he purchased so much that a truce was taken between the Kings of England and of France, their countries and heritages, to endure two years. To this truce all parties were agreed, but Brittany was clearly excepted, for the two ladies made still war one against the other.

Then the King of England and the queen returned into England, and the king made captain of Calais Sir Amery of Pavy, a Lombard born, whom the king had greatly advanced. Then the king sent from London thirty-six burgesses to Calais, who were rich and sage, and their wives and children, and daily increased the number, for the king granted there such liberties and franchises that men were glad to go and dwell there. The same time was brought to London Sir Charles de Blois, who called himself Duke of Brittany. He was put in courteous prison in the Tower of London with the King of Scots and the Earl of Moray; but he had not been there long but, at the request of the Queen of England, Sir Charles her

* Market.

cousin-german was received on his faith and troth, and rode all about London at his pleasure, but he might not lie past one night out of London without it were with the king or with the queen.

Also the same time there was prisoner in England the Earl of Eu and Guines, a right gentle knight. And his dealing was such that he was welcome wheresoever he came, and with the king and queen, lords, ladies and damosels.

Summary.   [Ch. 148-152]

THE truce was broken by brigands who won and plundered various towns and castles. The King of England returned privately to Calais, having learnt of a secret treaty to give up the town to the French party. The king fought under Sir Walter de Manny's banner. He took Sir Eustace de Ribemont prisoner and then set him free, having presented him with his own chaplet of pearls. The death of King Philip of France and the coronation of his son John took place in August and September, 1356. The Prince of Wales made an expedition to Carcassonne and Narbonne in 1355.

Of the assembly that the French king made to fight with the Prince of Wales who rode in Berry (1356).   [Ch. 157]

WHEN the French king had made his journey and reconquered towns and castles in base Normandy, pertaining as then to the King of Navarre whom he held in prison, and was gone back to the city of Paris, it was not long after but that he heard how the Prince of Wales, with a good number of men of war, was far entered in the country of Berry. Then the king said and sware that he would ride and fight with him wheresoever he found him. Then the king made again a special assembly of all nobles and such as held of him. His commandment was, that all manner of excuses laid apart his letters once seen, that every man, on pain of his displeasure, should draw and meet with him in the marches of Blois and Touraine, for the intent to fight with the Englishmen. And the king, to make the more haste, departed from Paris and rode to Chartres, to hear the better of surety what the Englishmen did. There he rested and daily men of war resorted thither from all parts, as of Auvergne, Berry, Burgundy, Lorraine, Hainault, Vermandois, Picardy, Brittany, and Normandy; and ever as they came they were set forward and made their musters, and lodged in the country, by the assignment of the marshals, the Lord John of Clermont and the Lord Arnold d'Audrehem. The king sent also great provision to all his fortresses and garrisons in Anjou, Poitou, Maine and Touraine, and into all the fortresses where he thought the Englishmen should pass, to the intent to close the passages from them and to keep them from victuals, that they should find no forage for them nor their horses.

Howbeit for all that, the prince and his company who were to the number of two thousand men of arms and six thousand archers, rode at their ease and had victuals enough, for they found the country of Auvergne right plentiful; but they would not tarry there but went forth to make war on their enemies. They burnt and exiled the country as much as they might, for when they were entered into a town and found it well replenished of all things, they tarried there a two or three days to refresh them. When they departed they would destroy all the residue, strike out the heads of the vessels of wine, and burn wheat, barley and oats, and all other things, to the intent that their enemies should have no aid thereof . . .
[The French tried to bar the Prince of Wales' escape route to Bordeaux at Romorantin. After a skirmish, the French took refuge in the castle.]

How the Prince of Wales took the castle of Romorantin (1356). [Ch. 158]

THE Prince of Wales heard how his foreriders were a-fighting; then he took that way and came into the town of Romorantin, wherein was much of his people studying how they might get the castle. Then the prince commanded the Lord Sir John Chandos to go and speak with them of the castle. Then Sir John went to the castle gate and made sign to speak with some person within. They that kept the watch there demanded what was his name and who did send him thither. He showed them. Then Sir Boucicault and the hermit of Chaumont came to the barriers. When Sir John saw them he saluted them courteously and said, 'Sirs, I am sent hither to you from my lord the prince, who will be right courteous unto his enemies as me thinketh. He saith that if ye will yield up this fortress to him and yield yourselves prisoners, he will receive you to mercy and keep you good company of arms.' The Lord Boucicault said, 'We are not in purpose to put ourselves in that case: it were great folly, since we have no need so to do. We think to defend ourselves.' So they departed, and the prince lodged there, and his men in the town without at their ease.

The next day every man was armed and under his banner, and began to assail the castle right fiercely. The archers were on the dykes, and shot so wholly together that none durst scant appear at their defences. Some swam over the dykes on boards and other things, with hooks and pikes in their hands, and mined at the walls. And they within cast down great stones and pots with lime. There was slain on the English party a squire called Remonde Derge du Lache. He was of the company of the Captal of Buch. This assault dured all the day without rest. At night the Englishmen drew to their lodgings, and so passed the night. In the morning when the sun was risen the marshals of the hosts sounded the trumpets. Then all such as were ordained to give the assault were ready apparelled, at the which assault the prince was personally, and by reason of his presence greatly encouraged the Englishmen; and not far from him there was a squire called Bernard slain with a stone. Then the prince sware that he would not depart thence till he had the castle and all them within at his pleasure.

Then the assault enforced on every part. Finally they saw that by assaults they could not win the castle, wherefore they ordained engines to cast in wildfire* into the base court. And so they did that all the base court was afire, so that the fire multiplied in such wise that it took into the covering of a great tower covered with reed. And when they within saw that they must either yield to the will of the prince or else perish by fire, then all three lords came down and yielded them to the prince, and so the prince took them with him as his prisoners and the castle was left void.

Of the great host that the French king brought to the battle of Poitiers (1356).   [Ch. 159]

AFTER the taking of the castle of Romorantin and of them that were therein, the prince then and his company rode as they did before, destroying the country approaching to Anjou and to Touraine. The French king, who was at Chartres, departed and came to Blois and there tarried two days, and then to Amboise and the next day to Loches. And then he heard how that the prince was at Touraine and how that he was returning by Poitou: ever the Englishmen was coasted by certain expert knights of France, who always made report to the king what the Englishmen did. Then the king came to La Haye in Touraine, and his men had passed the river of Loire, some at the bridge of Orleans and some at Meung, at Saumur, at Blois, and at Tours and whereas they might. They were in number a twenty thousand men of arms beside other; there were a twenty-six dukes and earls and more than sixscore banners, and the four sons of the king, who were but young, the Duke Charles of Normandy, the Lord Louis, that was from thenceforth Duke of Anjou, and the Lord John Duke of Berry, and the Lord Philip, who was after Duke of Burgundy.

The same season Pope Innocent the Sixth sent the Lord Bertrand, Cardinal of Périgord, and the Lord Nicholas, Cardinal of Urgel, into France to treat for a peace between the French king and all his enemies, first between him and the King of Navarre, who was in prison. And these cardinals oftentimes spake to the king for his deliverance during the siege at Bretuel, but they could do nothing in that behalf.

Then the Cardinal of Périgord went to Tours, and there he heard how the French king hasted sore to find the Englishmen. Then he rode to Poitiers, for he heard how both the hosts drew thitherward. The French king heard how the prince hasted greatly to return, and the king feared that he should escape him

* Greek fire.

and so departed from La Haye in Touraine, and all his company, and rode to Chauvigny where he tarried that Thursday in the town and without along by the river of Creuse; and the next day the king passed the river at the bridge there, weening that the Englishmen had been before him, but they were not. Howbeit they pursued after and passed the bridge that day more than threescore thousand horses, and divers other passed at Châtellerault, and ever as they passed they took their way to Poitiers.

On the other side the prince wist not truly where the Frenchmen were, but they supposed that they were not far off, for they could not find no more forage, whereby they had great fault in their host of victual; and some of them repented that they had destroyed so much as they had done before when they were in Berry, Anjou and Touraine, and in that they had made no better provision.

The same Friday three great lords of France, the Lord of Craon, the Lord Raoul of Coucy and the Earl of Joigny, tarried all day in the town of Chauvigny, and part of their companies. The Saturday they passed the bridge and followed the king, who was then a three leagues before, and took the way among bushes without a woodside to go to Poitiers. The same Saturday the prince and his company dislodged from a little village thereby, and sent before him certain currours to see if they might find any adventure and to hear where the Frenchmen were. They were in number a threescore men of arms well horsed, and with them was the Lord Eustace d'Aubrecicourt and the Lord John of Ghistelles; and by adventure the Englishmen and Frenchmen met together by the foresaid woodside.

The Frenchmen knew anon how they were their enemies. Then in haste they did on their helmets and displayed their banners and came a great pace towards the Englishmen; they were in number a two hundred men of arms. When the Englishmen saw them, and that they were so great a number, then they determined to fly and let the Frenchmen chase them, for they knew well the prince with his host was not far behind. Then they turned their horses and took the corner of the wood, and the Frenchmen after them crying their cries and made great noise. And as they chased, they came on the prince's battle or they were ware thereof themselves. The prince tarried there to have word again from them that he sent forth. The Lord Raoul of Coucy with his banner went so far forward that he was under the prince's banner: there was a sore battle and the knight fought valiantly. Howbeit, he was there taken, and the Earl of Joigny, the Viscount of Brosse, the Lord of Chauvigny and all the other taken or slain, but a few that escaped. And by the prisoners the prince knew how the French king followed* him in such wise that he could not eschew the battle. Then he assembled together all his men and commanded that no man should go before the marshals' banners.

Thus the prince rode that Saturday from the morning till it was against night, so that he came within two little leagues of Poitiers. Then the Captal de Buch,

* Barred his way.

Sir Aymenion of Pommiers, the Lord Bartholomew of Burghersh and the Lord Eustace d'Aubrecicourt, all these the prince sent forth to see if they might know what the Frenchmen did. These knights departed with two hundred men of arms well horsed. They rode so far that they saw the great battle of the king's, they saw all the fields covered with men of arms. These Englishmen could not forbear, but set on the tail of the French host and cast down many to the earth and took divers prisoners, so that the host began to stir, and tidings thereof came to the French king as he was entering into the city of Poitiers. Then he returned again and made all his host do the same, so that Saturday it was very late or he was lodged in the field.

The English currours returned again to the prince and showed him all that they saw and knew, and said how the French host was a great number of people. 'Well,' said the prince, 'in the name of God let us now study how we shall fight with them at our advantage.' That night the Englishmen lodged in a strong place among hedges, vines and bushes, and their host well-watched, and so was the French host.

Of the order of the Frenchmen before the battle of Poitiers (1356).   [Ch. 160]

ON the Sunday in the morning the French king, who had great desire to fight with the Englishmen, heard his mass in his pavilion and was houselled and his four sons with him. After mass there came to him the Duke of Orleans, the Duke of Bourbon, the Earl of Ponthieu, the Lord Jacques of Bourbon, the Duke of Athens, Constable of France, the Earl of Tancarville, the Earl of Sarrebruck, the Earl of Dammartin, the Earl of Ventadour, and divers other great barons of France and of other neighbours holding of France, as the Lord Clermont, the Lord Arnold d'Audrehem, Marshal of France, the Lord of Saint-Venant, the Lord John of Landas, the Lord Eustace Ribemont, the Lord Fiennes, the Lord Geoffrey of Charny, the Lord Châtillon, the Lord of Sully, the Lord of Nesle, Sir Robert Duras and divers other; all these with the king went to counsel.

Then finally it was ordained that all manner of men should draw into the field, and every lord to display his banner and to set forth in the name of God and Saint Denis. Then trumpets blew up through the host and every man mounted on horseback and went into the field, where they saw the king's banner with the wind. There might have been seen great noblesse of fair harness and rich armoury of banners and pennons, for there was all the flower of France: there was none durst abide at home without he would be shamed for ever.

Then it was ordained by the advice of the constable and marshals to be made three battles, and in each ward sixteen thousand men of arms all mustered and passed for men of arms. The first battle the Duke of Orleans to govern, with thirty-six banners and twice as many pennons; the second, the Duke of Normandy and his two brethren the Lord Louis and the Lord John; the third, the king himself. And while that these battles were setting in array, the king called to him the Lord Eustace Ribemont, the Lord John of Landas and the Lord Richard of Beaujeu and said to them, 'Sirs, ride on before to see the dealing of the Englishmen, and advise well what number they be and by what means we may fight with them, either afoot or a-horseback.' These three knights rode forth and the king was on a white courser and said a-high to his men, 'Sirs, among you, when ye be at Paris, at Chartres, at Rouen or at Orleans, then ye do threat the Englishmen and desire to be in arms out against them. Now ye be come thereto: I shall now show you them. Now show forth your evil will that ye bear them and revenge your displeasures and damages that they have done you, for without doubt we shall fight with them.' Such as heard him said, 'Sir, in God's name so be it, that would we see gladly.'

Therewith the three knights returned again to the king, who demanded of them tidings. Then Sir Eustace of Ribemont answered for all and said, 'Sir, we have seen the Englishmen: by estimation they be two thousand men of arms and four thousand archers and a fifteen hundred of other. Howbeit they be in a strong place, and as far as we can imagine they are in one battle. Howbeit they be wisely ordered, and along the way they have fortified strongly the hedges and bushes; one part of their archers are along by the hedge,* so that none can go nor ride that way but must pass by them, and that way must ye go an ye purpose to fight with them. In this hedge there is but one entry and one issue by likelihood that four horsemen may ride a-front. At the end of this hedge whereas no man can go nor ride, there be men of arms afoot and archers afore them in manner of a herse, so that they will not be lightly discomfited.' 'Well', said the king, 'what will ye then counsel us to do?' Sir Eustace said, 'Sir, let us all be afoot, except three hundred men of arms, well horsed, of the best in your host and most hardiest, to the intent they somewhat to break and to open the archers, and then your battles to follow on quickly afoot and so to fight with their men of arms hand to hand. This is the best advice I can give you: if any other think any other way better, let him speak.' The king said, 'Thus shall it be done.'

Then the two marshals rode from battle to battle and chose out a three hundred knights and squires of the most expert men of arms of all the host, every man well armed and horsed. Also it was ordained that the battles of Germans should abide still on horseback to comfort the marshals, if need were, whereof the Earl of Sarrebruck, the Earl of Nidau and the Earl of Nassau were captains. King John of France was there armed, and twenty other in his apparel; and he did put the guiding of his eldest son to the Lord of Saint-Venant, the Lord of Landas and the Lord Thibaut of Vaudenay; and the Lord Arnold of Cervolles, called the archpriest, was armed in the armour of the young Earl of Alençon.

---

* According to a better text, the archers were on both sides of the road.

How the Cardinal of Périgord treated to make agreement between the French king and the prince before the battle of Poitiers.   [Ch. 161]

WHEN the French king's battles was ordered and every lord under his banner among their own men, then it was commanded that every man should cut their spears to a five foot long and every man to put off their spurs. Thus as they were ready to approach, the Cardinal of Périgord came in great haste to the king. He came the same morning from Poitiers. He knelt down to the king and held up his hands and desired him for God's sake a little to abstain setting forward till he had spoken with him. Then he said, 'Sir, ye have here all the flower of your realm against a handful of Englishmen as to regard your company:* and, sir, if ye may have them accorded to you without battle, it shall be more profitable and honourable to have them by that manner rather than to adventure so noble chivalry as ye have here present. Sir, I require you in the name of God and humility, that I may ride to the prince and show him in what danger ye have him in.' The king said, 'It pleaseth me well, but return again shortly.'

The cardinal departed and diligently he rode to the prince, who was among his men afoot. Then the cardinal alighted and came to the prince, who received him courteously. Then the cardinal, after his salutation made, he said, 'Certainly, fair son, if you and your council advise justly the puissance of the French king, ye will suffer me to treat to make a peace between you, an I may.' The prince, who was young and lusty, said, 'Sir, the honour of me and of my people saved, I would gladly fall to any reasonable way.' Then the cardinal said, 'Sir, ye say well, and I shall accord you an I can, for it should be great pity if so many noble-men and other as be here on both parties should come together by battle.' Then the cardinal rode again to the king and said, 'Sir, ye need not to make any great haste to fight with your enemies, for they cannot fly from you though they would, they be in such a ground; wherefore, sir, I require you forbear for this day till tomorrow the sun-rising.' The king was loth to agree thereto, for some of his council would not consent to it, but finally the cardinal showed such reasons that the king accorded that respite. And in the same place there was pight up a pavilion of red silk fresh and rich, and gave leave for that day every man to draw to their lodgings, except the constable's and marshals' battles.

That Sunday all the day the cardinal travailed in riding from the one host to the other gladly to agree them: but the French king would not agree without he might have four of the principallest of the Englishmen at his pleasure, and the prince and all the other to yield themselves simply; howbeit there were many great offers made. The prince offered to render into the king's hands all that ever he had won in that voyage, towns and castles, and to quit all prisoners that he

* 'In comparison with your company'.

or any of his men had taken in that season, and also to swear not to be armed against the French king in seven year after; but the king and his council would none thereof. The uttermost that he would do was that the prince and a hundred of his knights should yield themselves into the king's prison, otherwise he would not: the which the prince would in no wise agree to.

In the mean season that the cardinal rode thus between the hosts in trust to do some good, certain knights of France and of England both rode forth the same Sunday, because it was truce for that day, to coast the hosts and to behold the dealing of their enemies. So it fortuned that the Lord John Chandos rode the same day coasting the French host, and in like manner the Lord of Clermont, one of the French marshals, had ridden forth and aviewed the state of the English host; and as these two knights returned towards their hosts they met together. Each of them bare one manner of device, a blue Lady embroidered in a sunbeam above on their apparel. Then the Lord Clermont said, 'Chandos, how long have ye taken on you to bear my device?' 'Nay, ye bear mine' said Chandos, 'for it is as well mine as yours.' 'I deny that', said Clermont, 'but an it were not for the truce this day between us, I should make it good on you incontinent that ye have no right to bear my device.' 'Ah, sir,' said Chandos, 'ye shall find me tomorrow ready to defend you and to prove by feat of arms that it is as well mine as yours.' Then Clermont said, 'Chandos, these be well the words of you Englishmen, for ye can devise nothing of new, but all that ye see is good and fair.' So they departed without any more doing, and each of them returned to their host.

The Cardinal of Périgord could in no wise that Sunday make any agreement between the parties, and when it was near night he returned to Poitiers. That night the Frenchmen took their ease, they had provision enough; and the English-men had great default: they could get no forage, nor they could not depart thence without danger of their enemies. That Sunday the Englishmen made great dykes and hedges about their archers to be the more stronger. And on the Monday in the morning the prince and his company were ready apparelled as they were before, and about the sun-rising in like manner were the Frenchmen.

The same morning betimes the cardinal came again to the French host and thought by his preaching to pacify the parties. But then the Frenchmen said to him, 'Return whither ye will, bring hither no more words of treaty nor peace; an ye love yourself depart shortly.' When the cardinal saw that he travailed in vain, he took leave of the king and then he went to the prince and said, 'Sir, do what ye can, there is no remedy but to abide the battle, for I can find none accord in the French king.' Then the prince said, 'The same is our intent and all our people. God help the right.' So the cardinal returned to Poitiers. In his company there were certain knights and squires, men of arms, who were more favourable to the French king than to the prince. And when they saw that the parties should fight, they stole from their masters and went to the French host; and they made their captain the Châtelain of Amposte, who was as then there with the cardinal, who knew nothing thereof till he was come to Poitiers.

The certainty of the order of the Englishmen was showed to the French king, except they had ordained three hundred men a-horseback, and as many archers a-horseback, to coast under covert of the mountain and to strike into the battle of the Duke of Normandy, who was under the mountain afoot. This ordinance they had made of new, that the Frenchmen knew not of. The prince was with his battle down among the vines, and had closed in the weakest part with their carriages. Now will I name some of the principal lords and knights that were there with the prince: the Earl of Warwick, the Earl of Suffolk, the Earl of Salisbury, the Earl of Oxford, the Lord John Chandos, the Lord Richard Stafford, the Lord Raynold Cobham, the Lord Spencer, the Lord James Audley, the Lord Peter his brother, the Lord Berkeley, the Lord Basset, the Lord Warin, the Lord Delaware, the Lord Mohun, the Lord Willoughby, the Lord Bartholomew de Burghersh, the Lord of Felton, the Lord Richard of Pembroke, the Lord Stephen of Cosington, the Lord Bradestan and other Englishmen; and of Gascons there was the Lord of Pommiers, the Lord of Languiran, the Captal of Buch, the Lord John of Caumont, the Lord de Lesparre, the Lord of Rauzan, the Lord of Condom, the Lord of Montferrand, the Lord of Landiras, the Lord Soudic of Latrau and other that I cannot name; and of Hainaulters the Lord Eustace d'Aubrecicourt, the Lord John of Ghistelles, and two other strangers, the Lord Daniel Pasele and the Lord Denis of Morbeke. All the prince's company passed not an eight thousand men one and other, and the Frenchmen were a sixty thousand fighting men, whereof there were more than three thousand knights.

Of the battle of Poitiers between the Prince of Wales and the French king (1356).   [Ch. 162]

WHEN the prince saw that he should have battle and that the cardinal was gone without any peace or truce making, and saw that the French king did set but little store by him, he said then to his men, 'Now, sirs, though we be but a small company as in regard to the puissance of our enemies, let us not be abashed therefor: for the victory lieth not in the multitude of people, but whereas God will send it. If it fortune that the journey be ours, we shall be the most honoured people of all the world. And if we die in our right quarrel, I have the king my father and brethren, and also ye have good friends and kinsmen; these shall revenge us. Therefore sirs, for God's sake, I require you do your devoirs this day, for if God be pleased and Saint George, this day ye shall see me a good knight.'

These words and such other that the prince spake comforted all his people. The Lord Sir John Chandos that day never went from the prince, nor also the Lord James Audley of a great season; but when he saw that they should needs fight, he said to the prince, 'Sir, I have served always truly my lord your father and you also, and shall do as long as I live. I say this because I made once a vow that the first battle that either the king your father or any of his children should be at, how that I would be one of the first setters on, or else to die in the pain. Therefore I require your Grace, as in reward for any service that ever I did to the king your father or to you, that you will give me licence to depart from you and to set myself thereas I may accomplish my vow.' The prince accorded to his desire and said, 'Sir James, God give you this day that grace to be the best knight of all other,' and so took him by the hand.

Then the knight departed from the prince and went to the foremost front of all the battles, all only accompanied with four squires, who promised not to fail him. This Lord James was a right sage and a valiant knight, and by him was much of the host ordained and governed the day before. Thus Sir James was in the front of the battle ready to fight with the battle of the marshals of France. In likewise the Lord Eustace d'Aubrecicourt did his pain to be one of the foremost to set on. When Sir James Audley began to set forward to his enemies, it fortuned to Sir Eustace d'Aubrecicourt as ye shall hear after. Ye have heard before how the Germans in the French host were appointed to be still a-horseback. Sir Eustace being a-horseback laid his spear in the rest and ran into the French battle. And then a knight of Germans called the Lord Louis of Recombes, who bare a shield silver, five roses gules, and Sir Eustace bare ermines, two humets of gules—when this German saw the Lord Eustace come from his company, he rode against him and they met so rudely that both knights fell to the earth. The German was hurt in the shoulder, therefore he rose not so quickly as did Sir Eustace, who when he was up and had taken his breath, he came to the other knight as he lay on the ground. But then five other knights of Germany came on him all at once and bare him to the earth, and so perforce there he was taken prisoner and brought to the Earl of Nassau who as then took no heed of him. And I cannot say whether they sware him prisoner or no, but they tied him to a cart and there let him stand.

Then the battle began on all parts, and the battles of the marshals of France approached, and they set forth that were appointed to break the array of archers. They entered a-horseback into the way where the great hedges were on both sides set full of archers. As soon as the men of arms entered, the archers began to shoot on both sides and did slay and hurt horses and knights, so that the horses when they felt the sharp arrows they would in no wise go forward, but drew aback and flung and took on so fiercely, that many of them fell on their masters, so that for press they could not rise again; insomuch that the marshals' battle could never come at the prince. Certain knights and squires that were well horsed passed through the archers and thought to approach to the prince, but they could not. The Lord James Audley with his four squires was in the front of that battle and there did marvels in arms, and by great prowess he came and fought with Sir

Arnold d'Audrehem under his own banner, and there they fought long together, and Sir Arnold was there sore handled.

The battle of the marshals began to disorder by reason of the shot of the archers with the aid of the men of arms, who came in among them and slew of them and did what they list. And there was the Lord Arnold d'Audrehem taken prisoner by other men than by Sir James Audley or his four squires, for that day he never took prisoner, but always fought and went on his enemies. Also on the French party, the Lord John Clermont fought under his own banner as long as he could endure, but there he was beaten down and could not be relieved nor ransomed, but was slain without mercy: some said it was because of the words that he had the day before to Sir John Chandos.

So within a short space the marshals' battles were discomfited, for they fell one upon another and could not go forth. And the Frenchmen that were behind and could not get forward reculed back and came on the battle of the Duke of Normandy, the which was great and thick, and were afoot. But anon they began to open behind, for when they knew that the marshals' battle was discomfited, they took their horses and departed, he that might best. Also they saw a rout of Englishmen coming down a little mountain a-horseback, and many archers with them, who brake in on the side of the duke's battle.

True to say, the archers did their company that day great advantage, for they shot so thick that the Frenchmen wist not on what side to take heed, and little and little the Englishmen won ground on them. And when the men of arms of England saw that the marshals' battle was discomfited and that the duke's battle began to disorder and open, they leapt then on their horses, the which they had ready by them. Then they assembled together and cried, 'Saint George! Guyenne!' And the Lord Chandos said to the prince, 'Sir, take your horse and ride forth, this journey is yours: God is this day in your hands. Get us to the French king's battle, for there lieth all the sore of the matter. I think verily by his valiantness he will not fly: I trust we shall have him by the grace of God and Saint George, so he be well fought withal; and Sir, I heard you say that this day I should see you a good knight.' The prince said, 'Let us go forth, ye shall not see me this day return back,' and said, 'Advance banner, in the name of God and of Saint George.' The knight that bare it did his commandment. There was then a sore battle and a perilous, and many a man overthrown, and he that was once down could not be relieved again without great succour and aid.

As the prince rode and entered in among his enemies, he saw on his right hand, in a little bush lying dead, the Lord Robert of Duras and his banner by him and a ten or twelve of his men about him. Then the prince said to two of his squires and to three archers, 'Sirs, take the body of this knight on a targe and bear him to Poitiers, and present him from me to the Cardinal of Périgord, and say how I salute him by that token.' And this was done. The prince was informed that the cardinal's men were on the field against him, the which was not pertaining to the right order of arms, for men of the church that cometh and goeth for treaty of peace ought not by reason to bear harness nor to fight for neither of the parties: they ought to be indifferent. And because these men had done so, the prince was displeased with the cardinal, and therefore he sent unto him his nephew the Lord Robert of Duras dead. And the Châtelain of Amposte was taken, and the prince would have had his head stricken off, because he was pertaining to the cardinal, but then the Lord Chandos said, 'Sir, suffer for a season. Intend to a great matter, and peradventure the cardinal will make such excuse that ye shall be content.' Then the prince and his company dressed them on the battle of the Duke of Athens, Constable of France: there was many a man slain and cast to the earth. As the Frenchmen fought in companies, they cried, 'Mountjoy! Saint Denis!' and the Englishmen, 'Saint George! Guyenne!'

Anon the prince with his company met with the battle of Germans, whereof the Earl of Sarrebruck, the Earl Nassau and the Earl Nidau were captains, but in a short space they were put to flight: the archers shot so wholly together that none durst come in their dangers. They slew many a man that could not come to no ransom; these three earls was there slain, and divers other knights and squires of their company, and there was the Lord d'Aubrecicourt rescued by his own men and set on horseback, and after he did that day many feats of arms and took good prisoners.

When the Duke of Normandy's battle saw the prince approach, they thought to save themselves, and so the duke and the king's children, the Earl of Poitiers and the Earl of Touraine, who were right young, believed their governors and so departed from the field, and with them more than eight hundred spears that struck no stroke that day. Howbeit the Lord Guichard d'Angle and the Lord John of Saintré, who were with the Earl of Poitiers, would not fly, but entered into the thickest press of the battle. The king's three sons took the way to Chauvigny, and the Lord John of Landas and the Lord Thibaut of Vaudenay, who were set to await on the Duke of Normandy, when they had brought the duke a long league from the battle, then they took leave of the duke and desired the Lord of Saint-Venant that he should not leave the duke but to bring him in safeguard, whereby he should win more thank of the king than to abide still in the field. Then they met also the Duke of Orleans and a great company with him, who were also departed from the field with clear hands. There were many good knights and squires, though that their masters departed from the field, yet they had rather have died than to have had any reproach.

Then the king's battle came on the Englishmen: there was a sore fight and many a great stroke given and received. The king and his youngest son met with the battle of the English marshals, the Earl of Warwick and the Earl of Suffolk, and with them the Gascons the Captal of Buch, the Lord of Pommiers, the Lord

Amery of Tastes, the Lord of Mussidan, the Lord of Languiran and the Lord de Latrau. To the French party there came time enough the Lord John of Landas and the Lord of Vaudenay; they alighted afoot and went into the king's battle. And a little beside fought the Duke of Athens, Constable of France, and a little above him the Duke of Bourbon and many good knights of Bourbonnais and of Picardy with him. And a little on the one side there were the Poitevins, the Lord de Pons, the Lord of Partenay, the Lord of Dammartin, the Lord of Tannay-Bouton, the Lord of Surgères, the Lord John Saintré, the Lord Guichard d'Angle, the Lord Argenton, the Lord of Linières, the Lord of Montendre and divers other, also the Viscount of Rochechouart and the Earl of Aunay; and of Burgundy, the Lord James of Beaujeu, the Lord de Château-Villain and other. In another part there was the Earl of Ventadour, and of Montpensier, the Lord James of Bourbon, the Lord John d'Artois and also the Lord James his brother, the Lord Arnold of Cervolles, called the archpriest, armed for the young Earl of Alençon. And of Auvergne there was the Lord of Mercoeur, the Lord de la Tour, the Lord of Chalençon, the Lord of Montaigu, the Lord of Rochfort, the Lord d'Acier, the Lord d'Acon; and of Limoges there was the Lord de Melval, the Lord of Mareuil, the Lord of Pierre-Buffière; and of Picardy there was the Lord William of Nesle, the Lord Arnold of Rayneval, the Lord Geoffrey of Saint-Dizier, the Lord of Chauny, the Lord of Helly, the Lord of Montsault, the Lord of Hangest and divers other. And also in the king's battle there was the Earl Douglas of Scotland, who fought a season right valiantly, but when he saw the discomfiture, he departed and saved himself, for in no wise he would be taken of the Englishmen, he had rather been there slain.

On the English part the Lord James Audley with the aid of his four squires fought always in the chief of the battle. He was sore hurt in the body and in the visage: as long as his breath served him he fought. At last at the end of the battle his four squires took and brought him out of the field, and laid him under a hedge-side for to refresh him, and they unarmed him and bound up his wounds as well as they could. On the French party King John was that day a full right good knight. If the fourth part of his men had done their devoirs as well as he did, the journey had been his by all likelihood. Howbeit they were all slain and taken that were there, except a few that saved themselves that were with the king.* There was slain the Duke Peter of Bourbon, the Lord Guichard of Beaujeu, the Lord of Landas, and the Duke of Athens, Constable of France, the Bishop of Chalons in Champagne, the Lord William of Nesle, the Lord Eustace of Ribemont, the Lord de la Tour, the Lord William of Montaigu, Sir Grismouton of Chambly, Sir Baudrin de la Heuse, and many other, as they fought by companies. And there were taken prisoners the Lord of Vaudenay, the Lord of Pompadour and the archpriest, sore hurt, the Earl of Vaudimont, the Earl of Mons, the Earl of Joinville, the

* Few escaped that stayed with the king.

Earl of Vendôme, Sir Louis of Melval, the Lord Pierre-Buffière and the Lord of Serignac. There were at that brunt slain and taken more than two hundred knights.

Of two Frenchmen that fled from the battle of Poitiers, and two Englishmen that followed them (1356). [Ch. 163]

Among the battles, recounterings, chases and pursuits that were made that day in the field, it fortuned so to Sir Oudart of Renty that when he departed from the field because he saw the field was lost without recovery, he thought not to abide the danger of the Englishmen: wherefore he fled all alone and was gone out of the field a league, and an English knight pursued him and ever cried to him, and said, 'Return again, sir knight, it is a shame to fly away thus.' Then the knight turned, and the English knight thought to have stricken him with his spear in the targe, but he failed, for Sir Oudart swerved aside from the stroke; but he failed not the English knight, for he struck him such a stroke on the helm with his sword, that he was astonied and fell from his horse to the earth and lay still. Then Sir Oudart alighted and came to him or he could rise, and said, 'Yield you, rescue or no rescue, or else I shall slay you.' The Englishman yielded and went with him, and afterward was ransomed.

Also it fortuned that another squire of Picardy called John de Hellenes was fled from the battle and met with his page, who delivered him a new fresh horse, whereon he rode away alone. The same season there was in the field the Lord Berkeley of England, a young lusty knight, who the same day had reared his banner; and he all alone pursued the said John of Hellenes. And when he had followed the space of a league, the said John turned again and laid his sword in the rest instead of a spear, and so came running toward the Lord Berkeley, who lift up his sword to have stricken the squire; but when he saw the stroke come, he turned from it, so that the Englishman lost his stroke and John struck him as he passed on the arm, that the Lord Berkeley's sword fell into the field. When he saw his sword down, he alighted suddenly off his horse and came to the place where his sword lay, and as he stooped down to take up his sword, the French squire did pike his sword at him and by hap struck him through both the thighs, so that the knight fell to the earth and could not help himself. And John alighted off his horse and took the knight's sword that lay on the ground, and came to him and demanded if he would yield him or not. The knight then demanded his name, 'Sir,' said he, 'I hight John of Hellenes, but what is your name?' 'Certainly,' said the knight, 'my name is Thomas, and am Lord of Berkeley, a fair castle on the river of Severn in the marches of Wales.' 'Well sir,' quoth the squire, 'then ye shall be my prisoner, and I shall bring you in safeguard and I shall see that you shall be healed of your hurt.' 'Well,' said the knight, 'I am content to be your prisoner, for ye have by law of arms won me.' There he sware to be his prisoner, rescue or no rescue. Then the squire drew forth the sword out of the knight's thighs and the wound was open. Then he wrapped and bound the wound and set him on his horse and so brought him fair and easily to Châtellerault, and there tarried more than fifteen days for his sake, and did get him remedy for his hurt. And when he was somewhat amended, then he got him a litter and so brought him at his ease to his house in Picardy. There he was more than a year till he was perfectly whole. And when he departed he paid for his ransom six thousand nobles, and so this squire was made a knight by reason of the profit that he had of the Lord Berkeley.

How King John was taken prisoner at the battle of Poitiers (1356). [Ch. 164]

OFTEN times the adventures of amours and of war are more fortunate and marvellous than any man can think or wish. Truly this battle, the which was near to Poitiers in the fields of Beauvoir and Maupertuis, was right great and perilous, and many deeds of arms there was done the which all came not to knowledge. The fighters on both parties endured much pain. King John with his own hands did that day marvels in arms: he had an axe in his hands wherewith he defended himself and fought in the breaking of the press. Near to the king there was taken the Earl of Tancarville, Sir James of Bourbon, Earl of Ponthieu, and the Lord John of Artois, Earl of Eu; and a little above that under the banner of the Captal of Buch was taken Sir Charles of Artois and divers other knights and squires. The chase endured to the gates of Poitiers. There were many slain and beaten down, horse and man, for they of Poitiers closed their gates and would suffer none to enter; wherefore in the street before the gate was horrible murder, men hurt and beaten down. The Frenchmen yielded themselves as far as they might know an Englishman. There was divers English archers that had four, five or six prisoners. The Lord of Pons, a great baron of Poitou, was there slain, and many other knights and squires; and there was taken the Earl of Rochechouart, the Lord of Dammartin, the Lord of Partenay; and of Saintonge the Lord of Montendre and the Lord John of Santré, but he was so sore hurt that he had never health after; he was reputed for one of the best knights in France. And there was left for dead among other dead men the Lord Guichard d'Angle, who fought that day by the king right valiantly, and so did the Lord of Charny, on whom was great press, because he bare the sovereign banner of the king's: his own banner was also in the field, the which was of gules, three scutcheons silver. So many Englishmen and Gascons came to that part, that perforce they opened the king's battle, so that the Frenchmen were so mingled among their enemies that sometime there was five men upon one gentleman. There was taken the Lord of Pompadour and the Lord

K

Bartholomew de Brunes, and there was slain Sir Geoffrey of Charny with the king's banner in his hands. Also the Lord Raynold Cobham slew the Earl of Dammartin. Then there was a great press to take the king, and such as knew him cried, 'Sir, yield you or else ye are but dead.' There was a knight of Saint-Omer, retained in wages with the King of England, called Sir Denis Morbeke, who had served the Englishmen five year before, because in his youth he had forfeited the realm of France for a murder that he did at Saint Omer. It happened so well for him that he was next to the king when they were about to take him. He stepped forth into the press, and by strength of his body and arms, he came to the French king, and said in good French, 'Sir, yield you.' The king beheld the knight and said, 'To whom shall I yield me? Where is my cousin the Prince of Wales? If I might see him, I would speak with him.' Denis answered and said, 'Sir, he is not here, but yield you to me and I shall bring you to him.' 'Who be you?' quoth the king. 'Sir,' quoth he, 'I am Denis of Morbeke, a knight of Artois, but I serve the King of England because I am banished the realm of France and I have forfeited all that I had there.' Then the king gave him his right gauntlet, saying, 'I yield me to you.' There was a great press about the king, for every man enforced him to say, 'I have taken him,' so that the king could not go forward with his young son the Lord Philip with him because of the press.

The Prince of Wales, who was courageous and cruel as a lion, took that day great pleasure to fight and to chase his enemies. The Lord John Chandos, who was with him, of all that day never left him nor never took heed of taking of any prisoner. Then at the end of the battle, he said to the prince, 'Sir, it were good that you rested here and set your banner a-high in this bush, that your people may draw hither, for they be sore spread abroad nor I can see no more banners nor pennons of the French party; wherefore, sir, rest and refresh you, for ye be sore chafed.' Then the prince's banner was set up a-high on a bush, and trumpets and clarions began to sound. Then the prince did off his bassenet, and the knights for his body and they of his chamber were ready about him, and a red pavilion pight up, and then drink was brought forth to the prince and for such lords as were about him, the which still increased as they came from the chase. There they tarried and their prisoners with them.

And when the two marshals were come to the prince, he demanded of them if they knew any tidings of the French king. They answered and said, 'Sir, we hear none of certainty, but we think verily he is either dead or taken, for he is not gone out of the battles.' Then the prince said to the Earl of Warwick and to Sir Raynold Cobham, 'Sirs, I require you go forth and see what ye can know, that at your return ye may show me the truth.' These two lords took their horses and departed from the prince, and rode up a little hill to look about them; then they perceived a flock of men of arms coming together right wearily. There was the French king afoot in great peril, for Englishmen and Gascons were his masters: they had taken him from Sir Denis Morbeke perforce. And such as were most of force said, 'I have taken him.' 'Nay,' quoth another, 'I have taken him': so they strove which should have him. Then the French king, to eschew that peril, said, 'Sirs, strive not, lead me courteously, and my son, to my cousin the prince, and strive not for my taking, for I am so great a lord to make you all rich.' The king's words somewhat appeased them. Howbeit ever as they went they made riot and brawled for the taking of the king.

When the two foresaid lords saw and heard that noise and strife among them, they came to them and said, 'Sirs, what is the matter that ye strive for?' 'Sirs,' said one of them, 'it is for the French king, who is here taken prisoner, and there be more than ten knights and squires that challengeth the taking of him and of his son.' Then the two lords entered into the press and caused every man to draw aback, and commanded them in the prince's name on pain of their heads to make no more noise nor to approach the king no nearer, without they were commanded. Then every man gave room to the lords, and they alighted and did reverence to the king, and so brought him and his son in peace and rest to the Prince of Wales.

Of the gift that the prince gave to the Lord Audley after the battle of Poitiers (1356).
[Ch. 165]

AS soon as the Earl of Warwick and the Lord Cobham were departed from the prince, as ye have heard before, then the prince demanded of the knights that were about him for the Lord Audley, if any knew anything of him. Some knights that were there answered and said, 'Sir, he is sore hurt and lieth in a litter here beside.' 'By my faith,' said the prince, 'of his hurts I am right sorry. Go and know if he may be brought hither, or else I will go and see him there as he is.' Then two knights came to the Lord Audley, and said, 'Sir, the Prince desireth greatly to see you. Either ye must go to him or else he will come to you.' 'Ah, sir,' said the knight, 'thank the prince, when he thinketh on so poor a knight as I am.' Then he called eight of his servants and caused them to bear him in his litter to the place whereas the prince was. Then the prince took him in his arms and kissed him and made him great cheer, and said, 'Sir James, I ought greatly to honour you, for by your valiance ye have this day achieved the grace and renown of us all, and ye are reputed for the most valiant of all other.' 'Ah, Sir,' said the knight, 'ye say as it pleaseth you. I would it were so, and if I have this day anything advanced myself to serve you and to accomplish the vow that I made, it ought not to be reputed to me of any prowess.' 'Sir James,' said the prince, 'I and all ours take you in this journey for the best doer in arms. And to the intent to furnish you the better to pursue the wars, I retain you for ever to be my knight, with five hundred marks of yearly revenues, the which I shall assign you on mine

heritage in England.' 'Sir,' said the knight, 'God grant me to deserve the great goodness that ye show me.' And so he took his leave of the prince, for he was right feeble,
and so his servants brought him to his lodging. And as soon as he was gone, the Earl
of Warwick and the Lord Cobham returned to the prince and presented to him the
French king. The prince made lowly reverence to the king and caused wine and
spices to be brought forth, and himself served the king in sign of great love.

How the Englishmen won greatly at the battle of Poitiers (1356).   [Ch. 166]

THUS this battle was discomfited, as ye have heard, the which was in the fields
of Maupertuis, a two leagues from Poitiers, the twenty-second day of September
the year of our Lord MCCCLVI. It began in the morning and ended at noon, but
as then all the Englishmen were not returned from the chase: therefore the prince's
banner stood on a bush to draw all his men together, but it was nigh night or all
came from the chase. And as it was reported, there was slain all the flower of
France, and there was taken with the king and the Lord Philip his son a seventeen
earls, beside barons, knights and squires, and slain a five or six thousand of one
and other. When every man was come from the chase, they had twice as many
prisoners as they were in number in all. Then it was counselled among them,
because of the great charge and doubt to keep so many, that they should put
many of them to ransom incontinent in the field: and so they did. And the prisoners
found the Englishmen and Gascons right courteous; there were many that day
put to ransom and let go, all only on their promise of faith and troth to return
again between that and Christmas to Bordeaux with their ransoms.

Then that night they lay in the field beside whereas the battle had been. Some
unarmed them but not all, and unarmed all their prisoners, and every man made
good cheer to his prisoner, for that day whosoever took any prisoner, he was clear
his, and might quit or ransom him at his pleasure. All such as were there with the
prince were all made rich with honour and goods, as well by ransoming of prisoners
as by winning of gold, silver, plate, jewels, that was there found; there was no man
that did set anything by rich harness, whereof there was great plenty, for the Frenchmen came thither richly beseen, weening to have had the journey for them.

How the Lord James Audley gave to his four squires the five hundred marks of revenues that the prince had given him (1356).   [Ch. 167]

WHEN Sir James Audley was brought to his lodging, then he sent for Sir Peter
Audley his brother and for the Lord Bartholomew of Burghersh, the Lord Stephen
of Cosington, the Lord of Willoughby and the Lord Ralph Ferrers: all these were

of his lineage.   And then he called before them his four squires, that had served
him that day well and truly.   Then he said to the said lords, 'Sirs, it hath pleased
my lord the prince to give me five hundred marks of revenues by year in heritage,
for the which I have done him but small service with my body.   Sirs, behold here
these four squires, who hath always served me truly, and specially this day; that
honour that I have is by their valiantness.   Wherefore I will reward them: I give
and resign into their hands the gift that my lord the prince hath given me of five
hundred marks of yearly revenues, to them and to their heirs for ever, in like
manner as it was given to me.   I clearly disherit me thereof and inherit them without
any repeal or condition.'   The lords and other that were there, every man beheld
other and said among themselves, 'It cometh of a great nobleness to give this gift.'
They answered him with one voice, 'Sir, be it as God will, we shall bear witness
in this behalf wheresoever we be come.'   Then they departed from him, and some
of them went to the prince, who the same night would make a supper to the French
king and to the other prisoners, for they had then enough to do with all of that
the Frenchmen brought with them, for the Englishmen wanted victual before,
for some in three days had no bread before.

How the prince made a supper to the French king the same day of the battle (1356).   [Ch. 168]

THE same day of the battle at night the prince made a supper in his lodging to
the French king and to the most part of the great lords that were prisoners.   The
prince made the king and his son, the Lord James of Bourbon, the Lord John
d'Artois, the Earl of Tancarville, the Earl de Etampes, the Earl Dammartin, the
Earl of Joinville, and the Lord of Partenay to sit all at one board, and other lords,
knights and squires at other tables.   And always the prince served before the king
as humbly as he could, and would not sit at the king's board for any desire that
the king could make, but he said he was not sufficient to sit at the table with so
great a prince as the king was.   But then he said to the king, 'Sir, for God's sake
make none evil nor heavy cheer, though God this day did not consent to follow
your will: for sir, surely the king my father shall bear you as much honour and
amity as he may do, and shall accord with you so reasonably that ye shall ever
be friends together after.   And sir, methink ye ought to rejoice, though the journey
be not as ye would have had it, for this day ye have won the high renown of prowess
and have passed this day in valiantness all other of your party.   Sir, I say not this
to mock you, for all that be on our party that saw every man's deeds, are plainly
accorded by true sentence to give you the prize and chaplet.'   Therewith the
Frenchmen began to murmur and said among themselves how the prince had
spoken nobly, and that by all estimation he should prove a noble man, if God
send him life, and to persevere in such good fortune.

How the prince returned to Bordeaux after the battle of Poitiers (1356).   [Ch. 169]

WHEN supper was done, every man went to his lodging with their prisoners. The same night they put many to ransom and believed them on their faiths and troths, and ransomed them but easily, for they said they would set no knight's ransom so high, but that he might pay at his ease and maintain still his degree. The next day when they had heard mass and taken some repast, and that everything was trussed and ready, then they took their horses and rode towards Poitiers.

The same night there was come to Poitiers the Lord of Roye with a hundred spears. He was not at the battle, but he met the Duke of Normandy near to Chauvigny, and the duke sent him to Poitiers to keep the town till they heard other tidings. When the Lord of Roye knew that the Englishmen were so near coming to the city, he caused every man to be armed and every man to go to his defence to the walls, towers and gates. And the Englishmen passed by without any approaching, for they were so laden with gold, silver and prisoners, that in their returning they assaulted no forts; they thought it a great deed if they might bring the French king, with their other prisoners and riches that they had won, in safeguard to Bordeaux. They rode but small journeys because of their prisoners and great carriages that they had; they rode in a day no more but four or five leagues and lodged ever betimes, and rode close together in good array, saving the marshals' battles, who rode ever before with five hundred men of arms to open the passages as the prince should pass, but they found no encounters, for all the country was so frayed that every man drew to the fortresses.

As the prince rode, it was showed him how the Lord Audley had given to his four squires the gift of the five hundred marks that he had given unto him. Then the prince sent for him, and he was brought in his litter to the prince, who received him courteously and said, 'Sir James, we have knowledge that the revenues that we gave you, as soon as ye came to your lodging, you gave the same to four squires. We would know why ye did so, and whether the gift was agreeable to you or not.' 'Sir,' said the knight, 'it is of truth that I have given it to them, and I shall show you why I did so. These four squires that be here present have a long season served me well and truly in many great businesses; and, sir, at this last battle they served me in such wise that an they had never done nothing else, I was bound to reward them, and before the same day they had never nothing of me in reward. Sir, I am but a man alone, but by the aid and comfort of them I took on me to accomplish my vow long before made. I had been dead in the battle an they had not been, wherefore, sir, when I considered the love that they bare unto me, I had not been courteous if I would not have rewarded them. I thank God I have had and shall have enough as long as I live. I will never be abashed for lack of good. Sir, if I have done this without your pleasure, I require you to pardon me, for sir, both I and my squires shall serve you as well as ever we did.' Then the prince said, 'Sir James, for anything that ye have done I cannot blame you, but can you good thank therefor; and for the valiantness of these squires whom ye praise so much, I accord to them your gift, and I will render again to you six hundred marks in like manner as ye had the other.'

Thus the prince and his company did so much that they passed through Poitou and Saintonge without damage and came to Blaye, and there passed the river of Gironde and arrived in the good city of Bordeaux. It cannot be recorded the great feast and cheer that they of the city with the clergy made to the prince and how honourably they were received. The prince brought the French king into the abbey of Saint Andrew's, and there they lodged both, the king in one part and the prince in the other. The prince bought of the lords, knights and squires of Gascony the most part of the earls of the realm of France, such as were prisoners, and paid ready money for them.

There was divers questions and challenges made between the knights and squires of Gascony for taking of the French king. Howbeit Denis Morbeke, by right of arms and by true tokens that he showed, challenged him for his prisoner. Another squire of Gascony called Bernard of Truttes said how he had right to him; there was much ado and many words before the prince and other lords that were there: and because these two challenged each other to fight in that quarrel, the prince caused the matter to rest till they came in England, and that no declaration should be made but afore the King of England his father. But because the French king himself aided to sustain the challenge of Denis Morbeke, for he inclined more to him than to any other, the prince therefore privily caused to be delivered to the said Sir Denis two thousand nobles to maintain withal his estate.

Anon after the prince came to Bordeaux, the Cardinal of Périgord came thither, who was sent from the Pope in legation, as it was said. He was there more than fifteen days or the prince would speak with him because of the Châtelain of Amposte and his men, who were against him in the battle of Poitiers. The prince believed that the cardinal sent them thither, but the cardinal did so much by the means of the Lord of Caumont, the Lord of Montferrand, and the Captal of Buch, who were his cousins, they showed so good reasons to the prince, that he was content to hear him speak. And when he was before the prince, he excused himself so sagely that the prince and his council held him excused, and so he fell again into the prince's love and redeemed out his men by reasonable ransoms. And the châtelain was set to his ransom of ten thousand francs, the which he paid after. Then the cardinal began to treat on the deliverance of the French king, but I pass it briefly because nothing was done. Thus the prince, the Gascons and Englishmen tarried still at Bordeaux till it was Lent in great mirth and revel, and spent foolishly the gold and silver that they had won. In England also there was great joy when they heard tidings of the battle of Poitiers, of the discomfiting of the Frenchmen and taking of the king. Great solemnities were made in all churches and great fires and wakes throughout all England. The knights and squires, such as were come home from that journey, were much made of and praised more than other.

How the three estates of France assembled together at Paris after the battle of Poitiers (1356).
[Ch. 170]

THE same season that the battle of Poitiers was, the Duke of Lancaster was in the county of Evreux and on the marches of Cotentin, and with him the Lord Philip of Navarre and the Lord Godfrey of Harcourt. They made war in Normandy and had done all that season in the title of the King of Navarre, whom the French king held in prison. These lords did all that they might to have been at the journey of Poitiers with the prince, but they could not, for all the passages on the river of Loire were so well kept that they might not pass. But when they heard how the prince had taken the French king at the battle of Poitiers, they were glad and brake up their journey, because the Duke of Lancaster and Sir Philip of Navarre would go into England: and so they did. And they sent Sir Godfrey of Harcourt to Saint-Sauveur-le-Vicomte to keep there frontier war.

Now let us speak of the French king's three sons, Charles, Louis and John, who were returned from the business at Poitiers. They were right young of age and of counsel. In them was but small recovery, nor there was none of them that would take on him the governance of the realm of France. Also the lords, knights and squires, such as fled from the battle, were so hated and blamed of the commons of the realm, that scant they durst abide in any good town. Then all the prelates of Holy Church being in France, bishops, abbots, and all other noble lords and knights, and the provost of the merchants, the burgesses of Paris, and the councils of other good towns, they all assembled at Paris, and there they would ordain how the realm should be governed till the king were delivered out of prison. Also they would know furthermore what was become of the great treasure that had been levied in the realm by dimes, maltotes, subsidies, forging of moneys, and in all other extortions whereby the people had been overlaid and troubled, and the soldiers evil-paid, and the realm evil-kept and defended: but of all this there were none that could give account.

Then they agreed that the prelates should choose out twelve persons among them, who should have power by them and by all the clergy to ordain and to advise all things convenable to be done. And the lords and knights to choose other twelve among them of their most sagest and discreet persons, to determine all causes; and the burgesses to choose other twelve for the commons: the which six-and-thirty persons should oftentimes meet at Paris and there to commune and to ordain for all causes of the realm, and every matter to be brought to them. And to these three estates all other prelates, lords and commons should obey.

So these persons were chosen out, but in the beginning there were divers in this election that the Duke of Normandy was not content withal, nor his council. First, these three estates defended ever more forging of money. Also they required the Duke of Normandy that he would arrest the chancellor of the king his father, the Lord Robert of Lorris, and the Lord Simon of Bucy and divers other masters of the accounts and other councillors of the king's, to the intent that they might make a true account of that they had taken and levied in the realm and by their counsels. When these masters and councillors heard of his matter, they departed out of the realm into other countries, to abide there till they heard other tidings.

How the three estates sent men of war against the Lord Godfrey of Harcourt (1356). [Ch. 171]

THESE three estates ordained and established in their names, receivers of all maltotes, dimes, subsidies and other rights pertaining to the king and to the realm. And they made new money to be forged of fine gold, called moutons. Also they would gladly that the King of Navarre had been delivered out of prison, whereas he was at the castle of Crèvecoeur in Cambrésis. It was thought by divers of the three estates that the realm of France should be the more stronger and the better defended if he would be true to the realm, for they saw well there were then but few nobles to maintain the realm, for they were nigh all taken and slain at the battle of Poitiers. Then they required the Duke of Normandy to deliver him out of prison, for they said how they thought he had great wrong to be kept in prison for they wist not why. The duke answered and said how he durst not take on him his deliverance, for the king his father put him in prison, he could not tell for what cause.

The same season there came tidings to the duke and to the three estates that the Lord Godfrey of Harcourt made sore war in Normandy, and overran the country two or three times in a week, sometime to the suburbs of Caen, of Saint Lô, Evreux, and Coutances. Then the duke and the three estates ordained a company of men of arms, of three hundred spears and five hundred of other, and made four captains . . .

These men of war departed from Paris and went to Rouen, and there they assembled on all parts. There were divers knights of Artois and of Vermandois . . . and also of Normandy there were many expert men of arms. And these lords rode to Coutances and there made their garrison.

Of the battle of Coutances between the Lord Godfrey of Harcourt and the Lord Louis of Ravenall (1356). [Ch. 172]

WHEN the Lord Godfrey of Harcourt, who was a right hardy knight and a courageous, knew that the Frenchmen were come to the city of Coutances, he assembled together as many men of war as he could get, archers and other, and said how he would ride and look on the Frenchmen, and so departed from Saint-Sauveur-le-Vicomte. He had about a seven hundred men, one and other.

The same day the Frenchmen also rode forth and sent before them their currours, who brought them word again that they had seen the Navarrais. Also Sir Godfrey had sent his currours, who had also well aviewed the Frenchmen and saw their banners and pennons and what number they were; and returned and showed it to Sir Godfrey, who said: 'Since we see our enemies we will fight with them.' Then he set his archers before and set his company in good order. And when Sir Louis of Ravenall saw their demeanour, he caused his company to alight afoot and to pavise them with their targes against the archers, and commanded that none should go forward without he commanded. The archers began to approach and shoot fiercely. The Frenchmen, who were well armed and pavised, suffered their shot: it did them no great hurt. So the Frenchmen stood still till the archers had spent all their arrows. Then they cast away their bows and resorted back to their men of arms who were arranged along by a hedge, and Sir Godfrey with his banner before them. Then the French archers began to shoot and gathered up the arrows that had been shot at them before, and also their men of arms began fiercely to approach. There was a sore fight when they met hand to hand, and Sir Godfrey's footmen kept none array but were soon discomfited. Then Sir Godfrey sagely withdrew himself down into a wing closed with hedges. When the Frenchmen saw that, they all alighted afoot and devised which way they might enter. They went all about to find a way and Sir Godfrey was ready ever to defend. There were many hurt and slain of the Frenchmen or they could enter at their pleasure. Finally they entered and then there was a sore fight and many a man overthrown. And Sir Godfrey's men kept no good array nor did not as they had promised: most part of them fled.

When Sir Godfrey saw that, he said to himself how he had rather there be slain than to be taken by the Frenchmen. Then he took his axe in his hands and set fast the one leg before the other to stand the more surely, for his one leg was a little crooked, but he was strong in the arms. There he fought valiantly and long, none durst well abide his strokes. Then two Frenchmen mounted on their horses and ran both with their spears at once at him, and so bare him to the earth. Then other that were afoot came with their swords and struck him into the body under his harness so that there he was slain. And all such as were with him were nigh all slain and taken, and such as escaped returned to Saint-Sauveur-le-Vicomte. This was about the feast of Saint Martin, in winter, the year of our Lord MCCCLVI.

How the Prince conveyed the French king from Bordeaux into England (1356).   [Ch. 173]

AFTER the death of this knight, Sir Godfrey of Harcourt, the Frenchmen returned to Coutances with their prisoners and pillage, and anon after they went into France to the Duke of Normandy, who as then was called Regent of France, and to the three estates, who received them right honourably. So from thenceforth Saint-Sauveur-le-Vicomte was English and all the lands pertaining to Sir Godfrey of Harcourt, for he had sold it to the King of England after his decease and disherited the Lord Louis of Harcourt his nephew, because he would not take his part.

As soon as the King of England heard tidings of the death of the Lord Godfrey of Harcourt, he was sorry thereof. Then he sent incontinent men of arms, knights, squires and archers more than three hundred by sea to go and take possession for him by Saint-Sauveur-le-Vicomte, the which was worth thirty thousand francs by year, and made captain of those lands the Lord John Lisle. The three estates all that season studied on the ordinance of the realm of France, and it was all governed by them.

The same winter the Prince of Wales and such of England as were with him at Bordeaux ordained for ships to convey the French king and his son and all other prisoners into England. And when the time of his departure approached, then he commanded the Lord d'Albret, the Lord of Mussidan, the Lord de Lesparre, the Lord of Pommiers and the Lord of Rauzan to keep the country there till his return again. Then he took the sea and certain lords of Gascony with him. The French king was in a vessel by himself, to be the more at his ease, accompanied with two hundred men of arms and two thousand archers: for it was showed the prince that the three estates by whom the realm of France was governed had laid in Normandy and Crotoy two great armies, to the intent to meet with him and to get the French king out of his hands, if they might; but there were no such that appeared, and yet they were on the sea eleven days, and on the twelfth day they arrived at Sandwich. Then they issued out of their ship and lay there all that night, and tarried there two days to fresh them. And on the third day they rode to Canterbury.

When the King of England knew of their coming, he commanded them of London to prepare them and their city to receive such a man as the French king was. Then they of London arrayed themselves by companies and the chief mesters' clothing different from the other. At Saint Thomas of Canterbury the French king and the prince made their offerings and there tarried a day, and then rode to Rochester and tarried there that day, and the next day to Dartford and the fourth day to London, where they were honourably received, and so they were in every good town as they passed. The French king rode through London on a white courser, well apparelled, and the prince on a little black hobby by him. Thus he was conveyed along the city till he came to the Savoy, the which house pertained to the heritage of the Duke of Lancaster. There the French king kept his house a long season, and thither came to see him the king and the queen oftentimes and made him great feast and cheer.

Anon after, by the commandment of Pope Innocent the Sixth, there came into England the Lord Talleyrand, Cardinal of Périgord, and the Lord Nicholas, Cardinal of Urgel. They treated for a peace between the two kings but they could bring nothing to effect; but at last by good means they procured a truce between the two kings and all their assisters, to endure till the feast of Saint John the Baptist in the year of our Lord MCCCLIX. And out of this truce was excepted the Lord Philip of Navarre and his allies, the Countess of Montfort and the Duchy of Brittany.

Anon after, the French king was removed from the Savoy to the castle of Windsor, and all his household, and went a-hunting and a-hawking thereabout at his pleasure, and the Lord Philip his son with him. And all the other prisoners abode still in London, and went to see the king at their pleasure, and were received all only on their faiths.

Of the beginning of the rising of the commons called Jacquerie, in Beauvoisin (1358). [Ch. 182]

ANON after the deliverance of the King of Navarre, there began a marvellous tribulation in the realm of France, as in Beauvoisin, in Brie, on the river of Marne in Laonnois, and about Soissons; for certain people of the common villages, without any head or ruler, assembled together in Beauvoisin. In the beginning they passed not a hundred in number. They said how the noblemen of the realm of France, knights and squires, shamed the realm, and that it should be a great wealth to destroy them all, and each of them said it was true, and said all with one voice, 'Shame have he that doth not his power to destroy all the gentlemen of the realm.'

Thus they gathered together without any other counsel, and without any armour saving with staves and knives, and so went to the house of a knight dwelling thereby, and broke up his house and slew the knight and the lady and all his children, great and small, and burnt his house. And then they went to another castle, and took the knight thereof and bound him fast to a stake, and then violated his wife and daughter before his face and then slew the lady and his daughter and all his other children, and then slew the knight by great torment and burnt and beat down the castle. And so they did to divers other castles and good houses. And they multiplied so that they were a six thousand, and ever as they went forward they increased, for suchlike as they were fell ever to them, so that every gentleman fled from them and took their wives and children with them, and fled ten or twenty leagues off to be in surety, and left their houses void and their goods therein.

These mischievous people thus assembled without captain or armour, robbed, burnt and slew all gentlemen that they could lay hands on, and forced and ravished ladies and damosels, and did such shameful deeds that no human creature ought to think on any such, and he that did most mischief was most praised with them and greatest master. I dare not write the horrible deeds that they did to ladies and damosels: among other they slew a knight and after did put him on a broach and roasted him at the fire in the sight of the lady his wife and his children; and after that the lady had been enforced and ravished with a ten or twelve, they made her perforce to eat of her husband, and after made her to die an evil death and all her children.

They made among them a king, one of Clermont in Beauvoisin. They chose him that was most ungraciousest of all other and they called him King Jaques Goodman, and so thereby they were called companions of the Jacquerie. They destroyed and burnt in the country of Beauvoisin about Corbie, Amiens and Montdidier, more than threescore good house sand strong castles. In like manner these unhappy people were in Brie and Artois, so that all the ladies, knights and squires of that country were fain to fly away to Meaux in Brie, as well the Duchess of Normandy and the Duchess of Orleans as divers other ladies and damosels, or else they had been violated and after murdered.

Also there were a certain of the same ungracious people between Paris and Noyon and between Paris and Soissons, and all about in the land of Coucy, in the county of Valois, in the bishopric of Laon, Noyon and Soissons. There were burnt and destroyed more than a hundred castles and good houses of knights and squires in that country.

How the provost of the merchants of Paris caused walls to be made about the city of Paris.
[Ch. 183]

WHEN the gentlemen of Beauvoisin, or Corbiois, of Vermandois and of other lands whereas these mischievous people were conversant, saw the woodness among them, they sent for succours to their friends into Flanders, to Brabant, to Hainault, and to Hesbaye. So there came from all parts, and so all these gentlemen, strangers with them of the country, assembled together and did set on these people where they might find them, and slew and hanged them upon trees by heaps. The King of Navarre on a day slew of them more than three thousand beside Clermont in Beauvoisin. It was time to take them up, for an they had been all together assembled they were more than a hundred thousand. And when they were demanded why they did so evil deeds, they would answer and say they could not tell, but that they did as they saw other do, thinking thereby to have destroyed all the nobles and gentlemen of the world.

In the same season the Duke of Normandy departed from Paris and was in doubt of the King of Navarre, and of the provost of the merchants and of his sect, for they were all of one accord. He rode to the bridge of Charenton on the river of Marne, and there he made a great summons of gentlemen, and then defied the provost of the merchants and all his aiders. Then the provost was in doubt of him, that he would in the night-time come and overrun the city of Paris, the which as then was not closed. Then he set workmen a-work as many as he could get, and made great dykes all about Paris, and began walls and gates. He had the space of one whole year a three hundred workmen continually working. It was a great deed to furnish an army, and to close with defence such a city as Paris: surely it was the best deed that ever any provost did there, for else it had been after divers times overrun and robbed by divers occasions.

Of the battle at Meaux in Brie, where the companions of the Jacquerie were discomfited by the Earl of Foix and the Captal of Buch (1358). [Ch. 184]

IN the season while these ungracious people reigned, there came out of Prussia the Earl of Foix and the Captal of Buch his cousin, and in their way they heard, as they should have entered into France, of the great mischief that fell among the noblemen by these unhappy people. And in the city of Meaux was the Duchess of Normandy and the Duchess of Orleans and a three hundred other ladies and damosels, and the Duke of Orleans also. Then the two said knights agreed to go and see these ladies and to comfort them to their powers; howbeit the captal was English, but as then it was truce between the two kings. They had in their company a threescore spears. And when they were come to Meaux in Brie, they were welcome to the ladies and damosels there. And when those of the Jacquerie understood that there was at Meaux such a number of ladies, young damosels and noble children, then they assembled together and with them they of Valois, and so came to Meaux. And also certain of Paris that heard thereof went to them, so that they were in all a nine thousand, and daily more resorted to them. So they came to the gates of the town of Meaux and the people of the town opened the gates and suffered them to enter, so that all the streets were full of them to the market-place, whereas these noble ladies were lodged in a strong place closed about with the river of Marne. There came such a number against them that the ladies were sore afraid.

Then these two knights and their company came to the gate of the market-place and issued out and set on those villains, who were but evil armed, the Earl of Foix's banner and the Duke of Orleans', and the captal's pennon. And when these villains saw these men of war well apparelled issued out to defend the place, the foremost of them began to recule back, and the gentlemen pursued them with their spears and swords; and when they felt the great strokes, they reculed all at once and fell for haste each on other. Then all the noblemen issued out of the barriers and anon won the place, and entered in among their enemies and beat them down by heaps and slew them like beasts and chased them all out of the

town, and slew so many that they were weary, and made many of them by heaps
to fly into the river. Briefly, that day they slew of them more than seven thousand,
and none had escaped if they would have followed the chase any further. And
when these men of arms returned again to the town, they set fire thereon and
burned it clean and all the villains of the town that they could close therein, because they took part with the Jacquerie. After this discomfiture thus done at
Meaux they never assembled again together after, for the young Enguerrand,
Lord of Coucy, had about him certain men of war, and they ever slew them as
they might meet with them without any mercy.

How Paris was besieged by the Duke of Nor-mandy, Regent of France (1358).   [Ch. 185]

ANON after this adventure, the Duke of Normandy assembled all the noblemen
together that he could get as well of the realm as of the Empire for his wages; so
that he had a three thousand spears, and so went and laid siege to Paris toward
Saint-Antoine along by the river of Seine, and was lodged himself at Saint-Maur
and his men thereabout, and every day they ran skirmishing to the walls of Paris.
And sometime the duke lay at Charenton and another season at Saint-Maur so
that nothing came to Paris on that side neither by land nor by water, for the duke
caused both the rivers of Seine and Marne to be surely kept, and burnt all the
villages about Paris, such as were not closed, the better thereby to chastise them
of Paris. And if Paris had not then been fortified with walls and dykes, it had
been destroyed. None durst go into Paris nor go out for fear of the duke's men
who rode on both sides the river of Seine at his pleasure; there were none to resist
them. The provost kept still in love the King of Navarre and took of him counsel,
and the commons day and night did work on the defence of the city and kept a
great number of men of war, Navarrais and English archers and other companions.
   There was in the city certain well-disposed persons, as John Maillart and Simon
his brother and divers of their lineage, that were sore displeased of the Duke of
Normandy's evil will. But the provost had so drawn to his opinion all manner
of men, that none durst say contrary to him without he were slain without mercy.
The King of Navarre seeing the variance between them of Paris and the Duke of
Normandy thought and supposed that the matter could not long endure in that
state and he had no great trust to the commonalty of Paris, and so he departed
thence as courteously as he might and went to Saint-Denis; and there he kept
with him a good number of soldiers at the wages of them of Paris.
   The Duke thus lay a six weeks at Charenton, and the King of Navarre at Saint-
Denis. They pilled and ate up the country on every side. Between these parties
entreated for a peace the Archbishop of Sens, the Bishop of Auxerre, the Bishop
of Beauvais, the Lord of Montmorency, the Lord of Fiennes and the Lord of

Saint-Venant. And so often they went between the parties and so sagely demeaned their business, that the King of Navarre with his own goodwill without constraint went to Charenton to the Duke of Normandy and excused himself of that he was had in suspect: first, of the death of the two knights and of master Simon Bucy, and of the despite that the provost had done to him in the palace of Paris. And there he sware that it was unknown to him, and there promised the duke to stick with him in good and evil, and there peace was made between them and the King of Navarre said how he would cause them of Paris to make amends for that they had done. The duke was content that the commons of Paris should have peace so that he might have the provost and twelve other burgesses such as he would chose within Paris, to correct them at his pleasure. All these things agreed, the King of Navarre returned to Saint-Denis and the duke went to Meaux in Brie and gave leave to all his men of war to depart.

Certain burgesses of Paris such as had hoped to make the said treaty desired the duke to come to Paris, saying how they should do him all the honour they might. The duke answered and said he would keep the peace made and that he had sworn unto without any breaking of his part; but to enter into Paris surely, he said, he would never till he had satisfaction of them that had displeased him. The provost of the merchants and his sect oftentimes visited the King of Navarre at Saint-Denis, and showed him how they were in the indignation of the Duke of Normandy for his sake, because they delivered him out of prison and brought him to Paris. Therefore they said to him, 'Sir, for God's sake have no great trust in the duke nor in his counsel.' The king said, 'Certainly friends ye shall have none evil but my part shall be therein. And seeing ye have as now the governance of Paris, I would counsel you to provide yourself of gold and silver, so that if ye have need, by that ye may ever help yourself; and hardly send it hither to Saint-Denis on the trust of me, and I shall keep it well, and shall always entertain men of war secretly, that if ye have need shall make war against your enemies.' So thus after this the provost two times a week sent ever to Saint-Denis two somers charged with florins to the King of Navarre, who received the money with glad cheer.

Of the death of the provost of the merchants of Paris.   [Ch. 187]

THE provost and his sect had among themselves divers councils secretly, to know how they should maintain themselves, for they could find by no means any mercy in the Duke of Normandy; for he sent word generally to all the commons of Paris that he would keep with them no longer peace, without he had delivered into his hands twelve of Paris, such as he would chose, to do with them his pleasure: the which thing greatly abashed the provost and his company. Finally, they saw well that it were better for them to save their lives, goods and friends, rather than to be destroyed, and that it were better for them to slay than to be slain. Then secretly they treated with Englishmen, such as made war against Paris, and they agreed between them that the provost and his sect should be at the gate Saint-Honoré and at the gate Saint-Antoine at the hour of midnight and to let in the Englishmen and the Navarrais provided ready to overrun the city and to destroy and rob it clean, except such houses as had certain signs limited among them, and in all other houses without such tokens to slay men, women and children. The same night that this should have been done, God inspired certain burgesses of the city, such as always were of the duke's party, as John Maillart and Simon his brother and divers other, who by divine inspiration, as it ought to be supposed, were informed that Paris should be that night destroyed. They incontinent armed them and showed the matter in other places to have more aid, and a little before midnight they came to the gate Saint-Antoine and there they found the provost of the merchants with the keys of the gates in his hands. Then John Maillart said to the provost, calling him by his name, 'Stephen, what do you here at this hour?' The provost answered and said, 'John, what would ye? I am here to take heed to the town, whereof I have the governing.' 'By God' said John, 'ye shall not go so. Ye are not here at this hour for any good, and that may be seen by the keys of the gates that ye have in your hands. I think it be to betray the town.' Quoth the provost, 'John, ye lie falsely.' 'Nay,' said John, 'Stephen, thou liest falsely like a traitor', and therewith struck at him, and said to his company, 'Slay the traitors.' Then every man struck at them. The provost would have fled, but John Maillart gave him with an axe on the head, that he fell down to the earth, and yet he was his gossip and left not till he was slain, and six of them that were there with him, and the other taken and put in prison. Then people began to stir in the streets, and John Maillart and they of his accord went to the gate Saint-Honoré, and there they found certain of the provost's sect, and there they laid treason to them, but their excuses availed nothing. There were divers taken and sent into divers places to prison, and such as would not be taken were slain without mercy. The same night they went and took divers in their beds, such as were culpable of the treason by the confession of such as were taken.

The next day John Maillart assembled the most part of the commons in the market hall, and there he mounted on a stage and showed generally the cause why he had slain the provost of the merchants. And there by the counsel of all the wise men, all such as were of the sect of the provost were judged to the death, and so they were executed by divers torments of death. Thus done, John Maillart, who was then greatly in the grace of the commons of Paris, and other of his adherents, sent Simon Maillart and two masters of the parliament, Sir Stephen Alphonse and Master John Pastourel, to the Duke of Normandy being at Charenton. They showed the duke all the matter, and desired him to come to Paris to aid and to counsel them of the city from thenceforth, saying that all his adversaries were dead. The duke said, 'With a right goodwill', and so he came to Paris, and with him Sir Arnold d'Audrehem, the Lord of Roye and other knights, and he lodged at [the] Louvre.

Summary.   [Ch. 187-236]

AFTER the Duke of Normandy had quelled the burgesses of Paris, the King of Navarre was forced to declare war on France. Peace was restored after some Navarrais successes. When the truce between England and France expired, Edward III invaded France once more and laid siege to Rheims. He then retired towards Paris where the Duke of Normandy agreed to the Treaty of Brétigny [1360] whereby the French king was released on payment of 600,000 crowns and delivery of hostages. Edward III renounced his claim to the throne of France. France was much troubled by the roving bands of discharged soldiers. Edward received the vast principality of Aquitaine which was given the Black Prince to govern. In 1363 one of John's sons, a hostage for the payment of the ransom, broke his parole and John felt bound by honour to return to captivity. The next year he died in London and the Duke of Normandy became King Charles V. Under him the fortunes of France prospered once more. Steadily he began with the help of Bertram de Guesclin to win back lost territories. The rivalry extended across the Pyrenees when Pedro the Cruel of Castile was driven out by his bastard half-brother, Henry of Trastamare, who had French support. Pedro appealed to the Black Prince to come to his aid. This brings us to the year 1367 and the Battle of Najera, a complete victory for the Black Prince.

How the prince commanded his people to be ready to fight, and how King Henry ordained his battles; and how they fought fiercely together, and of the comfort that King Henry did to his people (1367).   [Ch. 237]

THUS, as ye have heard, King Henry and Sir Bertram of Guesclin devised together of divers matters and left talking of the prince's letter, for it was King Henry's intention to have battle, and so intended to order his field and people. The Earl Don Tello and his brother Don Sancho were greatly renowned in their host for the journey that they had made before, as ye have heard. The prince, the Friday the second day of April, dislodged from Logrono and advanced forward arranged in battle ready to fight, for he knew well that King Henry was not far hence. And so that day he advanced two leagues, and at three of the day he came before Najera and there took his lodging. Then the prince sent forth his currours to aview his enemies and to know where they were lodged, and then they departed from the host and rode so forward that they saw all their enemy's host, who were lodged before Nazres. So they brought report thereof to the prince, and in the evening the prince caused secretly to be shown through all the host, that at the first sounding of the trumpets every man to apparel himself, and at the second to be armed, and at the third to leap a-horseback and to follow the marshal's banners with the pennon of Saint George; and that none on pain of death advance before them without he be commanded so to do.

In like manner as the prince had done the same Friday in sending out his currours, so did King Henry on his part to know where the prince was lodged. And when he had true report thereof, then the king called Sir Bertram of Guesclin and took counsel and advice how to persevere. Then they caused their people to sup and after to go to rest to be the more fresher, and at the hour of midnight to be ready apparelled and to draw to the field and to ordain their battles, for he knew well the next day he should have battle. So that night the Spaniards took their ease and rest, for they had well wherewith so to do, as plenty of victuals and other things. And the Englishmen had great default: therefore they had great desire to fight either to win or to lose all.

After midnight the trumpets sounded in King Henry's host. Then every man made him ready. At the second blast they drew out of their lodgings and ordered three battles. The first had Sir Bertram of Guesclin, Lord Robert of Roquebertin and the Earl Dune of Aragon; and there were all the strangers as well of France as of other countries, and there were two barons of Hainault, the Lord d'Antoing and Sir Alard, Lord of Briffeuil. There was also the Begue of Villaines, the Begue of Villiers, Sir John of Berguettes, Sir Gawain of Bailleul, the Alemant of Saint-Venant, who was there made knight, and divers other of France, Aragon and Provence and of the marches thereabout. There was well in that battle four thousand knights and squires well armed and dressed after the usage of France. The second battle had the Earl Don Tello and his brother the Earl Don Sancho, and in that battle with the genetours there were fifteen thousand afoot and a-horseback, and they drew them a little aback on the left hand of the first battle. The third battle, and the greatest of all, governed King Henry himself; and in his company there were a seven thousand horsemen and threescore thousand afoot, with the crossbows: so in all three battles he was a fourscore and six thousand a-horseback and afoot.

Then King Henry leapt on a strong mule after the usage of the country, and rode from battle to battle right sweetly, praying every man that day to employ themself to defend and keep their honour, and so he showed himself so cheerfully that every man was joyful to behold him. Then he went again to his own battle, and by that time it was daylight; and then about the sun-rising, he advanced forth toward Najera to find his enemies, in good order of battle ready to fight.

The Prince of Wales at the breaking of the day was ready in the field arranged in battle, and advanced forward in good order, for he knew well he should encounter his enemies. So there were none that went before the marshals' battles but such currours as were appointed. So thus the lords of both hosts knew by the report of their currours that they should shortly meet. So they went forward an hosting pace each toward other, and when the sun was rising up it was a great beauty to behold the battles and the armours shining against the sun. So thus they went forward till they approached near together. Then the prince and his company went over a little hill, and in the descending thereof they perceived clearly their enemies coming toward them. And when they were all descended down this mountain, then every man drew to their battles and kept them still, and so rested them, and every man dressed and apparelled himself ready to fight.

Then Sir John Chandos brought his banner rolled up together to the prince and said, 'Sir, behold here is my banner. I require you display it abroad, and give me leave this day to raise it; for, sir, I thank God and you, I have land and heritage sufficient to maintain it withal'. Then the prince and King Don Pedro took the banner between their hands and spread it abroad, the which was of silver, a sharp pile gules, and delivered it to him and said, 'Sir John, behold here your banner. God send you joy and honour thereof.' Then Sir John Chandos bare his banner to his own company, and said, 'Sirs, behold here my banner and yours. Keep it as your own.' And they took it and were right joyful thereof, and said that by the pleasure of God and Saint George, they would keep and defend it to the best of their powers. And so the banner abode in the hands of a good English squire called William Alery who bare it that day, and acquitted himself right nobly. Then anon after the Englishmen and Gascons alighted off their horses, and every man drew under their own banner and standard in array of battle ready to fight. It was great joy to see and consider the banners and pennons and the noble armoury that was there.

Then the battles began a little to advance, and then the Prince of Wales opened his eyes and regarded toward heaven, and joined his hands together and said, 'Very God, Jesu Christ, who hath formed and created me, consent by your benign grace that I may have this day victory of mine enemies, as that I do is in a rightful quarrel, to sustain and to aid this king chased out of his own heritage, the which giveth me courage to advance myself to re-establish him again into his realm.' And then he laid his right hand on King Don Pedro, who was by him, and said, 'Sir King, ye shall know this day if ever ye shall have any part of the realm of Castile or not. Therefore, advance banners, in the name of God and Saint George!' With those words the Duke of Lancaster and Sir John Chandos approached, and the duke said to Sir William Beauchamp, 'Sir William, behold yonder our enemies. This day ye shall see me a good knight, or else to die in the quarrel.' And therewith they approached their enemies.

And first the Duke of Lancaster's and Sir John Chandos' battle assembled with the battle of Sir Bertram of Guesclin and of the marshal Sir Arnold d'Audrehem, who were a four thousand men of arms. So ar the first brunt there was a sore encounter with spears and shields, and they were a certain space or any of them could get within other. There was many a deed of arms done, and many a man reversed and cast to the earth that never after was relieved. And when these two first battles were thus assembled, the other battles would not long tarry behind, but approached and assembled together quickly. And so the prince and his battle came on the Earl Don Sancho's battle, and with the prince was King Don Pedro of Castile and Sir Martin de la Carra, who represented the King of Navarre. And at the first meeting that the prince met with the Earl Don Sancho's battle, the earl and his brother fled away without order or good array, and wist not why, and a two thousand spears with him. So this second battle was opened and anon discomfited, for the Captal of Buch and the Lord Clisson and their company came on them afoot and slew and hurt many of them. Then the prince's battle with King Don Pedro came and joined with the battle of King Henry, whereas there were threescore thousand men afoot and a-horseback. There the battle began to be fierce and cruel on all parts, for the Spaniards and Castilians had slings wherewith they cast stones in such wise that therewith they clove and brake many a bassenet and helm, and hurt many a man and overthrew them to the earth. And the archers of England shot fiercely and hurt Spaniards grievously, and brought them to great mischief. The one part cried, 'Castile, for King Henry!' and the other part, 'Saint George! Guyenne!' And the first battle, as the Duke of Lancaster and Sir John Chandos and the two marshals Sir Guichard d'Angle and Sir Stephen Cosington, fought with Sir Bertram of Guesclin and with the other knights of France and of Aragon. There was done many a deed of arms, so it was hard for any of them to open either's battle. Divers of them held their spears in both their hands, foining and pressing each at other, and some fought with short swords and daggers. Thus at the beginning, the Frenchmen and they of Aragon fought valiantly, so that the good knights of England endured much pain.

That day Sir John Chandos was a good knight, and did under his banner many a noble feat of arms. He adventured himself so far that he was closed in among his enemies, and so sore overpressed that he was felled down to the earth. And on him there fell a great and a big man of Castile called Martin Ferrant, who was greatly renowned of hardiness among the Spaniards, and he did his intent to have slain Sir John Chandos, who lay under him in great danger. Then Sir John Chandos remembered of a knife that he had in his bosom, and drew it out and struck this Martin so in the back and in the sides, that he wounded him to death as he lay on him. Then Sir John Chandos turned him over and rose quickly on his feet, and his men were there about him, who had with much pain broken the press to come to him whereas they saw him felled.

The Saturday in the morning between Nazres and Najera was the battle right fell and cruel, and many a man brought to great mischief. There was done many a noble deed of arms by the prince and by the Duke of Lancaster his brother, and by Sir John Chandos, Sir Guichard d'Angle, the Captal of Buch, the Lord of Clisson, the Lord of Retz, Sir Hugh Calverley, Sir Matthew Gournay, Sir Louis Harcourt, the Lord of Pons, the Lord of Partenay. And of Gascons fought valiantly the Earl of Armagnac, the Lord d'Albret, the Lord of Pommiers and his brethren, the Lord of Mussidan, the Lord of Rauzan, the Earl of Périgord, the Earl of Comminges, the Earl of Caraman, the Lord of Condom, the Lord Lesparre, the Lord of Caumont, Sir Bertram of Terride, the Lord of Puycornet, Sir Bernard d'Albret, the Lord of Geronde, Sir Aymery of Tastes, the Soudic of Latrau, Sir Petiton of Curton, and divers other knights and squires acquitted themselves right nobly in arms to their powers. And under the pennon of Saint George and the banner of Sir John Chandos were all the companions to the number of twelve hundred pensels, and they were right hardy and valiant knights, as Sir Robert Cheyne, Sir Perducas d'Albret, Robert Briquet, Sir Garsis of the Castle, Sir Gaillard Vigier, Sir John Creswey, Naudan of Bageran, Aymenion d'Artigue, Perrot of Savoy, the Bourg Camus, the Bourg Lesparre, the Bourg Breteuil, Espiote and divers other.

On the French party Sir Bertram of Guesclin, Sir Arnold d'Audrehem, Sancho, Sir Gomez Carillo and other knights of France and of Aragon fought right nobly to their powers. Howbeit they had none advantage, for these companions were hardy and strong knights and well used and expert in arms, and also there were great plenty of knights and squires of England, under the banner of the Duke of Lancaster, and of Sir John Chandos. There was the Lord William Beauchamp, son to the Earl of Warwick, Sir Ralph Camoys, Sir Walter Urswick, Sir Thomas Dammery, Sir John Grandison, Sir John d'Ypres, Sir Amery of Rochechouart, Sir Gaillard de la Motte, and more than two hundred knights, the which I cannot name. And to speak truly, the said Sir Bertram de Guesclin and the Marshal d'Audrehem, the Begue of Villaines, the Lord d'Antoing, the Lord of Briffeuil, Sir Gawain of Bailleul, Sir John of Berguettes, the Begue of Villiers, the Alemant of Saint-Venant, and the good knights and squires of France that were there acquitted themselves nobly: for of truth, if the Spaniards had done their part as well as the Frenchmen did, the Englishmen and Gascons should have had much more to do and have suffered more pain than they did. The fault was not in King Henry that they did no better, for he had well admonished and desired them to have done their devoir valiantly, and so they had promised him to have done. The king bare himself right valiantly and did marvels in arms, and with good courage comforted his people, as when they were flying and opening he came in among them and said, 'Lords, I am your king: ye have made me King of Castile, and have sworn and promised that to die ye will not fail me. For God's sake keep your promise that ye have sworn and acquit you against me, and I shall acquit me against you, for I shall not fly one foot as long as I may see you do your devoir.' By these words and such other full of comfort King Henry brought his men together again three times the same day, and with his own hands he fought valiantly, so that he ought greatly to be honoured and renowned.

This was a marvellous dangerous battle and many a man slain and sore hurt. The commons of Spain, according to the usage of their country, with their slings they did cast stones with great violence and did much hurt, the which at the beginning troubled greatly the Englishmen; but when their cast was past and that they felt the sharp arrows light among them, they could no longer keep their array. With King Henry in his battle were many noble men of arms, as well of Spain as of Lisbon, of Aragon and of Portugal, who acquitted them right nobly and gave it not up so lightly, for valiantly they fought, with spears, javelins, archegayes and swords. And on the wing of King Henry's battle there were certain well-mounted, who always kept the battle in good order, for if the battle opened or broke array in any side, then they were ever ready to help to bring them again into good order. So these Englishmen and Gascons, or they had the advantage they bought it dearly, and won it by noble chivalry and great prowess of arms. And for to say truth, the prince himself was the chief flower of chivalry of all the world, and had with him as then right noble and valiant knights and squires. And a little beside the prince's battle was the King of Majorca and his company fighting and acquitting themselves right valiantly. And also there was the Lord Martin de la Carra representing the King of Navarre, who did right well his devoir. I cannot speak of all them that did that day right nobly, but about the prince in his battle there were divers good knights, as well of England as of Gascony, as Sir Richard Pontchardon, Sir Thomas Spenser, Sir Thomas Holland, Sir Nigel Loring, Sir Hugh and Sir Philip Courtenay, Sir John Trivet, Sir Nicholas Bond, Sir Thomas Trivet, and divers other, as the Seneschal of Saintonge, Sir Baldwin of Freville, the Seneschal of Bordeaux, of Rochelle, of Poitou, of Angoulême, of Rouergue, of Limoges and of Périgord, and Sir Louis Melval, Sir Raymond Mareuil and divers other. There was none that feigned to fight valiantly, and also they had good cause why: for there were of Spaniards and of Castile more than a hundred thousand men in harness, so that by reason of their great number it was long or they could be overcome. King Don Pedro was greatly chafed, and much desired to meet with the bastard his brother, and said, 'Where is that whore's son that calleth himself King of Castile?' And the same King Henry fought right valiantly whereas he was, and held his people together right marvellously, and said, 'Ah! ye good people, ye have crowned me king, therefore help and aid me to keep the heritage that you have given me.' So that by these words and such other as he spake that day, he caused many to be right hardy and valiant, whereby they abode on the field, so that because of their honour they would not fly from the place.

How Sir Bertram of Guesclin was discomfited, he taken, and King Henry saved himself, and of the Spaniards that fled, and of the number of the dead, and of the cities that yielded them up to King Don Pedro, and of the answers that he made to the prince (1367).   [Ch. 238]

THE battle that was best fought and longest held together was the company of Sir Bertram of Guesclin, for there were many noble men of arms who fought and held together to their powers, and there was done many a noble feat of arms. And on the English part, specially there was Sir John Chandos, who that day did like a noble knight and governed and counselled that day the Duke of Lancaster in like manner as he did before the prince at the battle of Poitiers, wherein he was greatly renowned and praised, the which was good reason; for a valiant man and a good knight acquitting himself nobly among lords and princes, ought greatly to be recommended, for that day he took no heed for taking of any prisoner with his own hands, but always fought and went forward. But there was taken by his company under his banner divers good knights and squires of Aragon and of France, and specially Sir Bertram of Guesclin, Sir Arnold d'Audrehem, Sir Begue of Villaines, and more than threescore prisoners.

So thus finally the battle of Sir Bertram of Guesclin was discomfited and all that were therein taken and slain, as well they of France as of Aragon. There was slain the Begue of Villiers and taken the Lord Antoing of Hainault, the Lord Briffeuil, Sir Gawain of Bailleul, Sir John of Berguettes, Sir Alemant of Saint-Venant and divers other. Then drew together these banners: the banner of the Duke of Lancaster, of Sir John Chandos and of the two marshals, and the pennon of Saint George, and went altogether on the battle of King Henry and cried with a high voice, 'Saint George! Guyenne!' Then the Spaniards and their company were sore put aback. The Captal of Buch and the Lord Clisson fought valiantly, and also Sir Eustace d'Aubrecicourt, Sir Hugh Calverley, Sir Soudic, Sir John Devereux and other acquitted themselves that day right nobly. The prince showed himself like a noble knight and fought valiantly with his enemies. On the other side King Henry acquitted himself right valiantly, and recovered and turned again his people that day three times. For after that the Earl Don Tello and a three thousand horsemen with him were departed from the field, the other began then greatly to be discomfited and were ever ready to fly after their company, but then ever King Henry was before them and said, 'Fair lords, what do you? Wherefore will ye thus forsake and betray me? Since ye have made me king and set the crown on my head, and put the heritage of Castile into my hands, return and help to keep and defend me, and abide with me, for by the grace of God, or it be night, all shall be ours.' So that these words, or suchlike, encouraged his people in such wise that it made them to abide longer in the field, for they durst not fly for shame when they saw their king and their lord so valiantly fight and speak so amiably: so that there died more than a thousand and five hundred persons, that might well have saved themselves and have taken the time to their advantage, an the love that they had to their lord and king had not been.

When the battle of the marshals were passed through their enemies, and had discomfited the greatest number of them, so that the Spaniards could not sustain nor defend them any longer, but began to fly away in great fear without any good array or order toward the city of Nazres, and so passed by the great river, so that for any words that King Henry could say they would not return, and when the king saw the mischief and discomfiture of his people and that he saw no recovery: then he called for his horse and mounted thereon and put himself among them that fled, but he took not the way to Nazres for fear of enclosing, but then took another way eschewing all perils, for he knew well that if he were taken he should die without mercy. Then the Englishmen and Gascons leapt a-horseback and began to chase the Spaniards, who fled away sore discomfited to the great river. And at the entry of the bridge of Nazres there was a hideous shedding of blood, and many a man slain and drowned, for divers leapt into the water the which was deep and hideous: they thought they had as lief to be drowned as slain. And in this chase among other there were two valiant knights of Spain, bearing on them the habit of religion, the one called the Great Prior of Saint James and the other the Great Master of Calatrava. They and their company to save themselves entered into Nazres, and they were so near chased at their back by Englishmen and Gascons that they* won the bridge, so that there was a great slaughter. And the Englishmen entered into the city after their enemies, who were entered into a strong house of stone. Howbeit, incontinent it was won by force and the knights taken and many of their men slain, and all the city overrun and pilled, the which was greatly to Englishmen's profit. Also they won King Henry's lodging, wherein they found great riches of vessel, and jewels of gold and silver, for the king was come thither with great nobleness, so that when they were discomfited they had no leisure for to return thither again to save what they had left there. So this was a hideous and a terrible discomfiture, and specially on the river side there was many a man slain. And it was said, as I heard after reported of some of them that were there present, that one might have seen the water that ran by Nazres to be of the colour of red, with the blood of men and horse that were there slain. This battle was between Nazres and Nàjera in Spain, the year of the incarnation of our Lord Jesu Christ, a thousand three hundred threescore and seven, the 3rd day of April, the which was on a Saturday.

After the discomfiture of the battle of Nazres, which was done by noon, the prince caused his banner to be raised up a-high upon a bush on a little hill, to

* i.e. the English and Gascons.

the intent to draw his people thither. And so thither drew all those that came from the chase: thither came the Duke of Lancaster, Sir John Chandos, the Lord Clisson, the Captal of Buch, the Earl of Armagnac, the Lord d'Albret and divers other barons, and had raised up on high their banners to draw their people thither; and ever as they came they ranged them in the field. Also there was James King of Majorca, his banner before him, whereunto his company drew. And a little there beside was Sir Martin de la Carra with the banner of his lord the King of Navarre, with divers other earls and barons, the which was a goodly thing to regard and behold. Then came thither King Don Pedro, right sore chafed, coming from the chase on a great black courser, his banner beaten with the arms of Castile before him. And as soon as he saw the prince's banner, he alighted and went thither, and when the prince saw him coming he went and met him and did him great honour. There the King Don Pedro would have kneeled down to have thanked the prince, but the prince made great haste to take him by the hand, and would not suffer him to kneel. Then the king said, 'Dear and fair cousin, I ought to give you many thanks and praises for this fair journey that I have attained this day by your means.' Then the prince said, 'Sir, yield thanks to God and give him all the praise, for the victory hath come by him all only and not by me.'

Then the lords of the prince's council drew together and communed of divers matters, and so long the prince was still there till all his people were returned from the chase. Then he ordained four knights and four heralds to go search the fields, to know what people were taken and the number of them that were slain, and also to know the truth of King Henry, whom they called bastard, whether he were alive or dead. And then the prince and his lords went to the lodging of King Henry and of the Spaniards, where they were well and easily lodged, for it was great and large and well replenished of all things necessary. So then they supped that night in great joy, and after supper the knights and heralds that went to visit the field returned, and there they reported that there were slain of their enemies, of men of arms a five hundred and threescore, and of commons about a seven thousand and five hundred beside them that were drowned, whereof the number was unknown. And of their own company there was no more slain but four knights, whereof two were Gascons, the third a German and the fourth an Englishman, and of other commons not past a forty. But they showed how they could not find King Henry, whereof King Don Pedro was right sorry. So this Saturday at night they rested themselves and made good cheer, for they had well wherewith, for there they found plenty of wine and other victuals, and so refreshed them there all the Sunday, the which was Palm Sunday.

The Sunday in the morning, when the Prince was up and ready apparelled, then he issued out of his pavilion, and then came to him the Duke of Lancaster his brother, the Earl of Armagnac, the Lord d'Albret, Sir John Chandos, the Captal of Buch, the Lord of Pommiers, Sir Guichard d'Angle, the King of Majorca, and a great number of other knights and squires. And then anon after came to the prince the King Don Pedro, to whom the prince made great honour and reverence. Then the King Don Pedro said, 'Dear and fair cousin, I pray and require you that ye will deliver to me the false traitors of this country, as my bastard brother Don Sancho, and such other, and I shall cause them to lose their heads, for they have well deserved it.'

Then the prince advised him well and said, 'Sir king, I require you in the name of love and lineage that ye will grant me a gift and a request.' The king, who in no wise would deny his request, said, 'Good cousin, all that I have is yours: therefore I am content, whatsoever ye desire, to grant it.' Then the prince said, 'Sir, I require you to give pardon to all your people in your realm, such as hath rebelled against you, by the which courtesy ye shall abide in the better rest and peace in your realm, except Gomez Carillo, for of him I am content ye take your pleasure.' The King Don Pedro accorded to his desire, though it were against his will, but he durst not deny the prince, he was so much bounden to him, and said, 'Fair cousin, I grant your request with a good heart.' Then the prisoners were sent for and the prince accorded them with the king their lord, and caused him to forgive all his evil will to his brother the Earl Sancho and to all other, so that they should make covenant, and swear fealty, homage and service, to hold of him truly for ever, and to become his men and to acknowledge him for their lord and king for ever. This courtesy with divers other did the prince to the king, the which after was but smally rewarded, as ye shall hear after in this history.

And also the prince showed great courtesy to the barons of Spain such as were prisoners, for if King Don Pedro had taken them in his displeasure, they had all died without mercy. And then Sir Gomez Carillo was delivered to the king, whom he hated so sore, that he would take no ransom for him but made his head to be stricken off before his lodging.

Then King Don Pedro mounted on his horse, and the Earl Sancho his brother and all those that were become his men, and his marshals, Sir Guichard d'Angle and Sir Stephen Cosington, and a five hundred men of arms, and they departed from the prince's host and rode to Burgos and so came thither the Monday in the morning. And they of Burgos, who were well informed how the journey of Nazres was achieved and how that King Henry was discomfited, they thought not to keep the town against Don Pedro, but divers of the richest of the town, and of the most notablest, issued out of the town and presented the keys of the city to him and received him to their lord, and so brought him and all his men into the city of Burgos with great joy and solemnity. And all the Sunday the prince abode still in the lodgings they had won. And on the Monday after evensong, he dislodged and went and lodged at Briviesca, and there tarried till it was Wednesday, and then they went all to the city of Burgos. And there the prince entered into the town with great reverence, and with him the Duke of Lancaster, the Earl of

Armagnac, and divers other great lords. And their people made their lodgings without the town, for they could not all have been lodged within at their ease. And when the prince was at his lodging there, he gave and rendered judgments of arms and of all things thereto appertaining, and there kept field and wage of battle: wherefore it might well be said that all Spain was come that day in his hands and under his obeisance.

The Prince of Wales and King Don Pedro held their Easter in the town of Burgos, and there tarried a three weeks and more. And on Easter Day they of Asturias, of Toledo, of Lisbon, of Cordoba, of Galicia, of Seville and of all the other marches and limitations of the realm of Castile, came thither and made homage to King Don Pedro, and were glad to see the prince and Don Ferrant of Castro, and so there was great cheer made between them. And when King Don Pedro had tarried there the term that I have showed you and more, and saw that there were no more that rebelled against him but every man to him obeisant, then the prince said to him, 'Sir king, ye are now, thanked be God, peaceably king of this your own realm, without any rebellion or let, and sir, I and my company tarry here at a great charge and expense: therefore we require you to provide for money to pay the wages to them that hath helped to bring you again into your realm, and in fulfilling of your promise whereunto ye have sworn and sealed. And, sir, the shortlier that ye do it, the greater thanks we shall give you and the more shall be your profit, for ye know well men of war must be paid to live withal, or else they will take it whereas they may get it.' Then the king answered and said, 'Cousin, we will hold, keep, and accomplish to our power that we have sworn and sealed unto. But, sir, as for this present time we have no money, wherefore we will draw us to the marches of Seville, and there we will so procure for money that we will satisfy every party. And, sir, ye shall abide still here in Valladolid, the which is a plentiful country, and sir, we shall return again to you in as short time as we conveniently can or may, and at the farthest by Whitsuntide.' This answer was right pleasant to the prince and to his council. And shortly after the King Don Pedro departed from the prince and rode toward Seville to the intent to get money to pay his men of war, as he had promised. And the prince went and lodged in Valladolid, and all his lords and people spread abroad in the country to get victuals more plentiful for them and for their horses. There thus they sojourned to a small profit to the country, for the companions could not abstain themselves from robbing and pilling of the country.

Summary.   [**Ch. 239-266**]

PEDRO the Cruel did not enjoy his success long for two years later Henry of Trastamare treacherously killed him at a meeting between them. War broke out again between France and England.

How Queen Philippa of England trespassed out of this mortal life, and of the three gifts that she desired of the king her husband or she died (1369). [Ch. 267]

IN the mean season while the noblemen of France were thus assembled before Tornehem, of whom the Duke of Burgundy was chief and sovereign and the Duke of Lancaster with the Englishmen on the other part, there fell in England a heavy case and a common: howbeit it was right piteous for the king, his children, and all his realm, for the good Queen of England, that so many good deeds had done in her time and so many knights succoured and ladies and damosels comforted, and had so largely departed of her goods to her people, and naturally loved always the nation of Hainault, the country whereas she was born, she fell sick in the castle of Windsor; the which sickness continued on her so long, that there was no remedy but death. And the good lady, when she knew and perceived that there was with her no remedy but death, she desired to speak with the king her husband. And when he was before her, she put out of her bed her right hand and took the king by his right hand, who was right sorrowful at his heart. Then she said, 'Sir, we have in peace, joy, and great prosperity, used all our time together. Sir, now I pray you at our departing, that ye will grant me three desires.' The king, right sorrowfully weeping, said, 'Madam, desire what ye will, I grant it.' 'Sir,' said she, 'I require you first of all, that all manner of people such as I have dealt withal in their merchandise, on this side the sea or beyond, that it may please you to pay everything that I owe to them or to any other. And secondly, sir, all such ordinance and promises as I have made to the churches, as well of this country as beyond the sea, whereas I have had my devotion, that it may please you to accomplish and to fulfill the same. Thirdly, sir, I require you that it may please you to take none other sepulture, whensoever it shall please God to call you out of this transitory life, but beside me in Westminster.' The king all weeping said, 'Madam, I grant all your desire.' Then the good lady and queen made on her the sign of the cross and commended the king her husband to God, and her youngest son Thomas who was there beside her. And anon after she yielded up the spirit, the which I believe surely the holy angels received with great joy up to heaven, for in all her life she did neither in thought nor deed thing whereby to lose her soul, as far as any creature could know.

Thus the good Queen of England died, in the year of our Lord MCCCLXIX in the vigil of our Lady, in the midst of August. Of whose death tidings came to Tornehem in the English host, whereof every creature was sore displeased and right sorrowful, and specially her son the Duke of Lancaster. Howbeit there is no sorrow but it behoveth at length to be borne and forgotten: therefore the Englishmen left not their order, but remained a long space before the Frenchmen . . .

How Sir Bertram of Guesclin made great war in the county of Limoges, and how they took the castle of Saint-Yrieix (1369-70). [Ch. 282]

THE same season that Sir Robert Knowles made thus his viage and that the Prince of Wales and his two brethren lay before the city of Limoges, Sir Bertram of Guesclin and his company, the which were to the number of two hundred spears, he rode by the one side of the country of Limoges. But he lay not in the field never a night for fear of the Englishmen, but every night lay in a fortress, such as were turned French, pertaining to Sir Louis of Melval and to Sir Raymond of Makevil, and to other. Howbeit every day they rode forth and did great pain to conquer towns and fortresses.

The prince was well advertised of this journey that Sir Bertram made, and daily complaints came to him; howbeit in no wise he would break up his siege. Then Sir Bertram of Guesclin entered into the vicomté of Limoges, a country that was yielded, and did hold of the Duke of Brittany, the Lord John of Montfort, and there Sir Bertram began to make great war in the name of the lady, wife to the Lord Charles of Blois, to whom the same inheritance sometime belonged. There he made great war for none came against him, for the Duke of Brittany thought full little that Sir Bertram would have made any war against him. And so Sir Bertram came before the town of Saint-Yrieix, wherein there was never a gentleman to defend the town: wherefore they were so afraid that they yielded them up to the obeisance of the lady of Brittany, in whose name Sir Bertram made war. And so of Saint-Yrieix the Bretons made a great garrison, whereby they won divers other towns in Limousin.

Now let us return to the Prince of Wales.

How the Prince took the city of Limoges, and how four companions did marvels in arms (1370). [Ch. 283]

ABOUT the space of a month or more was the Prince of Wales before the city of Limoges and there was neither assault nor skirmish, but daily they mined. And they within knew well how they were mined, and made a countermine there against to have destroyed the English miners, but they failed of their mine. And when the prince's miners saw how the countermine against them failed, they said to the prince, 'Sir, whensoever it shall please you, we shall cause a part of the wall to fall into the dykes, whereby ye shall enter into the city at your ease without any danger.' Which words pleased greatly the prince and said, 'I will that tomorrow betimes ye show forth and execute your work.' Then the miners set fire into their mine, and so the next morning as the prince had ordained, there fell down a great pane of the wall and filled the dykes, whereof the Englishmen were glad, and were ready armed in the field to enter into the town. The foot-men might well enter at their ease, and so they did, and ran to the gate and beat down the fortifying and barriers, for there was no defence against them: it was down so suddenly that they of the town were not ware thereof.

Then the prince, the Duke of Lancaster, the Earl of Cambridge, the Earl of Pembroke, Sir Guichard d'Angle, and all the other with their companies entered into the city, and all other foot-men ready apparelled to do evil and to pill and rob the city, and to slay men, women and children, for so it was commanded them to do. It was great pity to see the men, women and children that kneeled down on their knees before the prince for mercy, but he was so inflamed with ire that he took no heed to them, so that none was heard but all put to death as they were met withal, and such as were nothing culpable. There was no pity taken of the poor people who wrought never no manner of treason, yet they bought it dearer than the great personages, such as had done the evil and trespass. There was not so hard a heart within the city of Limoges, an if he had any remembrance of God, but that wept piteously for the great mischief that they saw before their eyes, for more than three thousand men, women and children were slain and beheaded that day. God have mercy on their souls, for I trow they were martyrs. And thus entering into the city a certain company of Englishmen entered into the bishop's palace, and there they found the bishop. And so they brought him to the prince's presence, who beheld him right fiercely and felly, and the best word that he could have of him was how he would have his head stricken off, and so he was had out of his sight.

Now let us speak of the knights that were within the city, as Sir John of Villemur, Sir Hugh de la Roche, Roger Beaufort, son to the Earl of Beaufort, captains of the city. When they saw the tribulation and pestilence that ran over them and their company, they said one to another, 'We are all dead without we defend ourselves. Therefore let us sell our lives dearly, as good knights ought to do.' Then Sir John of Villemur said to Roger Beaufort, 'Roger, it behoveth that ye be made a knight.' Then Roger answered and said, 'Sir, I am not as yet worthy to be a knight. I thank you, sir, of your goodwill.' So there was no more said: they had not the leisure to speak long together. Howbeit they assembled them together in a place against an old wall and there displayed their banners. So they were to the number of eighty persons. Thither came the Duke of Lancaster, the Earl of Cambridge and their companies, and so alighted afoot, so that the Frenchmen could not long endure against the Englishmen, for anon they were slain and taken. Howbeit the Duke of Lancaster himself fought long hand to hand against Sir John of Villemur, who was a strong knight and a hardy. And the Earl of Cambridge fought against Sir Hugh de la Roche, and the Earl of Pembroke against Roger Beaufort, who was as then but a squire. These three Frenchmen did many feats of arms: their men were occupied otherwise. The prince in his chariot came by them and beheld them gladly, and appeased himself in beholding of them. So long they fought together that the three Frenchmen, by one accord, beholding their swords said, 'Sirs, we be yours, ye have conquered us. Do with us according to right of arms.' 'Sir,' quoth the Duke of Lancaster, 'we look for nothing else, therefore we receive you as our prisoners.' And thus the foresaid three Frenchmen were taken, as it was informed me.

How the city of Limoges was burnt and destroyed and the bishop delivered from death, and how Sir Bertram of Guesclin was chosen constable (1370).   [Ch. 284]

THUS the city of Limoges was pilled, robbed and clean burnt and brought to destruction. Then the Englishmen departed with their conquest and prisoners and drew to Cognac, where my lady the princess was. Then the prince gave leave to all his men of war to depart and did no more that season, for he felt himself not well at ease, for always his sickness increased, whereof his brethren and people were sore dismayed.

Now shall I show you of the Bishop of Limoges, who was in great peril of losing of his head. The Duke of Lancaster desired of the prince to give him the bishop to do with him at his pleasure. The prince was content and caused him to be delivered to the duke. The bishop had friends and they had newly informed the Pope, who was as then at Avignon, of the bishop's taking, the which fortuned well for the bishop for else he had been dead. Then the Pope by sweet words entreated the Duke of Lancaster to deliver to him the said bishop. The duke would not deny the Pope but granted him and sent him to Avignon, whereof the Pope was right glad.

Now let us speak of the adventures of France. The French king was informed of the destruction and conquest of the city of Limoges, and how it was left clean void as a town of desert, wherewith he was sore displeased and took it in great passion, the damage and annoy of the inhabitants of the same. Then was it advised in France by counsel of the nobles, prelates and commons of all the realm, that it was necessary that the Frenchmen should have a chief and a governor, called the constable, for Sir Moreau of Fiennes would leave and give up his office, who was a right valiant man of his hands and a great enterpriser of deeds of arms. So that all things considered and imagined, by a common accord they chose Sir Bertram of Guesclin, so that he would take it on him, as the most valiant knight, most virtuous and most able to execute that office, and most fortunate that they knew as then that bare arms for the crown of France. Then the king wrote and sent certain messengers to him, that he should come and speak with him at Paris. The messengers found him in the county of Limoges, whereas he took fortresses and castles and made them to yield to the Lady of Brittany, wife to Sir Charles of Blois. And as then he had newly taken a town called Brantôme and was riding towards another. And when the king's messengers were come to him he received them joyously and right sagely, as he that could do it right well. Then the messenger delivered to him the king's letter and did his message. And when Sir Bertram saw the commandment of the king, he would make none excuse, but concluded to go and know the king's pleasure. And so departed as soon as he might, and sent the most part of his men into garrisons such as he had conquered, and he made sovereign and keeper of them Sir Oliver of Manny his nephew.

Then he rode forth so long by his journeys that he came to Paris, where he found the king and great number of lords of his council, who received him right joyously and did him great reverence. And there the king showed him how he and his council had chosen him to be Constable of France. Then he excused himself right sagely and said, 'Sir, I am not worthy. I am but a poor knight as in regard of your other great lords and valiant men in France, though it be so that fortune hath a little advanced me.' Then the king said, 'Sir, it is for nothing that ye excuse you. It behoveth you to take it, for it is so ordained and determined by all the council of France, the which in no wise I will break.' Then Sir Bertram excused himself again by another way and said, 'Right dear sir and noble king, I may not nor dare not withsay your noble pleasure: howbeit, sir, it is of truth that I am but a poor man, and too low of blood to come to the office of Constable of France, the which is so great and so noble an office. For it is convenient that he that will exercise and acquit himself well in that office must command as well, and rather the great men than the small personages. And, sir, behold here my lords your brethren, your nephews, and your cousins, who hath charge of many men of war in your host and journeys. Sir, how durst I then be so bold as to command them? Certainly, sir, envy is so great that I ought to fear it. Therefore, sir, I require your Grace pardon me and give this office to some other that would gladlier have it than I, and that may better execute the office.' Then the king answered and said, 'Sir Bertram, excuse you not by that way, for I have neither brother, cousin nor nephew, earl nor baron in my realm, but that shall obey you: and if any do the contrary I shall so anger him that he shall perceive well my displeasure. Therefore, sir, take joyously the office I require you.' Sir Bertram saw well that any excusations that he could make should not avail. Then finally he accorded to the opinion of the king right sore against his will. So then with great joy Sir Bertram of Guesclin was made Constable of France, and further to his advancement the king caused him to sit at his table, and showed all the tokens of love that he could devise, and gave him with the office divers gifts and great lands and heritage to him and to his heirs for ever. To this promotion did help greatly the Duke of Anjou.

M

Summary.   [Ch. 285-380]

THE Black Prince died in 1576 and his father, Edward III the next year. Due to the unceasing efforts of Charles II of France, the great gains of the Treaties of Calais and Brétigny were gradually whittled away. Richard II of England was a minor and there was no strong direction to the English war policy. Then in 1380 Charles II died, also leaving his realm to a minor, Charles VI. England however had its internal problems: the Peasants' Revolt which is described in the following pages. This was due partly to the fact that a new stronger class of peasantry had arisen and partly to the repressive measures passed to keep the peasants in order after the labour shortages caused by the outbreaks of the Black Death.

How the Earl of Cambridge departed out of England to go into Portugal; and how the commons of England rebelled against the noblemen (1381).   [Ch. 381]

. . . . . IN the mean season while this treaty was, there fell in England great mischief and rebellion of moving of the common people, by which deed England was at a point to have been lost without recovery. There was never realm nor country in so great adventure as it was in that time, and all because of the ease and riches that the common people were of which moved them to this rebellion; as sometime they did in France, the which did much hurt, for by such incidents the realm of France hath been greatly grieved. It was a marvellous thing and of poor foundation that this mischief began in England, and to give ensample to all manner of people, I will speak thereof as it was done, as I was informed, and of the incidents thereof.

There was a usage in England and yet is in divers countries, that the noblemen hath great franchises over the commons and keepeth them in service, that is to say, their tenants ought by custom to labour the lords' lands, to gather and bring home their corns, and some to thresh and to fan, and by servage to make their hay, and to hew their wood and bring it home. All these things they ought to do by servage, and there be more of these people in England than in any other realm. Thus the noblemen and prelates are served by them and specially in the counties of Kent, Essex, Sussex and Bedford. These unhappy people of these said countries began to stir, because they said they were kept in great servage, and in the beginning of the world they said there were no bondmen, wherefore they maintained that none ought to be bond, without he did treason to his lord, as Lucifer did to God. But they said they could have no such battle,* for they were neither angels nor spirits, but men formed to the similitude of their lords, saying, why should

* Lord Berners' text had 'bataille' instead of 'taille'–nature.

they then be kept so under like beasts, the which they said they would no longer suffer, for they would be all one; and if they laboured or did anything for their lords, they would have wages therefor as well as other. And of this imagination was a foolish priest in the country of Kent, called John Ball, for the which foolish words he had been three times in the Bishop of Canterbury's prison. For this priest used oftentimes on the Sundays after mass, when the people were going out of the minster, to go into the cloister and preach and made the people to assemble about him, and would say thus, 'Ah! ye good people, the matters goeth not well to pass in England, nor shall not do till everything be common, and that there be no villeins nor gentlemen, but that we may be all united together, and that the lords be no greater masters than we be. What have we deserved, or why should we be kept thus in servage? We be all come from one father and one mother, Adam and Eve: whereby can they say or show that they be greater lords than we be, saying by that they cause us to win and labour for that they dispend? They are clothed in velvet and camlet furred with grise, and we be vestured with poor cloth. They have their wines, spices and good bread, and we have the drawing out of the chaff, and drink water. They dwell in fair houses, and we have the pain and travail, rain and wind in the fields; and by that that cometh of our labours they keep and maintain their estates. We be called their bondmen, and without we do readily them service, we be beaten; and we have no sovereign to whom we may complain, nor that will hear us nor do us right. Let us go to the king, he is young, and show him what servage we be in, and show him how we will have it otherwise, or else we will provide us of some remedy. And if we go together all manner of people that be now in any bondage will follow us, to the intent to be made free, and when the king seeth us we shall have some remedy, either by fairness or otherwise.' Thus John Ball said on Sundays when the people issued out of the churches in the villages, wherefore many of the mean people loved him, and such as intended to no goodness said how he said truth. And so they would murmur one with another in the fields and in the ways as they went together, affirming how John Ball said truth.

The Archbishop of Canterbury, who was informed of the saying of this John Ball, caused him to be taken and put in prison a two or three months to chastise him. Howbeit it had been much better at the beginning that he had been condemned to perpetual prison, or else to have died, rather than to have suffered him to have been again delivered out of prison: but the bishop had conscience to let him die. And when this John Ball was out of prison, he returned again to his error as he did before. Of his words and deeds there were much people in London informed, such as had great envy at them that were rich and such as were noble. And then they began to speak among them and said how the realm of England was right evil governed, and how that gold and silver was taken from them by them that were named noblemen. So thus these unhappy men of London began to rebel and assembled together, and sent word to the foresaid countries that they should come to London, and bring their people with them, promising how they should find London open to receive them and the commons of the city to be of the same accord, saying how they would do so much to the king that there should not be one bondman in all England.

This promise moved so them of Kent, of Essex, of Sussex, of Bedford, and of the countries about, that they rose and came towards London to the number of sixty thousand. And they had a captain called Water Tyler and with him in company was Jack Straw and John Ball. These three were chief sovereign captains, but the head of all was Water Tyler and he was indeed a tiler of houses, an ungracious patron.

When these unhappy men began thus to stir, they of London, except such as were of their band, were greatly afraid. Then the Mayor of London and the rich men of the city took counsel together, and when they saw the people thus coming on every side, they caused the gates of the city to be closed and would suffer no man to enter into the city. But when they had well imagined, they advised not so to do, for they thought they should thereby put their suburbs in great peril to be burnt, and so they opened again the city; and there entered in at the gates in some place a hundred, two hundred, by twenty and by thirty. And so when they came to London they entered and lodged, and yet of truth the third part* of these people could not tell what to ask or demand, but followed each other like beasts, as the shepherds did of old time, saying how they would go conquer the Holy Land, and at last all came to nothing.† In likewise these villains and poor people came to London a hundred mile off, sixty mile, fifty mile, forty mile and twenty mile off, and from all countries about London, but the most part came from the countries before named. And as they came they demanded ever for the king. The gentlemen of the countries, knights and squires, began to doubt, when they saw the people began to rebel, and though they were in doubt, it was good reason: for a less occasion they might have been afraid. So the gentlemen drew together as well as they might.

The same day that these unhappy people of Kent were coming to London, there returned from Canterbury the king's mother, Princess of Wales, coming from her pilgrimage. She was in great jeopardy to have been lost, for these people came to her carriage and dealt rudely with her, whereof the good lady was in great doubt lest they would have done some villainy to her or to her damosels. Howbeit, God kept her, and she came in one day from Canterbury to London, for she never durst tarry by the way. The same time King Richard her son was at the Tower of London. There his mother found him, and with him there was the Earl of Salisbury, the Archbishop of Canterbury, Sir Robert of Namur, the

* 'three-fourths' in the original.
† A reference to the Pastoureaux of 1320, destroyed at Aigues-Mortes on their way to the Holy Land.

Lord of Gommegnies and divers other, who were in doubt of these people that thus gathered together and wist not what they demanded. This rebellion was well-known in the king's court or any of these people began to stir out of their houses, but the king nor his council did provide no remedy therefor, which was great marvel. And to the intent that all lords and good people, and such as would nothing but good, should take ensample to correct them that be evil and rebellious, I shall show you plainly all the matter as it was.

The evil deeds that these commons of England did to the king's officers, and how they sent a knight to speak with the king (1381). [Ch. 382]

THE Monday before the feast of Corpus Christi, the year of our Lord God a thousand three hundred and eighty-one, these people issued out of their houses to come to London to speak with the king to be made free, for they would have had no bondman in England. And so first they came to Saint Thomas of Canterbury, and there John Ball had thought to have found the Bishop of Canterbury, but he was at London with the king. When Wat Tyler and Jack Straw entered into Canterbury, all the common people made great feast for all the town was of their assent. And there they took counsel to go to London to the king, and to send some of their company over the river of Thames into Essex, into Sussex, and into the counties of Stafford and Bedford, to speak to the people that they should all come to the farther side of London, and thereby to close London round about so that the king should not stop their passages, and that they should all meet together on Corpus Christi day. They that were at Canterbury entered into Saint Thomas' church and did there much hurt, and robbed and brake up the bishop's chamber. And in robbing and bearing out their pillage they said, 'Ah! this Chancellor of England hath had a good market to get together all this riches. He shall give us now account of the revenues of England and of the great profits that he hath gathered since the king's coronation.'

When they had this Monday thus broken the abbey of Saint Vincent, they departed in the morning and all the people of Canterbury with them, and so took the way to Rochester and sent their people to the villages about. And in their going they beat down and robbed houses of advocates and of the procurors of the king's court and of the archbishop, and had mercy of none. And when they were come to Rochester, they had there good cheer, for the people of that town tarried for them, for they were of the same sect. And then they went to the castle there and took the knight that had the rule thereof: he was called Sir John Newton. And they said to him, 'Sir, it behoveth you to go with us and you shall be our sovereign captain, and to do what we will have you.' The knight excused himself honestly and showed them divers considerations and excuses, but all availed him nothing, for they said unto him, 'Sir John, if ye do not as we will have you, ye are but dead.' The knight seeing these people in that fury and ready to slay him, he then doubted death and agreed to them, and so they took him with them against his inward will. And in likewise did they of other countries in England, as Essex, Sussex, Stafford, Bedford, and Norfolk even to Lynn, for they brought the knights and gentlemen into such obeisance that they caused them to go with them whether they would or not, as the Lord Morley, a great baron, Sir Stephen of Hales and Sir Thomas of Cosington and other.

Now behold the great fortune. If they might have come to their intents, they would have destroyed all the noblemen of England, and thereafter all other nations would have followed the same and have taken foot and ensample by them and by them of Ghent and Flanders, who rebelled against their lord. The same year the Parisians rebelled in likewise and found out the mallets of iron, of whom there were more than twenty thousand, as ye shall hear after in this history, but first we will speak of them of England.

When these people thus lodged at Rochester departed and passed the river and came to Dartford, alway keeping still their opinions, beating down before them and all about the places and houses of advocates and procurors, and striking off the heads of divers persons; and so long they went forward until they came within a four mile of London, and there lodged on a hill called Blackheath. And as they went, they said ever they were the king's men and the noble commons of England. And when they of London knew that they were come so near to them, the mayor, as ye have heard before, closed the gates and kept straitly all the passages: this order caused the mayor, who was called William Walworth, and divers other rich burgesses of the city who were not of their sect, but there were in London of their unhappy opinions more than thirty thousand. Then these people thus being lodged on Blackheath determined to send their knight to speak with the king, and to show him how all that they have done or will do is for him and his honour, and how the realm of England hath not been well governed a great space for the honour of the realm nor for the common profit by his uncles and by the clergy, and specially by the Archbishop of Canterbury his chancellor, whereof they would have account. This knight durst do none otherwise but so came by the river of Thames to the Tower. The king and they that were with him in the Tower, desiring to hear tidings, seeing this knight coming, made him way, and was brought before the king into a chamber. And with the knight was the princess his mother and his two brethren, the Earl of Kent and the Lord John Holland, the Earl of Salisbury, the Earl of Warwick, the Earl of Oxford, the Archbishop of Canterbury, the Lord of Saint John's, Sir Robert of Namur, the Lord of Vertaing, the Lord of Gommegnies, Sir Henry of Senzeille, the Mayor of London and divers other notable burgesses. This knight Sir John Newton, who was well known among them for he was one of the king's officers, he kneeled down before the king and said, 'My right redoubted lord, let it not displease your Grace the message that I must needs show you, for, dear sir, it is by force and against my will.' 'Sir John,' said the king, 'say what ye will, I hold you excused.' 'Sir, the commons of this your realm hath sent me to you to desire you to come and speak with them on Blackheath, for they desire to have none but you. And, sir, ye need not to have any doubt of your person, for they will do you no hurt, for they hold and will hold you for their king; but, sir, they say they will show you divers things the which shall be right necessary for you to take heed of when they speak with you, of the which things, sir, I have no charge to show you. But, sir, an it may please you to give me an answer such as may appease them, and that they may know for truth that I have spoken with you, for they have my children in hostage till I return again to them and without I return again they will slay my children in- continent.' Then the king made him an answer and said, 'Sir, ye shall have an answer shortly.' Then the king took counsel what was best for him to do, and it was anon determined that the next morning the king should go down the river by water, and without fail to speak with them. And when Sir John Newton heard that answer he desired nothing else, and so took his leave of the king and of the lords and returned again into his vessel, and passed the Thames and went to Blackheath where he had left more than threescore thousand men. And there he answered them that the next morning they should send some of their council to the Thames, and there the king would come and speak with them. This answer greatly pleased them, and so passed that night as well as they might. And the fourth part* of them fasted for lack of victual, for they had none, wherewith they were sore displeased, which was good reason.

All this season the Earl of Buckingham was in Wales, for there he had fair heritages by reason of his wife, who was daughter to the Earl of Northumberland and Hereford; but the voice was all through London how he was among these people, and some said certainly how they had seen him there among them. And all was because there was one Thomas in their company, a man of the county of Cambridge, that was very like the earl. Also the lords that lay at Plymouth to go into Portugal were well informed of this rebellion, and of the people that thus began to rise, wherefore they doubted lest their viage should have been broken, or else they feared lest the commons about Southampton, Winchester, and Arundel would have come on them. Wherefore they weighed up their anchors and issued out of the haven with great pain, for the wind was sore against them, and so took the sea and there cast anchor abiding for the wind. And the Duke of Lancaster, who was in the marches of Scotland between Moorlane and Roxburgh entreating with the Scots, where it was showed him of the rebellion, whereof he was in doubt, for he knew well that he was but little beloved with the commons of England. Howbeit, for all those tidings yet he did sagely demean himself as touching the treaty with the Scots.

* 'Four-fifths of them'.

The Earl Douglas, the Earl of Moray, the Earl of Sutherland and the Earl Thomas Erskine, and the Scots that were there for the treaty knew right well the rebellion in England, how the common people in every part began to rebel against the noblemen; wherefore the Scots thought that England was in great danger to be lost, and therefore in their treaties they were the more stiffer against the Duke of Lancaster and his council.

Now let us speak of the commons of England and how they persevered.

How the commons of England entered into London, and of the great evil that they did, and of the death of the Bishop of Canterbury and divers other (1381).   [Ch. 383]

IN the morning on Corpus Christi day King Richard heard mass in the Tower of London, and all his lords, and then he took his barge with the Earl of Salisbury, the Earl of Warwick, the Earl of Oxford, and certain knights, and so rowed down along Thames to Rotherhithe, whereas was descended down the hill a ten thousand men to see the king and to speak with him. And when they saw the king's barge coming they began to shout and made such a cry as though all the devils in hell had been among them. And they had brought with them Sir John Newton, to the intent that if the king had not come they would have stricken him all to pieces, and so they had promised him. And when the king and his lords saw the demeanour of the people, the best assured of them were in dread, and so the king counselled by his barons not to take any landing there, but so rowed up and down the river. And the king demanded of them what they would, and said how he was come thither to speak with them. And they said all with one voice, 'We would that ye should come a-land, and then we shall show you what we lack.' Then the Earl of Salisbury answered for the king and said, 'Sirs, ye be not in such order nor array that the king ought to speak with you'; and so with those words no more said. And then the king was counselled to return again to the Tower of London, and so he did. And when these people saw that, they were inflamed with ire and returned to the hill where the great band was, and there showed them what answer they had and how the king was returned to the Tower of London.

Then they cried all with one voice, 'Let us go to London,' and so they took their way thither. And in their going they beat down abbeys and houses of advocates and of men of the court, and so came into the suburbs of London, which were great and fair, and there beat down divers fair houses, and specially they brake up the king's prisons, as the Marshalsea and other, and delivered out all the prisoners that were within and there they did much hurt. And at the bridge foot they threat them of London because the gates of the bridge were closed, saying how they would burn all the suburbs and so conquer London by force, and to slay and burn all the commons of the city. There were many within the city of their accord, and so they drew together and said, 'Why do we not let these good people enter into the city? They are our fellows and that that they do is for us.' So therewith the gates were opened, and then these people entered into the city and went into houses and sat down to eat and drink. They desired nothing but it was incontinent brought to them, for every man was ready to make them good cheer and to give them meat and drink to appease them.

Then the captains, as John Ball, Jack Straw and Wat Tyler, went throughout London, and a twenty thousand with them, and so came to the Savoy in the way to Westminster, which was a goodly house and it pertained to the Duke of Lancaster. And when they entered they slew the keepers thereof and robbed and pilled the house, and when they had so done, then they set fire on it and clean destroyed and burnt it. And when they had done that outrage, they left not therewith but went straight to the fair hospital of the Rhodes called Saint John's, and there they burnt house, hospital, minster and all. Then they went from street to street and slew all the Flemings that they could find, in church or in any other place: there was none respited from death. And they brake up divers houses of the Lombards and robbed them and took their goods at their pleasure, for there was none that durst say them nay. And they slew in the city a rich merchant called Richard Lyon, to whom before that time Wat Tyler had done service in France; and on a time this Richard Lyon had beaten him while he was his varlet, the which Wat Tyler then remembered, and so came to his house and struck off his head and caused it to be borne on a spear-point before him all about the city. Thus these ungracious people demeaned themselves, like people enraged and wood, and so that day they did much sorrow in London.

And so against night they went to lodge at Saint Katherine's before the Tower of London, saying how they would never depart thence till they had the king at their pleasure, and till he had accorded to them all that they would ask accounts of the Chancellor of England, to know where all the good was become that he had levied through the realm; and without he made a good account to them thereof, it should not be for his profit. And so when they had done all these evils to the strangers all the day, at night they lodged before the Tower.

Ye may well know and believe that it was great pity for the danger that the king and such as were with him were in. For some time these unhappy people shouted and cried so loud, as though all the devils of hell had been among them.

In this evening the king was counselled by his brethren and lords, and by Sir William Walworth, Mayor of London, and divers other notable and rich burgesses, that in the night-time they should issue out of the Tower and enter into the city, and so to slay all these unhappy people while they were at their rest and asleep, for it was thought that many of them were drunken, whereby they should be slain like flies; also of twenty of them there was scant one in harness. And surely the good men of London might well have done this at their ease, for they had in their houses secretly their friends and servants ready in harness. And also Sir Robert Knowles was in his lodging, keeping his treasure, with a sixscore ready at his commandment. In likewise was Sir Perducas d'Albret, who was as then in London, insomuch that there might well [have] assembled together an eight thousand men ready in harness. Howbeit there was nothing done, for the residue of the commons of the city were sore doubted, lest they should rise also, and the commons before were a threescore thousand or more. Then the Earl of Salisbury and the wise men about the king said, 'Sir, if ye can appease them with fairness, it were best and most profitable, and to grant them everything that they desire: for if we should begin a thing the which we could not achieve, we should never recover it again, but we and our heirs ever to be disherited.' So this counsel was taken and the mayor countermanded, and so commanded that he should not stir; and he did as he was commanded, as reason was. And in the city with the major there were twelve aldermen, whereof nine of them held with the king and the other three took part with these ungracious people, as it was after well-known, the which they full dearly bought.

And on the Friday in the morning, the people being at Saint Katherine's near to the Tower, began to apparel themselves and to cry and to shout and said, without the king would come out and speak with them, they would assail the Tower and take it by force and slay all them that were within. Then the king doubted these words, and so was counselled that he should issue out to speak with them. And then the king sent to them that they should all draw to a fair plain place, called Mile End, whereas the people in the city did sport them in the summer season, and there the king to grant them that they desired. And there it was cried in the king's name that whosoever would speak with the king, let him go to the said place, and there he should not fail to find the king.

Then the people began to depart, specially the commons of the villages, and went to the same place. But all went not thither, for they were not all of one condition; for there were some that desired nothing but riches and the utter destruction of the noblemen, and to have London robbed and pilled: that was the principal matter of their beginning, the which they well showed, for as soon as the Tower gate opened and that the king was issued out with his two brethren and the Earl of Salisbury, the Earl of Warwick, the Earl of Oxford, Sir Robert of Namur, the Lord of Vertaing, the Lord Gommegnies and divers other, then Wat Tyler, Jack Straw, and John Ball and more than four hundred, entered into the Tower and brake up chamber after chamber; and at last found the Archbishop of Canterbury, called Simon, a valiant man and a wise, and chief Chancellor of England, and a little before he had said mass before the king. These gluttons took him and struck off his head, and also they beheaded the Lord of Saint John's, and a friar minor, master in medicine pertaining to the Duke of Lancaster. They slew him in despite of his master and a sergeant-at-arms, called John Leg. And these four heads were set on four long spears and they made them to be borne before them through the streets of London and at last set them a-high on London Bridge, as though they had been traitors to the king and to the realm. Also these gluttons entered into the princess' chamber and brake her bed, whereby she was so sore afraid that she swooned, and there she was taken up and borne to the waterside and put into a barge and covered, and so conveyed to a place called the Queen's Wardrobe. And there she was all that day and night, like a woman half dead, till she was comforted with the king her son, as ye shall hear after.

How the nobles of England were in great peril to have been destroyed, and how these rebels were punished and sent home to their own houses (1381).   [Ch. 384]

WHEN the king came to the said place of Mile End without London, he put out of his company his two brethren, the Earl of Kent and Sir John Holland, and the Lord of Gommegnies, for they durst not appear before the people. And when the king and his other lords were there, he found there a threescore thousand men of divers villages and of sundry countries in England. So the king entered in among them and said to them sweetly, 'Ah! ye good people, I am your king. What lack ye? What will ye say?' Then such as understood him said, 'We will that ye make us free for ever, ourselves, our heirs and our lands, and that we be called no more bond, nor so reputed.' 'Sirs,' said the king 'I am well agreed thereto. Withdraw ye home into your own houses and into such villages as ye came from, and leave behind you of every village two or three, and I shall cause writings to be made and seal them with my seal, the which they shall have with them, containing everything that ye demand. And to the intent that ye shall be the better assured, I shall cause my banners to be delivered into every bailiwick, shire, and counties.'

These words appeased well the common people, such as were simple and good plain men, that were come thither and wist not why. They said, 'It was well said, we desire no better.' Thus these people began to be appeased and began to withdraw them into the city of London. And the king also said a word, the which greatly contented them. He said, 'Sirs, among you good men of Kent, ye shall have one of my banners with you, and ye of Essex another, and ye of Sussex, of Bedford, of Cambridge, of Yarmouth, of Stafford, and of Lynn, each of you one; and also I pardon everything that ye have done hitherto, so that ye follow my banners and return home to your houses.' They all answered how they would do so. Thus these people departed and went into London.

Then the king ordained more than thirty clerks the same Friday to write with all diligence letters patent, and sealed with the king's seal, and delivered them to these people. And when they had received the writing they departed and returned to their own countries. But the great venom remained still behind, for Wat Tyler, Jack Straw and John Ball said, for all that these people were thus appeased, yet they would not depart so, and they had of their accord more than thirty thousand. So they abode still and made no press to have the king's writing nor seal, for all their intents was to put the city to trouble in such wise as to slay all the rich and honest persons and to rob and pill their houses. They of London were in great fear of this, wherefore they kept their houses privily with their friends and such servants as they had, every man according to his puissance. And when these said people were this Friday thus somewhat appeased, and that they should depart as soon as they had their writings, every man home into his own country, then King Richard came into the Royal* where the queen his mother was, right sore afraid. So he comforted her as well as he could and tarried there with her all that night.

Yet I shall show you of an adventure that fell by these ungracious people, before the city of Norwich, by a captain among them called William Lister of Stafford. The same day of Corpus Christi that these people entered into London and burnt the Duke of Lancaster's house, called the Savoy, and the Hospital of Saint John's and brake up the king's prisons and did all this hurt, as ye have heard before, the same time there assembled together they of Stafford, of Lynn, of Cambridge, of Bedford and of Yarmouth, and as they were coming towards London, they had a captain among them called Lister. And as they came they rested them before Norwich, and in their coming they caused every man to rise with them, so that they left no villeins behind them. The cause why they rested before Norwich I shall show you.

There was a knight, captain of the town, called Sir Robert Sale. He was no gentlemen born, but he had the grace to be reputed sage and valiant in arms, and for his valiantness King Edward made him knight. He was of his body one of the biggest knights in all England. Lister and his company thought to have had this knight with them and to make him their chief captain, to the intent to be the more feared and beloved. So they sent to him that he should come and speak with them in the field, or else they would burn the town. The knight considered that it was better for him to go and speak with them rather than they should do that outrage to the town. Then he mounted on his horse and issued out of the town all alone, and so came to speak with them. And when they saw him, they made him great cheer and honoured him much, desiring him to alight off his horse and to speak with them. And so he did, wherein he did great folly, for when he was alighted they came round about him and began to speak fair to him and said, 'Sir Robert, ye are a knight and a man greatly beloved in this country, and renowned a valiant man. And though ye be thus, yet we know you well: ye be no gentleman born, but son to a villein such as we be. Therefore come you

* A palace near Blackfriars where the Queen's Wardrobe was.

with us and be our master, and we shall make you so great a lord that one quarter of England shall be under your obeisance.' When the knight heard them speak thus it was greatly contrarious to his mind, for he thought never to make any such bargain, and answered them with a felonous regard, 'Fly away, ye ungracious people, false and evil traitors that ye be. Would you that I should forsake my natural lord for such a company of knaves as ye be, to my dishonour for ever? I had rather ye were all hanged, as ye shall be, for that shall be your end.' And with those words he had thought to have leapt again upon his horse, but he failed of the stirrup and the horse started away. Then they cried all at him, and said, 'Slay him without mercy.'

When he heard those words he let his horse go and drew out a good sword and began to skirmish with them, and made a great place about him, that it was pleasure to behold him. There was none that durst approach near him. There were some that approached near him but at every stroke that he gave he cut off either leg, head or arm: there was none so hardy but that they feared him. He did there such deeds of arms that it was marvel to regard, but there were more than forty thousand of these unhappy people. They shot and cast at him, and he was unarmed. To say truth, if he had been of iron or steel, yet he must needs have been slain; but yet, or he died, he slew twelve out of hand, beside them that he hurt. Finally he was stricken to the earth, and they cut off his arms and legs and then struck his body all to pieces. This was the end of Sir Robert Sale, which was great domage, for which deed afterward all the knights and squires of England were angry and sore displeased when they heard thereof.

Now let us return to the king. The Saturday the king departed from the Wardrobe in the Royal, and went to Westminster and heard mass in the church there, and all his lords with him. And beside the church there was a little chapel with an image of our Lady, which did great miracles and in whom the Kings of England had ever great trust and confidence. The king made his orisons before this image and did there his offering, and then he leapt on his horse and all his lords, and so the king rode toward London. And when he had ridden a little way, on the left hand there was a way to pass without London.

The same proper morning Wat Tyler, Jack Straw and John Ball had assembled their company to commune together in a place called Smithfield, whereas every Friday there is a market of horses. And there were together all of affinity more than twenty thousand, and yet there were many still in the town, drinking and making merry in the taverns, and paid nothing, for they were happy that made them best cheer. And these people in Smithfield had with them the king's banners the which were delivered them the day before, and all these gluttons were in mind to overrun and to rob London the same day, for their captains said how they had done nothing as yet: 'These liberties that the king hath given us is to us but a small profit: therefore let us be all of one accord, and let us overrun this rich and puissant city or they of Essex, of Sussex, of Cambridge, of Bedford, of Arundel, of Warwick, of Reading, of Oxford, of Guildford, of Lynn, of Stafford, of Yarmouth, of Lincoln, of York and of Durham do come hither, for all these will come hither; Baker and Lister will bring them hither. And if we be first lords of London and have the possession of the riches that is therein, we shall not repent 'us, for if we leave it, they that come after will have it from us.'

To this counsel they all agreed. And therewith the king came the same way unaware of them, for he had thought to have passed that way without London, and with him a forty horse. And when he came before the abbey of Saint Bartholomew and beheld all these people, then the king rested and said how he would go no farther till he knew what these people ailed, saying if they were in any trouble how he would re-appease them again. The lords that were with him tarried also, as reason was when they saw the king tarry. And when Wat Tyler saw the king tarry he said to his people, 'Sirs, yonder is the king, I will go and speak with him. Stir not from hence without I make you a sign, and when I make you that sign come on and slay all them except the king. But do the king no hurt, he is young, we shall do with him what we list and shall lead him with us all about England, and so shall we be lords of all the realm without doubt.'

And there was a doublet-maker of London called John Tycle, and he had brought to these gluttons a sixty doublets, the which they wore. Then he demanded of these captains who should pay him for his doublets: he demanded thirty mark. Wat Tyler answered him and said, 'Friend, appease yourself, thou shalt be well paid or this day be ended. Keep thee near me, I shall be your creditor.' And therewith he spurred his horse and departed from his company, and came to the king, so near him that his horse's head touched the croup of the king's horse. And the first word that he said was this, 'Sir king, seest thou all yonder people?' 'Yea, truly,' said the king, 'wherefore sayest thou?' 'Because', said he, 'they be all at my commandment, and have sworn to me faith and troth to do all that I will have them.' 'In a good time,' said the king 'I will well it be so.' Then Wat Tyler said, as he that nothing demanded but riot, 'What believest thou, king, that these people, and as many more as be in London at my commandment, that they will depart from thee thus without having thy letters?' 'No,' said the king, 'ye shall have them; they be ordained for you, and shall be delivered every one each after other. Wherefore, good fellows, withdraw fair and easily to your people and cause them to depart out of London, for it is our intent that each of you by villages and townships shall have letters patent as I have promised you.' With these words Wat Tyler cast his eyes on a squire that was there with the king bearing the king's sword, and Wat Tyler hated greatly the same squire, for the same squire had displeased him before for words between them. 'What!' said Tyler, 'art thou there? Give me thy dagger.' 'Nay,' said the squire, 'that will I not do. Wherefore should I give it thee?' The king beheld the squire and said, 'Give it him, let him have it.' And so the squire took it him sore against his will. And when this Wat Tyler had it he began to play therewith and turned it in his hand, and said again to the squire, 'Give me also that sword.' 'Nay,' said the squire, 'it is the king's sword. Thou art not worthy to have it, for thou art but a knave, and if there were no more here but thou and I, thou durst not speak those words for as much gold in quantity as all yonder abbey!' 'By my faith,' said Wat Tyler, 'I shall never eat meat till I have thy head!' And with those words the Mayor of London came to the king with a twelve horses well armed under their coats, and so he brake the press, and saw and heard how Wat Tyler demeaned himself, and said to him, 'Ha! thou knave, how art thou so hardy in the king's presence to speak such words? It is too much for thee so to do.' Then the king began to chafe and said to the mayor, 'Set hands on him.' And while the king said so, Tyler said to the mayor, 'A God's name, what have I said to displease thee?' 'Yes, truly' quoth the mayor, 'thou false stinking knave, shalt thou speak thus in the presence of the king my natural lord? I commit never to live, without thou shalt dearly abye it.' And with those words the mayor drew out his sword and struck Tyler so great a stroke on the head that he fell down at the feet of his horse. And as soon as he was fallen, they environed him all about, whereby he was not seen of his company. Then a squire of the king's alighted, called John Standish, and he drew out his sword and put it into Wat Tyler's belly, and so he died. Then the ungracious people there assembled, perceiving their captain slain, began to murmur among themselves and said, 'Ah! Our captain is slain, let us go and slay them all.' And therewith they arranged themselves on the place in manner of battle, and their bows before them.

Thus the king began a great outrage; howbeit all turned to the best, for as soon as Tyler was on the earth, the king departed from all his company and all alone he rode to these people, and said to his own men, 'Sirs, none of you follow me; let me alone.' And so when he came before these ungracious people, who put themselves in ordinance to revenge their captain then the king said to them, 'Sirs, what aileth you? Ye shall have no captain but me. I am your king. Be all in rest and peace.' And so the most part of the people that heard the king speak and saw him among them, were shamefaced and began to wax peaceable and to depart. But some, such as were malicious and evil, would not depart, but made semblance as though they would do somewhat. Then the king returned to his own company and demanded of them, what was best to be done. Then he was counselled to draw into the field, for to fly away was no boot. Then said the mayor, 'It is good that we do so, for I think surely we shall have shortly some comfort of them of London and of such good men as be of our part, who are purveyed and have their friends and men ready armed in their houses.' And in this meantime, voice and bruit ran through London how these unhappy people were likely to slay the king and the mayor in Smithfield, through the which noise all manner of good men of the king's party issued out of their houses and lodgings well armed, and so came all to Smithfield and to the field where the king was; and they were anon to the number of seven or eight thousand men well armed. And first thither same Sir Robert Knowles and Sir Perducas d'Albret, well accompanied, and divers of the aldermen of London, and with them a six hundred men in harness, and a puissant man of the city who was the king's draper called Nicholas Bramber, and he brought with him a great company. And ever as they came they ranged them afoot in order of battle, and on the other part these unhappy people were ready ranged, making semblance to give battle, and they had with them divers of the king's banners.

There the king made three knights, the one the Mayor of London Sir William Walworth, Sir John Standish, and Sir Nicholas Bramber. Then the lords said among themselves, 'What shall we do? We see here our enemies who would gladly slay us if they might have the better hand of us.' Sir Robert Knowles counselled to go and fight with them and slay them all, yet the king would not consent thereto but said, 'Nay, I will not so. I will send to them commanding them to send me again my banners, and thereby we shall see what they will do. Howbeit, either by fairness or otherwise, I will have them.' 'That is well said, sir,' quoth the Earl of Salisbury. Then these new knights were sent to them, and these knights make token to them not to shoot at them, and when they came so near them that their speech might be heard, they said, 'Sirs, the king commandeth you to send again his banners, and we think he will have mercy on you.' And incontinent they delivered again the banners and sent them to the king. Also they were commanded on pain of their heads, that all such as had letters of the king to bring them forth and to send them again to the king; and so many of them delivered their letters, but not all. Then the king made them to be all torn in their presence. And as soon as the king's banners were delivered again these unhappy people kept none array, but the most part of them did cast down their bows, and so brake their array and returned into London. Sir Robert Knowles was sore displeased in that he might not go to slay them all, but the king would not consent thereto, but said he would be revenged of them well enough, and so he was after.

Thus these foolish people departed, some one way and some another; and the king and his lords and all his company right ordinately entered into London with great joy. And the first journey that the king made he went to the lady princess his mother, who was in a castle in the Royal called the Queen's Wardrobe, and there she had tarried two days and two nights right sore abashed, as she had good reason. And when she saw the king her son, she was greatly rejoiced and said, 'Ah! fair son, what pain and great sorrow that I have suffered for you this day.' Then the king answered and said, 'Certainly, madam, I know it well; but now rejoice yourself and thank God for now it is time. I have this day recovered mine heritage and the realm of England, the which I had near lost.' Thus the king tarried that day with his mother, and every lord went peaceably to their own lodgings.

Then there was a cry made in every street in the king's name that all manner of men, not being of the city of London and have not dwelt there the space of one year, to depart; and if any such be found there the Sunday by the sun-rising, that they should be taken as traitors to the king and to lose their heads. This cry thus made, there was none that durst break it, and so all manner of people departed and sparkled abroad every man to their own places.

John Ball and Jack Straw were found in an old house hidden, thinking to have stolen away, but they could not for they were accused by their own men. Of the taking of them the king and his lords were glad, and then struck off their heads, and Wat Tyler's also, and they were set on London Bridge, and the valiant men's heads taken down that they had set on the Thursday before. These tidings anon spread abroad, so that the people of the strange countries, which were coming towards London, returned back again to their own houses and durst come no further.

How the Duke of Lancaster kept himself still in Scotland, for fear of this rebellion; and how the king punished of these traitors the chief masters (1381).   [Ch. 385]

NOW let us speak how the Duke of Lancaster in the mean season of this rebellion was in the marches of Scotland, treating for a peace with the Earl Douglas and the other lords of Scotland. The Scots knew right well of this rebellion in England, and in likewise so did the Duke of Lancaster; howbeit, he never made any semblance thereof to the Scots, but was as sore in his treaty as though England had been in good rest and peace. So long this treaty was debated among them that at last a truce was taken to endure three year between England and Scotland. And when this truce was thus accorded, the lords of each party made good cheer each to other.

Then the Earl Douglas said to the Duke of Lancaster, 'Sir, we know right well of the rebellion of the common people in England, and the peril that the realm of England is in by that incidence. Sir, we repute and take you for right sage and a valiant man, since ye have continued your treaty so freely as ye have done, for ye would never make any semblance thereof. Sir, we say to you that we offer ourselves, if ye have need, to be ready to aid you with five or six hundred spears and to do you service.' 'By my faith,' said the duke 'fair lords I thank you, I will not refuse your offer: howbeit I think verily that the king my lord hath so good counsel that the matter shall right well come to pass. Howbeit, I desire you to have a safe-conduct for me and mine to return into your country, if need be, till

N

the matter be appeased.' The Earl Douglas and the Earl Moray who had the king's authority, granted him his desire, and so then they departed.

The Scots returned to Edinburgh and the duke and his went to Berwick, weening to the duke to have entered into the town, for when he passed that way, there he left all his provision. But the captain of the town, called Sir Matthew Redmayne, refused to him the entry and closed the gates against him and his, saying how he was so commanded by the Earl of Northumberland, who as then was principal and sovereign of all the marches and frontiers of Northumberland. And when the duke heard those words he was sore displeased and said, 'How, Sir Matthew Redmayne, is there in Northumberland a greater sovereign than I am, that shall let me to pass this way, and left all my provision with you? What meaneth these tidings?' 'By my faith, sir,' said the knight, 'this is true that I say, and by the commandment of the king. Sir, this that I do to you is right sore against my will; howbeit I must needs do it. Therefore, sir, for God's sake hold me excused, for I am thus commanded on pain of my life, that ye shall not enter into this town, nor none of yours.'

Ye may well know that the Duke of Lancaster had great marvel and was sore displeased with these words, but not with the knight all only, but with them that ordained that matter; saying that he had travailed for the business of England, and then to have him in such suspect as to stop from him the first town between England and Scotland. And so imagined greatly in himself and discovered not all that he thought in his courage, and so he made no more press on the knight, and thought well the knight would not so do without some express commandment, and so brake out of that matter and said, 'Sir Redmayne, have you any knowledge of the tidings in England?' 'Sir,' said he, 'I know none but that the country is sore moved, and the king our sovereign lord hath written to all the lords, knights and good towns of this country to be all ready to come to him whensoever he sendeth for them, and [to] all constables and keepers of cities, towns and castles in Northumberland, he hath sent straight commandment on pain of death to suffer no man to enter into any place under their rules, and to take good heed of their charge. And as for the common people that rebelleth about London, I know no certain word of them, but that the officers of the Bishopric of Lincoln, of Cambridge, of Stafford, of Bedford and of Norwich, have written how that the common people under them have great desire that the matter should go evil, and that there should be trouble in England.' 'Yea', said the duke 'What hear you of our countries of Lancaster, Derby, and Leicester? Hear you of any rebellion there?' 'Sir,' said the knight, 'I hear nothing that they pass Lincoln.' Then the duke mused a little, and departed from the knight and took his way to Roxburgh, and there he was received of the constable, for when he passed he set him there.

Then the Duke of Lancaster was counselled, because he knew not surely how the matters did in England nor of whom he was beloved nor hated, that he should send to the lords of Scotland desiring them to send a quantity of men of war to convey him into Scotland with a safe-conduct . . .

Then it was marvel to regard the evils of these unhappy people, how in malice and hatred they spake of this duke without cause. The voice and bruit ran about in England, the time of this rebellion, how that the Duke of Lancaster was a traitor to the king and how he was become Scottish; but anon after it was found false and contrary. But these ungracious people, to bring the realm into trouble, sowed abroad these words, and that they acknowledged at the hour when they were executed to death: that is to say Lister, Wat Tyler, Jack Straw, Baker, and John Ball. These five were throughout all the realm chief and sovereign captains, for in five parts of the realm they were masters and governors. And specially they had in hatred the Duke of Lancaster, and that they well showed, for at their first entering into London they burnt his house of the Savoy clean to the earth. And beside that they had spread abroad in England by their false words how the duke was of the Scottish party, and in divers places they turned his arms upside-down like a traitor, the which was after dearly bought, for they that did it lost their heads for their labour.

Now I shall show you the vengeance that the King of England took of these ungracious people, in the mean season while the Duke of Lancaster was in Scotland.

When these people were re-appeased, and that Baker was executed to death, and Lister at Stafford, Wat Tyler, Jack Straw, John Ball and divers other at London, then the king was counselled to go visit his realm, through every shire, bailiwick and village, to purge and punish all the said evildoers, and to get again all such letters as by force he had given them in divers places, and so to bring again his realm in good order. Then the king sent secretly for a certain number of men of arms to come to him at a day appointed, and so they did to the number of a five hundred spears and as many archers. And when they were all come as the king had devised, the king departed from London with his household men all only and took the way into Kent, whereas first these ungracious people began to stir. And these foresaid men of war followed after the king, and coasted him, but they rode not in his company. The king entered into Kent and came to a village called Ospringe and called the mayor and all the men of the town before him. And when they were all come into a fair place, the king made to be showed by one of his council how they had erred against the king, and how they had near turned all England to tribulation and to loss. And because that the king knew well that this business was begun by some of them, and not by all, wherefore it were better that some did bear the blame than all, therefore he commanded them that they should show what they were that were culpable, on pain to be for ever in the king's indignation and to be reputed as traitors against him. And when they that were there assembled heard that request, and saw well that such as were culpable should excuse all the other, then they beheld each other and at last said, 'Sir, behold him here by whom this town was first moved'. Incontinent he was taken and hanged, and so there were hanged to the number of seven. And the letters that the king had given them were demanded again and so they were delivered again, and torn and broken before all the people. And it was said to them all, 'Sirs, ye that be here assembled, we command you in the king's name on pain of death, every man to go home to his own house peaceably, and never to grudge nor rise against the king nor none of his officers. And this trespass that ye have done, the king doth pardon you thereof.' Then they cried all with one voice: 'God thank the King's grace, and all his council!'

In like manner as the king did at Ospringe he did at Canterbury, at Sandwich, at Yarmouth, at Orwell and in other places in Kent.* In likewise he did in all other places of his realm whereas any rebellion had been, and there were hanged and beheaded more than fifteen hundred.

Then the king was counselled to send for his uncle the Duke of Lancaster out of Scotland, so the king sent for him by a knight out of his house called Sir Nicholas Carnefell. The knight rode so long that he came to Edinburgh, and there he found the duke and his company and delivered his letters of credence from the king. The duke obeyed, as it was reason, and also gladly he would return into England to his own heritage, and so took his way to come to Roxburgh. And at his departing he thanked the lords of Scotland of the comfort that they had done to him, as in sustaining him in their realm as long as it pleased him. The Earl Douglas, the Earl Moray and other of Scotland brought him to the abbey of Melrose. Thus the duke came to Roxburgh and to Newcastle-upon-Tyne, and so to Durham and to York, and in every place he found cities and towns ready apparelled, as it was reason.

And the same season there died in London a knight called Sir Guichard d'Angle, Earl of Huntingdon and master to the king. He was reverently buried in the Friars Preachers in London. And on the day of his obsequy there was the king, his two brethren, the princess his mother, and a great number of prelates, barons and ladies of England, and there did him great honour. And truly this gentle knight was well worthy to have honour, for in his time he had all noble virtues that a knight ought to have: he was merry, true, amorous, sage, secret, large, prewe, hardy, adventurous and chivalrous. Thus ended the gentle knight Sir Guichard d'Angle.

The selections from Lord Berners' first volume end here.

---

* 'in Kent' was added by Berners.

VOLUME TWO*

How Sir John Froissart, author of this chronicle, departed out of France and went to the Earl of Foix, and the manner of his voyage (1388).

[Ch. 21]

IT is long now since I made any mention of the businesses of far countries, for the businesses nearer home hath been so fresh that I left all other matters to write thereof. Howbeit, all this season valiant men desiring to advance themselves in the realm of Castile and Portugal, in Gascony, in Rouergue, in Quercy, in Limousin and in Bigorre, every day they imagined by what subtlety they could get one of another, by deeds of arms or by stealing of towns, castles and fortresses. And therefore I, John Froissart, who have taken on me to chronicle this present history at the request of the high renowned prince Sir Guy of Châtillon, Earl of Blois, Lord of Avesnes, Beaumont, Schoonhove, and of la Goude, my sovereign master and good lord, considering in myself how there was no great deeds of arms likely toward in the parts of Picardy or Flanders, seeing the peace was made between the duke and them of Ghent, and it greatly annoyed me to be idle, for I knew well that after my death this noble and high history should have his course, wherein divers noble men should have great pleasure and delight and as yet, I thank God, I have understanding and remembrance of all things past, and my wit quick and sharp enough to conceive all things showed unto me touching my principal matter, and my body as yet able to endure and to suffer pain: all things considered, I thought I would not let to pursue my said first purpose. And to the intent to know the truth of deeds done in far countries, I found occasion to go to the high and mighty Prince Gaston, Earl of Foix and of Béarn, for I knew well that if I might have that grace to come into his house and to be there at leisure, I could not be so well informed to my purpose in none other place of the world, for thither resorted all manner of knights and strange squires, for the great nobleness of the said earl. And as I imagined, so I did, and showed to my redoubted lord the Earl of Blois mine intent, and he gave me letters of recommendations to the Earl of Foix. And so long I rode without peril or damage, that I came to his

---

* The extracts from here to the end are taken from Volume II of Lord Berners' translation.

house called Orthez in the country of Bearn on Saint Katharine's day, the year of grace, one thousand three hundred fourscore and eight. And the said earl, as soon as he saw me, he made me good cheer and, smiling, said how he knew me: and yet he never saw me before, but he had often heard speaking of me. And so he retained me in his house to my great ease, with the help of the letters of credence that I brought unto him, so that I might tarry there at my pleasure. And there I was informed of the business of the realms of Castile, Portugal, Navarre and Aragon, yea, and of the realm of England and country of Bourbonnais and Gascony. And the earl himself, if I did demand anything of him, he did show me all that he knew, saying to me how the history that I had begun should hereafter be more praised than any other, and the reason he said why, was this: how that fifty year past there had been done more marvellous deeds of arms in the world than in three hundred year before that.

Thus was I in the court of the Earl of Foix, well cherished and at my pleasure. It was the thing that I most desired to know news as touching my matter, and I had at my will lords, knights and squires, ever to inform me, and also the gentle earl himself. I shall now declare in fair language all that I was informed of, to increase thereby my matter and to give example to them that list to advance themselves. Herebefore I have recounted great deeds of arms, taking and assaulting towns and castles, and battles and hard encounterings, and yet hereafter ye shall hear of many more, the which by the grace of God I shall make just narration. . . .

Of the great virtuousness and largesse that was in the Earl of Foix, and the manner of the piteous death of Gaston, the Earl's son (1388). [Ch. 26]

THE next day we departed and rode to dinner to Bourgaber, and so to Arthez, and there we drank, and by sun-setting we came to Orthez. The knight alighted at his own lodging and I alighted at the Moon, where dwelt a squire of the earl's, Ernaulton du Puy, who well received me because I was of France. Sir Espang of Lyon went to the castle to the earl and found him in his gallery, for he had but dined a little before, for the earl's usage was always that it was high noon or he arose out of his bed, and supped ever at midnight. The knight showed him how I was come thither and incontinent I was sent for to my lodging, for he was the lord of all the world the most desired to speak with strangers, to hear tidings.

When the earl saw me, he made me good cheer and retained me as of his house, where I was more than twelve weeks and my horse well treated. The acquaintance of him and of me was because I had brought with me a book which I made at the contemplation of Wenceslas of Bohemia, Duke of Luxembourg and of Brabant, which book was called the *Meliador*, containing all the songs, ballads, rondeaux and virelays which the gentle duke had made in his time, which by imagination

I had gathered together, which book the Earl of Foix was glad to see. And every night after supper I read thereon to him, and while I read there was none durst speak any word, because he would I should be well understood, wherein he took great solace. And when it came to any matter of question then he would speak to me, not in Gascon, but in good and fair French. And of his estate and house I shall somewhat record, for I tarried there so long that I might well perceive and know much.

This Earl Gaston of Foix with whom I was, at that time he was of a fifty year of age and nine: and I say I have in my time seen many knights, kings, princes and other, but I never saw none like him of personage, nor of so fair form, nor so well made. His visage fair, sanguine and smiling, his eyes grey and amorous whereas he list to set his regard, in everything he was so perfect that he cannot be praised too much. He loved that ought to be beloved, and hated that ought to be hated. He was a wise knight, of high enterprise, and of good counsel. He never had miscreant with him. He said many orisons every day: a nocturne of the psalter, matins of our Lady, of the Holy Ghost, and of the Cross, and Vigiles every day. He gave five florins in small money at his gate to poor folk for the love of God. He was large and courteous in gifts; he could right well take where it pertained to him, and to deliver again whereas he ought. He loved hounds of all beasts, winter and summer he loved hunting. He never loved folly outrage, nor folly largesse; every month he would know what he spended. He took in his country to receive his revenues and to serve him, notable persons, that is to say twelve receivers, and ever from two months to two months, two of them should serve for his receipt: for at the two months' end he would change and put other two into that office, and one that he trusted best should be his controller and to him all other should account, and the controller should account to him by rolls and books written, and the accounts to remain still with the earl. He had certain coffers in his chamber out of the which ofttimes he would take money to give to lords, knights and squires, such as came to him, for none should depart from him without some gift, and yet daily multiplied his treasure to resist the adventures and fortunes that he doubted. He was of good and easy acquaintance with every man, and amorously would speak to them. He was short in counsel and answers. He had four secretaries and at his rising they must ever be ready at his hand without any calling. And when any letter were delivered him and that he had read it, then he would call them to write again, or else for some other thing. In this estate the Earl of Foix lived.

And at midnight when he came out of his chamber into the hall to supper, he had ever before him twelve torches burning borne by twelve varlets standing before his table all supper. They gave a great light, and the hall ever full of knights and squires, and many other tables dressed to sup who would. There was none should speak to him at his table but if he were called. His meat was lightly wild fowl, the legs and wings only, and in the day he did but little eat and drink. He had great pleasure in harmony of instruments: he could do it right well himself. He would have songs sung before him. He would gladly see conceits and fantasies at his table, and when he had seen it, then he would send it to the other tables.

Briefly, all this I considered and advised. And or I came to his court I had been in many courts of kings, dukes, princes, earls, and great ladies, but I was never in none that so well liked me, nor there was none more rejoiced deeds of arms than the earl did. There was seen in his hall, chamber and court, knights and squires of honour going up and down and talking of arms and of amours. All honour there was found, all manner of tidings of every realm and country there might be heard, for out of every country there was resort for the valiantness of this earl. There I was informed of the most part of the deeds of arms that was done in Spain, in Portugal, in Aragon, in Navarre, in England and in Scotland, and in the frontiers and limitations of Languedoc, for I saw come thither to the earl while I was there knights and squires of all nations, and so I was informed by them and by the earl himself of all things that I demanded. There I enquired how Gaston the earl's son died, for Sir Espang de Lyon would not show me anything thereof. And so much I enquired that an ancient squire and a notable man showed the matter to me, and began thus: 'True it is' quoth he, 'that the Earl of Foix and my lady of Foix his wife agreeth not well together, nor have not done of a long season. And the discord between them first moved by the King of Navarre, who was brother to the lady, for the King of Navarre pledged himself for the Lord d'Albret, whom the Earl of Foix had in prison, for the sum of fifty thousand francs, and the Earl of Foix, who knew that the King of Navarre was crafty and malicious, in the beginning would not trust him, whereat the Countess of Foix had great displeasure and indignation against the earl her husband, and said to him: "Sir, ye repute but small honour in the King of Navarre my brother when ye will not trust him for fifty thousand francs. Though ye have no more of the Armagnacs nor of the d'Albrets than ye have, it ought to suffice. And also, sir, ye know well ye should assign out of my dower which mounteth to fifty thousand francs, which ye should put into the hands of my brother the King of Navarre. Wherefore, sir, ye cannot be evil paid." "Dame", quoth he, "ye say truth, but if I thought that the King of Navarre would stop the payment for that cause, the Lord d'Albret should never have gone out of Orthez, and so I should have been paid to the last penny, and since ye desire it I will do it, not for the love of you but for the love of my son." So by these words and by the King of Navarre's obligation, who became debtor to the Earl of Foix, the Lord d'Albret was delivered quit, and became French and was married in France to the sister of the Duke of Bourbon, and paid at his ease to the King of Navarre the sum of fifty thousand francs for his ransom, for the which sum the king was bound to the Earl of Foix, but he would not send it to the earl. Then the Earl of Foix said to his wife, "Dame, ye must go into Navarre to the king your brother and show him how I am not well content with him, that he will not send me that he hath received of mine." The lady answered how she was ready to go at his commandment; and so she departed and rode to Pamplona to the king her brother, who received her with much joy. The lady did her message from point to point. Then the king answered, "Fair sister, the sum of money is yours, the earl should give it for your dower. It shall never go out of the realm of Navarre since I have it in possession." "Ah! Sir", quoth the lady, "by this ye shall set great hate between the earl my husband and you, and if ye hold your purpose I dare not return again into the county of Foix, for my husband will slay me, he will say I have deceived him." "I cannot tell," quoth the king, "what ye will do, either tarry or depart, but as for this money I will not depart from it: it pertaineth to me to keep it for you, but it shall never go out of Navarre." The countess could have none other answer of the king her brother, and so she tarried still in Navarre and durst not return again. The Earl of Foix, when he saw the dealing of the King of Navarre, he began to hate his wife and was evil content with her. Howbeit she was in no fault but that she returned not again when she had done her message, but she durst not for she knew well the earl her husband was cruel where he took displeasure. Thus the matter standeth.

'The earl's son, called Gaston, grew and waxed goodly, and was married to the daughter of the Earl of Armagnac, a fair lady, sister to the earl that now is, the Lord Bertrand of Armagnac. And by the conjunction of that marriage there should have been peace between Foix and Armagnac. The child was a fifteen or sixteen year of age and resembled right well to his father. On a time he desired to go into Navarre to see his mother and his uncle the King of Navarre, which was in an evil hour for him and for all this country. When he was come into Navarre, he had there good cheer and tarried with his mother a certain space and then took his leave; but for all that he could do he could not get his mother out of Navarre, to have gone with him into Foix, for she demanded if the earl had commanded him so to do or no, and he answered that when he departed the earl spake nothing thereof. Therefore the lady durst not go thither but so tarried still. Then the child went to Pamplona to take his leave of the king his uncle. The king made him great cheer and tarried him there a ten days, and gave to him great gifts, and to his men. Also the last gift the king gave him was his death: I shall show you how.

'When this gentleman should depart, the king drew him apart into his chamber and gave him a little purse full of powder, which powder was such that if any creature living did eat thereof he should incontinent die without remedy. Then the king said, "Gaston, fair nephew, ye shall do as I shall show to you. Ye see how the Earl of Foix your father wrongfully hath your mother my sister in great hate, whereof I am sore displeased, and so ought ye to be. Howbeit, to perform all the matter, and that your father should love again your mother, to that intent

ye shall take a little of this powder, and put it on some meat that your father may
eat it, but beware that no man see you. And as soon as he hath eaten it, he shall
intend to nothing but to have again his wife, and so to love her ever after, which
ye ought greatly to desire. And of this that I show you let no man know, but keep
it secret or else ye lose all the deed." The child, who thought all that the king
said to him had been true, said, "Sir, it shall be done as ye have devised." And
so departed from Pamplona and returned to Orthez.

'The earl his father made him good cheer and demanded tidings of the King
of Navarre, and what gifts he had given him, and the child showed him how he
had given him divers and showed him all except the purse with the powder. Oft-
times this young Gaston and Yvain his bastard brother lay together, for they
loved together like brethren and were like arrayed and apparelled, for they were
near of a greatness and of one age. And it happened on a time as their clothes
lay together on their beds, Yvain saw a purse at Gaston's coat and said, "What
thing is this that ye bear ever about you?" whereof Gaston had no joy, and said,
"Yvain, give me my coat, ye have nothing to do therewith." And all that day
after Gaston was pensive. And it fortuned a three days after, as God would that
the earl should be saved, Gaston and his brother Yvain fell out together playing
at tennis and Gaston gave him a blow, and the child went into his father's chamber
and wept. And the earl as then had heard mass, and when the earl saw him weep
he said, "Son Yvain, what ailest thou?" "Sir," quoth he, "Gaston hath beaten
me, but he were more worthy to be beaten than I." "Why so?" quoth the earl,
and incontinent suspected something. "By my faith, sir," quoth he, "since he
returned out of Navarre he beareth privily at his breast a purse full of powder, I
wot not what it is nor what he will do therewith, but he hath said to me once or
twice that my lady his mother should shortly be again in your grace, and better
beloved than ever she was." "Peace" quoth the earl, "and speak no more, and
show this to no man living." "Sir," quoth he, "no more I shall." Then the earl
entered into imagination, and so came to the hour of his dinner and washed and
sat down at his table in the hall. Gaston his son was used to set down all his service
and to give the says.* And when he had set down the first course the earl cast
his eyes on him and saw the strings of the purse hanging at his bosom. Then his
blood changed, and said, "Gaston, come hither, I will speak with thee in thine
ear." The child came to him and the earl took him by the bosom and found out
the purse and with his knife cut it from his bosom. The child was abashed and
stood still and spake no word, and looked as pale as ashes for fear and began to
tremble. The Earl of Foix opened the purse and took of the powder and laid it
on a trencher of bread and called to him a dog and gave it him to eat, and as soon
as the dog had eaten the first morsel he turned his eyes in his head and died incontinent. And when the earl saw that he was sore displeased, and also he had

* Taste the meat.

good cause, and so rose from the table and took his knife and would have stricken his son. Then the knights and squires ran between them and said, "Sir, for God's sake have mercy, and be not so hasty. Be well informed first of the matter, or ye do any evil to your child." And the first word that the earl said was, "Ah! Gaston, traitor, for to increase thine heritage that should come to thee I have had war and hatred of the French king, of the King of England, of the King of Spain, of the King of Navarre, and of the King of Aragon, and as yet I have borne all their malices, and now thou wouldst murder me. It moveth of an evil nature, but first thou shalt die with this stroke." And so stepped forth with his knife and would have slain him, but then all the knights and squires kneeled down before him weeping and said, "Ah! Sir, have mercy for God's sake, slay not Gaston your son, remember ye have no more children. Sir, cause him to be kept and take good information of the matter: peradventure he knew not what he bare, and peradventure is nothing guilty of the deed." "Well," quoth the earl, "incontinent put him in prison and let him be so kept that I may have a reckoning of him." Then the child was put into the tower, and the earl took a great many of them that served his son and some of them departed, and as yet the Bishop of Lescar is [still] at Pau out of the country, for he was had in suspect and so were divers other. The earl caused to be put to death a fifteen right horribly, and the cause that the earl laid to them was, he said, it could be none otherwise but that they knew of the child's secrets, wherefore they ought to have showed it to him and to have said, "Sir Gaston, your son beareth a purse at his bosom". Because they did not thus they died horribly, whereof it was great pity, for some of them were as fresh and as jolly squires as were any in all the country, for ever the earl was served with good men. This thing touched the earl near to the heart and that he well showed, for on a day he assembled at Orthez all the nobles and prelates of Foix and of Béarn and all the notable persons of his country, and when they were all assembled he showed them wherefore he sent for them, as how he had found his son in this default for the which, he said, his intent was to put him to death, as he had well deserved. Then all the people answered to that case with one voice and said, "Sir, saving your grace, we will not that Gaston should die. He is your heir and ye have no more." And when the earl heard the people how they desired for his son, he somewhat refrained his ire. Then he thought to chastise him in prison a month or two, and then to send him on some voyage for two or three year till he might somewhat forget his evil will, and that the child might be of greater age and of more knowledge. Then he gave leave to all the people to depart but they of Foix would not depart from Orthez till the earl should assure them that Gaston should not die, they loved the child so well. Then the earl promised them, but he said he would keep him in prison a certain space to chastise him. And so upon this promise every man departed, and Gaston abode still in prison. These tidings spread abroad into divers places. And at that time Pope Gregory the Eleventh was at Avignon. Then he sent the Cardinal of Amiens in legation into Béarn, to have come to the Earl of Foix for that business. And by that time he came to Beziers, he heard such tidings that he needed not to go any further for that matter, for there he heard how Gaston, son to the Earl of Foix, was dead. Since I have showed you so much, now I shall show you how he died.

'The Earl of Foix caused his son to be kept in a dark chamber in the tower of Orthez a ten days. Little did he eat or drink, yet he had enough brought him every day, but when he saw it he would go therefrom and set little thereby. And some said that all the meat that had been brought him stood whole and entire the day of his death, wherefore it was great marvel that he lived so long, for divers reasons. The earl caused him to be kept in the chamber alone without any company either to counsel or comfort him. And all that season the child lay in his clothes as he came in, and he argued in himself and was full of melancholy, and cursed the time that he was born and engendered to come to such an end.

'The same day that he died they that served him of meat and drink, when they came to him, they said, "Gaston, here is meat for you." He made no care thereof and said, "Set it down there." He that served him regarded and saw in the prison all the meat stand whole as it had been brought him before, and so departed and closed the chamber door, and went to the earl and said, "Sir, for God's sake have mercy on your son Gaston, for he is near famished in prison. There he lieth, I think he never did eat anything since he came into prison, for I have seen there this day all that ever I brought him before lying together in a corner." Of those words the earl was sore displeased, and without any word speaking went out of his chamber and came to the prison where his son was. And in an evil hour he had the same time a little knife in his hand to pare withal his nails. He opened the prison door and came to his son and had the little knife in his hand, not an inch out of his hand, and in great displeasure he thrust his hand to his son's throat, and the point of the knife a little entered into his throat into a certain vein, and said, "Ah! Traitor, why dost not thou eat thy meat?" And therewith the earl departed without any more doing or saying and went into his own chamber. The child was abashed and afraid of the coming of his father and also was feeble of fasting, and the point of the knife a little entered into a vein of his throat, and so fell down suddenly and died. The earl was scant in his chamber but the keeper of the child came to him and said, "Sir, Gaston your son is dead." "Dead!" quoth the earl. "Yea, truly sir" quoth he. The earl would not believe it, but sent thither a squire that was by him, and he went, and came again and said, "Sir, surely he is dead." Then the earl was sore displeased and made great complaint for his son and said, "Ah! Gaston, what a poor adventure is this for thee and for me. In an evil hour thou wentest to Navarre to see thy mother. I shall never have the joy that I had before." Then the earl caused his barber to shave him, and clothed himself in black, and all his house, and with much sore weeping the child was borne to the Friars in Orthez and there buried. Thus, as I have showed you, the Earl of Foix slew Gaston his son, but the King of Navarre gave the occasion of his death.'

How Sir Peter of Béarn had a strange disease, and of the Countess of Biscay, his wife.

[Ch. 27]

WHEN I had heard this tale of the death of Gaston, son to the Earl of Foix, I had great pity thereof, for the love of the earl his father, whom I found a lord of high recommendation, noble, liberal and courteous, and also for love of the country that should be in great strife for lack of an heir. Then I thanked the squire and so departed from him. But after I saw him divers times in the earl's house and talked oftentimes with him. And on a time I demanded of him of Sir Peter of Béarn, bastard brother to the Earl of Foix, because he seemed to me a knight of great valour, whether he were rich and married or no. The squire answered and said: 'Truly he is married, but his wife and children be not in his company.' 'And why, sir?' quoth I. 'I shall show you,' quoth the squire. 'This Sir Peter of Béarn hath an usage that in the night-time while he sleepeth, he will rise and arm himself, and draw out his sword and fight all about the house, and cannot tell with whom, and then goeth to bed again. And when he is waking his servants show him how he did, and he would say he knew nothing thereof and how they lied. Sometime his servants would leave none armour nor sword in his chamber, and when he would thus rise and find none armour he would make such a noise and rumour as though all the devils of hell had been in his chamber.'

Then I demanded if he had great lands by his wife. 'Yes, truly, sir,' quoth he, 'but the lady by whom cometh the land joyeth of the profits thereof: this Sir Peter of Béarn hath but the fourth part.' 'Sir,' quoth I, 'where is his wife?' 'Sir,' quoth he, 'she is in Castile with the king her cousin. Her father was Earl of Biscay and was cousin-german to King Don Pedro who slew him, and also he would have had the lady to have put her in prison, and he took the possession of all the land, and as long as he lived the lady had nothing there. And it was said to this lady, who was Countess of Biscay, after the decease of her father: "Madam, save yourself, for King Don Pedro, if he may get you, will cause you to die or else put you in prison. He is so sore displeased with you because he saith you should report and bear witness that he caused the queen his wife to die in her bed, who was sister to the Duke of Bourbon and sister to the French queen. And your words, he saith, are believed rather than another because you were privy to her chamber." And for this cause the Lady Florence, Countess of Biscay, departed out of her country with a small company, as the common usage is, to fly from death as near as men can. So she went into the country of Basques and passed through it, and so came hither to Orthez to the earl and showed him all her adventure. The earl who had ever pity of ladies and damosels retained her, and so she abode with the lady of Corasse, a great lady in his country.

'As then this Sir Peter of Béarn his brother was but a young knight, and had not then this usage to rise a-nights, as he doth now. The earl loved him well and married him to this lady, and recovered her lands. And so Sir Peter had by this lady a son and a daughter, but they be with their mother in Castile, who be as yet but young, therefore the lady would not leave them with their father.' 'Ah! Saint Mary,' quoth I, 'How did Sir Peter of Béarn take this fantasy, first that he dare not sleep alone in his chamber, and that when he is asleep riseth thus and maketh all that business? They are things to be marvelled at.' 'By my faith,' quoth the squire, 'he hath been often demanded thereof, but he saith he cannot tell whereof it cometh. The first time that ever he did so was a night after that he had been on a day a-hunting in the woods of Biscay, and chased a marvellous great bear, and the bear had slain four of his hounds and hurt divers so that none durst come near him. Then Sir Peter took a sword of Bordeaux and came in great ire for because of his hounds, and assailed the bear and fought long with him, and was in great peril and took great pain or he could overcome him. Finally he slew the bear and then returned to his lodging to the castle of Lenguidendon in Biscay, and made the bear to be brought with him. Every man had marvel of the greatness of the beast and of the hardness of the knight, how he durst assail the bear. And when the Countess of Biscay his wife saw the bear, she fell in a swoon and had great dolour, and so she was borne into her chamber. And so all that day, the night after and the next day, she was sore discomforted and would not show what she ailed. On the third day she said to her husband, "Sir, I shall not be whole till I have been a pilgrimage at Saint James. Sir, I pray you give me leave to go thither, and to have with me my son, and Adrienne my daughter." Her husband agreed thereto. She took all her gold, jewels and treasure with her, for she thought never to return again, whereof her husband took no heed. So the lady did her pilgrimage and made an errand to go and see the King of Castile, her cousin, and the queen. They made her good cheer, and there she is yet, and will not return again nor send her children.

'And so thus the next night that this Sir Peter had thus chased the bear and slain him, while he slept in his bed this fantasy took him. And it was said that the countess his wife knew well, as soon as she saw the bear, that it was the same that her father did once chase, and on his chasing he heard a voice and saw nothing, that said to him, "Thou chasest me, and I would thee no hurt, therefore thou shalt die an evil death." Of this the lady had remembrance when she saw the bear, by that she had heard her father say before, and she remembered well how King Don Pedro struck off her father's head without any cause, and therefore she swooned in presence of her husband, and in likewise she feared her husband.

And yet she saith and maintaineth that he shall die of an evil death, and that he doth nothing as yet to that he shall do hereafter.

'Now, sir, I have showed you of Sir Peter of Béarn as ye have demanded of me, and this is a true tale, for thus it is, and thus it befell. How think you' quoth he 'thereby?' And I, who mused on the great marvel, said, 'Sir, I believe it well, that it is as ye have said. Sir, we find in old writing that anciently such as were called gods and goddesses at their pleasure would change and transform men into beasts and into fowls, and in likewise women. And it might be so that this bear was before some knight chasing in the forest of Biscay, and peradventure displeased in that time some god or goddess, whereby he was transformed into a bear, to do there his penance, as anciently Acteon was changed into a hart.' 'Acteon?' quoth the squire, 'I pray you show me that story. I would fain hear it.' 'Sir,' quoth I, 'according to the ancient writings we find how Acteon was a jolly and an expert knight, and loved the sport of hunting above all games. And on a day he chased in the woods and a hart rose before him, marvellous great and fair. He hunted him all the day, and lost all his company, servants, and hounds. And he was right desirous to follow his prey and followed the fewe of the hart till he came into a little meadow closed round about with woods and high trees, and in the meadow there was a fair fountain in which Diana goddess of chastity was bathing herself, and her damosels about her. The knight came suddenly on them or he was aware, and he was so far forward that he could not go back. And the damosels were abashed to see a stranger and ran to their lady and showed her, who was ashamed because she was naked. And when she saw the knight she said, "Acteon, they that sent thee hither loved thee but little. I will not that when thou art gone hence in other places, that thou shouldest report that thou hast seen me naked, and my damosels. And for the outrage that thou hast done, thou mayest have penance: therefore I will that thou be transformed in the likeness of the same hart that thou hast chased all this day." And incontinent Acteon was turned into a hart, who naturally loveth the water. In likewise it might be of the bear of Biscay, and how that the lady knew peradventure more than she would speak of at that time. Therefore she ought the better to be excused.' The squire answered and said, 'Sir, it may well be.' Then we left our talkings for that time.

Of the great solemnity that the Earl of Foix made at the feast of Saint Nicholas, and the tale that the Bascot of Mauleon showed to Sir John Froissart.   [Ch. 28]

AMONG other solemnities that the Earl of Foix kept on the high feasts of the year, he kept ever the feast of Saint Nicholas in great solemnity, he and all his land, as great as at the feast of Easter. And this was showed me by a squire of his house the third day that

I came hither, and I saw it myself right well apparent, for I was there on the same day. First all the clergy of the town of Orthez, and all the people, men, women and children, with procession came to the castle to fetch the earl, who all afoot departed from his castle and went with the clergy a procession to the church of Saint Nicholas, and there the clergy sang a psalm of the psalter, *Benedictus Dominus Deus meus, qui docet manus meas ad praelium, et digitos meos ad bellum, etc.* And when this psalm was sung, then they began to sing as they did on Christmas Day or Easter Day in the Pope's chapel or in the French king's, for he had with him many singers. The Bishop of Pamiers sang the mass, and there I heard as good playing at organs as ever I heard in any place. To speak briefly and according to reason, the Earl of Foix then was right perfect in all things, and as sage and as perceiving as any high prince in his days. There was none could compare with him in wit, honour, nor in largesse. At the feasts of Christmas, which he kept ever right solemn, came to his house many knights and squires of Gascony, and to every man he made good cheer. There I saw the Bourg of Spain, who laid the wood and the ass on the fire together, of whom Sir Espang de Lyon showed of his force, and I was glad to see him, and the Earl of Foix made him good semblant. There I saw also knights of Aragon and of England, of the Duke of Lancaster's house, who as then lay at Bordeaux. The earl made them good cheer and gave them great gifts.

I acquainted myself with those knights and by them I was informed of many things that fell in Castile, in Navarre and in Portugal, of the which I shall speak of when time requireth hereafter. And on a day I saw a squire of Gascony, called the Bascot of Mauleon, a man of a fifty year of age, an expert man of arms and a hardy beseeming. He alighted at my lodging in Orthez at the sign of the Moon, at Ernaulton du Puy's. He brought with him his somers and carriages as though he had been a great baron, and was served both he and his servants in silver vessel. And when I heard his name and saw the Earl of Foix and every man do him so much honour, then I demanded of Sir Espang de Lyon and said, 'Sir, is not this the squire that departed from the castle of Trigalet, when the Duke of Anjou lay at siege before Malvoisin?' 'Yes, truly' quoth he, 'it is the same, and he is a good man of arms and a good captain.' And so then I fell in acquaintance with him, for he was lodged there as I was. And a cousin of his called Ernaulton, captain of Carlat in Auvergne, with whom I was well acquainted, helped me to be acquainted with him, and in likewise so did the Bourg of Campagne. And at a time as we were talking and devising of arms, sitting by the fire abiding for midnight that the earl should go to supper, then this squire's cousin began to reckon up his life and of the deeds of arms that he had been at, saying how he had endured as much loss as profit. Then he demanded of me, and said, 'Sir John, have ye in your history anything of these matters that I speak of?' And I answered and said, 'I could not tell till I hear them. Show forth your matter and I will gladly hear you, for peradventure I have heard somewhat, but not all.' 'That is true' quoth the squire. Then he began to say thus: 'The first time that I bare armour was under the Captal of Buch at the battle of Poitiers. And as it was my hap, I had that day three prisoners, a knight and two squires, of whom I had one with another four hundred thousand francs. The next year after I was in Prussia with the Earl of Foix and the captal his cousin, under whom I was. And at our return at Meaux in Brie we found the Duchess of Normandy that was then, and the Duchess of Orleans, and a great number of ladies and damosels who were closed in and besieged by them of the Jacquerie, and if God had not helped them they had been enforced and defiled, for they were of great puissance and in number more than ten thousand, and the ladies were alone. And so we in the aid of those ladies did set on them, and there were slain of the Jacquerie more than six thousand, and they rebelled never since.

'At that time it was truce between France and England, but the King of Navarre made war in his own quarrel against the French king and regent. The Earl of Foix returned into his own country, but my master the captal and I, and other, abode still with the King of Navarre for his wages. And then we and other that aided us made great war in France, and specially in Picardy, and took many towns and castles in the bishopric, these of Beauvais and Amiens, and as then we were lords of the fields and rivers and conquered great finance. And when the truce failed between England and France, then the King of Navarre ceased his war and took a peace between the regent and him. Then the King of England with a great puissance passed the sea and came and laid siege to the town of Rheims. Then the King of England sent for my master who was at Clermont in Beauvoisin, and there made war for the king against all the country. Then we came to the King of England and to his children. And then', quoth the squire to me, 'Sir John, I think ye know already all that matter, and how the King of England wedded his wife and how he came before Chartres, and how the peace was made there between these two kings.' 'That is true, sir,' quoth I, 'In writing I have it, and the content of all the treaties.' Then the Bascot of Mauleon spake again and said: 'When this peace was thus made between these two kings, it was ordained that all men of war and companions should avoid and leave their fortresses and castles that they held. Then all manner of men of war and poor companions drew together and the captains took counsel what they should do. And then they said, "Though these two kings have taken peace together, yet we must live." Then they went into Burgundy, and there were captains of all nations, English, Gascons, Spaniards, Navarrais, Germans, Scots, and of all manner of nations, and there I was as a captain. And there we found in Burgundy and about the river of Loire of our company a twelve thousand of one and other, and in the same company there were a three or four thousand of good and chosen men of war, and as subtle in all deeds of arms as might be, and apt to advise a battle and to take their advantage, and as hardy to scale and assail town or castle. And that was well seen at the battle of Brignais

o

whereas we overthrew the Constable of France and the Earl of Forez, and two thousand spears, knights and squires. This battle did great profit to the companions, for before they were but poor, and then they were all rich by reason of good prisoners, towns, and castles that they won in the bishopric of Lyon and on the river of Rhône. And when they had the Pont-Saint-Esprit, they departed their war and made war to the Pope and to the cardinals, who could not be quit of them, nor had not been till they found another remedy. The Pope sent into Lombardy for the Marquis of Montferrat, a right valiant knight who had war with the Lord of Milan. When he came to Avignon, the Pope and the cardinals spake to him in such wise that he entreated with the captains, English, Gascons and Germans, for threescore thousand francs that the Pope and cardinals should pay to certain of these captains and to their companies, as Sir John Hawkwood, a valiant English knight, Sir Robert Briquet, Creswey, Naudan de Bageran, the Bourg Camus and divers other; and so then went into Lombardy and gave up the Pont-Saint-Esprit, and of all their routs they took but the sixth part [out of seven]. But we tarried behind, Sir Seguin of Badefol, Sir John Jouel, Sir James Planchin, Sir John Aymery, the Bourg of Périgord, Espiote, Louis Robaut, Limoges, Jacques Tiquerel, I and divers other. And we kept still and lay at Saint-Clement, at Arbresle, at Tarare, at Brignais, at the Pont-Saint-Denis, at the Hospital of Rochfort, for we had more than sixty fortresses and houses in the countries of Forez, Velay, base-Burgundy, and on the river of Loire, and we ransomed all the country: they could not be quit of us neither for paying well nor otherwise. And in a night we took the fortress of Charité, and there we abode a year and a half, and all was ours from Charité to Puy in Auvergne.

'Sir Seguin of Badefol had left his garrison of Anse and held Brioude in Auvergne, whereby he had great profit, what there and in the country to the value of a hundred thousand francs. And on the river of Loire to Orleans and the river of Alliers was all ours. And the archpriest who was captain of Nevers and was good French, could not remedy the country, but in that he knew many of the companions, and so by his desire sometime the less hurt was done. And the archpriest did the same time much good in Nivernais for he caused the city of Nevers to be closed, else it had been overrun and robbed divers times, for we had in those marches towns and castles more than twenty-six. There was neither knight nor squire nor rich man without he were agreed with us that durst look out of his house: and this war we made in the title of the king of Navarre.'

How divers captains, English and other, were discomfited before the town of Sancerre by the Frenchmen.   [Ch. 29]

. . . 'THEN the war renewed between the French king and the prince. Then we had much ado for we had sore war, and many captains, English and Gascons, were slain; and yet, I thank God, I am alive. There died Sir Robert Briquet between the land of the Duke of Orleans and the country of Blois in a place called Olivet, and there he and all his company were overthrown by a squire of Hainault, a valiant man of arms and a good captain called Alars Doustienes, surnamed Barbason, for he was of that lineage. He was as then governor of Blois and keeper of all the country, set there by the lords thereof as Louis, John and Guy. So it was his fortune to encounter with Sir Robert Briquet and Sir Robert Cheyne, and they and all their company were slain, for there were none taken to ransom. And at the battle of Niort in Saintonge, Creswey was slain by Sir Bertram of Guesclin and a seven hundred Englishmen were slain there. And at Saint-Sever were slain other English captains as Richard Gilles and Richard Holme. I knew but few except myself but that were slain.

'I have held frontier and made war for the King of England, for my heritage lieth in Bordelais. Sometime I have been so overthrown and pulled down that I had not wherewith to leap a-horseback, and another time I have been rich enough when good fortunes came. And in a season I and Raymond Lespes were companions together, and we had in Toulouse on the frontiers of Bigorre the castle of Malvoisin, the castle of Trigalet, and the castle of Lutillous, which as then did us great profit. Then the Duke of Anjou took them from us by force of puissance, but then Raymond Lespes turned French and I abide still good English, and shall do while I live. True it was, when I had lost the castle of Trigalet and was conducted to the castle of Culier, and that the duke was gone back again into France, I determined to do somewhat, either to get some profit or else to lose all, or to die in the pain. I caused by spial the town and castle of Terry in Albigeois to be well aviewed, which castle after availed to me, what by good fortunes and pacifying of the country, a hundred thousand francs. I shall show you how I won it.

'Without the town there is a fair fountain, and of usage every morning the women of the town would come thither with pots and other vessels on their heads to fetch of the clear water there. Then I took fifty companions of the garrison of Culier and we rode all a day through woods and bushes. And the next night about midnight I set a bushment near to Terry, and I and six other all only did on us women's array and with pots in our hands. And so we came to a meadow right near to the town and hid ourselves behind great cocks of hay that were there standing, for it was about the feast of Saint John when they make hay. And when the hour came that the gate was opened to let the women go out for water, we seven took our pots and filled them at the fountain, and went toward the town, our faces wrapped in kerchieves so that we could not be known. The women that we met going for water said to us, "Ah! Saint Mary, gossips, ye were up betimes." We answered in their language with a faint* voice, "That is true," and so passed by them and came to the gate, and we found nobody there but a sowter dressing

* Feigned.

forth his baggage. Then one of us blew a horn to draw hither our company out of the bushment. The sowter took no heed, but when he heard the horn blow he demanded of them, "What is this? Who was that blew the horn?" One answered and said, "It was a priest went into the fields." "Ah, that is true" quoth the sowter, "it was Francis, our priest. Gladly he goeth a mornings to seek for an hare." Then our company came, and we entered into the town where we found no man to draw his sword to make any defence. Thus I took the town and castle of Terry, whereby I have had great profit yearly, more than the castle of Trigalet with the appurtenance is worth. But as now I wot not what to do, for I am in a treaty with the Earl of Armagnac and with the Dolphin of Auvergne, who hath express authority by the French king to buy all towns and fortresses of the companions, such as they hold in their hands wheresoever they be, either in Auvergne, Rouergue, Limousin, Quercy, Périgord, Albigeois, Agen, and of all such as hath or doth make any war in the King of England's title. And many are departed and have rendered their fortresses: I cannot tell if I will render mine or not.' With that word, said the Bourg of Campagne, 'Cousin, it is true, for of Carlat, which I hold in Auvergne, I am come hither to hear some tidings, for Sir Louis of Sancerre, Marshal of France, will be here shortly; he is now at Tarbes, as I have heard of such as come thence.' With these words they called for wine and drank. Then the Bascot said to me, 'Sir John, are ye well informed of my life? Yet I have had other adventures, which I have not showed nor will not speak of all.' 'Sir,' quoth I, 'I have well heard you.'

How a squire called Limousin turned French, and how he caused Louis Robaut, his companion in arms, to be taken.   [Ch. 30]

Then again I demanded of him where Robaut, an expert squire and a great captain of men of war was become, because I saw him once in Avignon in great array. 'I shall show you,' quoth the Bascot of Mauléon.

'In time past, when Sir Seguin of Badefol held Brioude in Velay, a ten mile from Puy in Auvergne, and that he had made war in the country and conquered much, then he returned into Gascony and gave to Louis Robaut and to another companion of his called Limousin, Brioude and Anse on the water of Saône. The country as then was so desolate and full of companions in every quarter that none durst go out of their houses. And between Brioude in Auvergne and Anse is more than twenty-seven mile, a country full of mountains. And when Louis Robaut would ride for his pleasure from Brioude to Anse, he rode without doubt or fear, for he held divers fortresses in the county of Forez and thereabout, where he refreshed him; for as then the gentlemen of Auvergne, of Forez, of Velay and the frontiers, were sore travailed and overlaid with the war. They were so taken and ransomed that they doubted the war, for there was none of the great lords of France that sent any men of war into the country, for the French king was young and had much ado in divers parts of the realm, for in every part the companions and companies rode and did much hurt, so that the realm could not be quit of them. And also divers of the lords of France were in England in hostage, and in the mean season their countries and men were pilled and robbed, and had no remedy, for the men of the country were without courage to defend themselves. And so it was that Robaut and Limousin, who were companions in arms, fell out. I shall show you how.

'Louis Robaut had at Brioude a fair woman to his lover, whom he loved perfectly, and when he rode from Brioude to Anse he commanded Limousin to take good heed to her, and Limousin, who was his companion in arms and in whom he most trusted, he took so good heed to the damosel that he had his pleasure of her when he list, so that Louis Robaut was informed thereof, and he could suffer it no longer. So that he took such a hate against his companion that he caused him to be taken by his servants and made him to be driven all naked save a breech about the town, and beaten with scourges and trumpets to be blown before him, and at certain places his deed to be openly cried, and then banished the town like a traitor and, in a simple coat, put out.

'This despite did Louis Robaut to Limousin, which despite Limousin took grievously and said how he would be revenged if ever it lay in his power, as he was anon after. And this Limousin, while he was in prosperity, in riding between Brioude and Anse, he ever forbore the lands of the Lord of Voulte, dwelling on the river of Rhône, for he had served him in his youth. Then he thought to go to him and to cry him mercy and to desire him to make his peace in France. And so in his coat afoot he went to Voulte, for he knew right well the way, and so went into a house. And when he saw his time he went to the castle, and the porter would not suffer him to enter, but at last he spoke so fair that the porter did let him in, and commanded him to go no farther in without he were commanded, and he obeyed.

'When the lord was up, he went down into the court to sport him and so came to the gate. Then Limousin fell down on his knees and said, "Sir, do ye not know me?" "By my faith" quoth the lord, "no." He thought little it should have been Limousin. And when he had well advised him he said, "Thou resemblest well Limousin who was once my servant." "Sir" quoth he, "Limousin I am, and your servant." Then he cried him mercy for all things past before, and showed him from point to point all his business and how Louis Robaut and dealt with him at the end. Then the lord said, "Limousin, is it that thou sayest and that thou wilt become good French? I shall make thy peace." "By my faith, sir," quoth he, "I never did so much hurt to the realm of France but I shall do again more profit thereto." "That would I see gladly" quoth the Lord of Voulte. The lord kept him in his house till he had made his peace in every place, and when Limousin might in surety ride, then the Lord of Voulte armed him and brought him to the Seneschal of Velay and acquainted him there. And there he was examined of the state of Brioude and of Louis Robaut, and when he rideth what way he taketh. And then he said, "When Louis rideth he hath not with him past a thirty or a forty spears, and the ways that he keepeth I know them by heart, for with him and without him I have ridden them oft-times. And, sir, if ye will send forth a company of men of arms, on jeopardy of my head, ye shall have him within fifteen days."

'The captains there took heed to his saying and sent out spies, and Robaut was spied as he was riding from Brioude to Anse beside Lyon on the river of Rhône. When Limousin knew it, he showed it to the Lord of Voulte and said, "Sir, Louis Robaut is now at Anse, and at his returning I shall bring you to a strait whereas he must needs pass by." Then the Lord of Voulte made an assembly and was captain himself, and sent for the Bailey of Velay, the Lord of Montclare, Sir Guerrot of Salyers and his son Sir Plouserat of Vernet, the Lord of Villeneuve and for other men of arms thereabout, so that he was a three hundred spears. And they all assembled at Annonnay, and by the counsel of Limousin they made two bushments. The Viscount of Polignac and the Lord of Chalons had the rule of the one, and the Lord Voulte and the Lord of Montclare had the guiding of the other bushment, and with them Sir Louis of Tournon and the Lord of Salyers; and they had equally divided their company. The first company kept the pass near Saint-Rambert in Forez whereas Louis Robaut should pass the river of Loire, or else he must have gone [at a ford above Le Puy]. And when Louis Robaut had done that, he came for to Anse. He departed with a forty spears, and thought not to have any encounter and doubted nothing of Limousin: it was the least thought he had. And lightly ever the way that he rode outward he would not come homeward. And as he came outward he came by Saint-Rambert, and at his return he took another way and took the mountains above Lyon and above Vienne and under the village of Argental and rode straight toward le Monastier, a three little mile from Puy. And he had passed between the castle of Monistrol and Montfaucon, and so came about the country toward a village called Vaucance between Annonnay and Saint-Julien. And in the wood there was a straight passage which he must needs pass or else to go by Annonnay, at which strait lay the Lord of Voulte with two hundred spears, and Louis Robaut took no heed till he was among them.

'Then the Lord of Voulte, who was ready to do his enterprise, laid the spear in the rest and came crying "La Voulte!" and dashed in among the companions who rode abroad without good array. And so at the first meeting many of them were overthrown to the earth, and Louis Robaut was stricken from his horse by a squire of Auvergne called Amblardon, and so he took him prisoner, and all other taken or slain: none escaped. And there they found in boiettes a three thousand francs which Louis Robaut had received at Anse for tribute of certain villages thereabout, whereof they were glad for every man had his part. And when Limousin saw Robaut thus trapped, he came before him and said in reproach, "Louis, Louis, here faulteth company; remember ye the blame and shame that ye did put me to at Brioude for your mistress? I would have thought little for a woman ye would have put me to that ye did; for if ye had done as much to me I would not have been so angry, for two such companions in arms as we were might have passed our time well enough with one woman." With those words the lords laughed, but Louis Robaut had no sport thereat.

'By the taking thus of this Louis Robaut, Brioude was delivered to the Seneschal of Auvergne, for after they had lost their captain and the chief men they had, they would keep it no longer. And in likewise so did they of Anse and other fort-resses in Velay and Forez that was on their part, for they within any of these fortresses were right joyous to yield up their holds to save their lives. Then Louis Robaut was brought to Annonnay and there set in prison, and the French king had great joy of his taking. And, as I heard reported, he was beheaded at Villeneuve beside Avignon. Thus Louis Robaut died. God have mercy on him.

'Thus, sir,' quoth the Bascot of Mauléon, 'I have held you with talking to pass away the night. Howbeit, sir, all that I have said is true.' 'Sir', quoth I, 'With all my heart I thank you. Sir, I trust your sayings shall not be lost, for, sir, an God suffer me to return into mine own country, all that I have heard you say and all that I have seen and found in my voyage, I shall put it in remembrance in the noble chronicle that the Earl of Blois hath set me a-work on; for I shall write it and chronicle it by the grace of God to the intent it shall be in perpetual remembrance.'

Then the Bourg of Campagne, called Ernalton, began to speak and would gladly that I should perceive by him that he would I should record his life and of the Bourg English his brother, and how they had done in Auvergne and other places. But as then he had no leisure for the watch of the castle sounded to assemble all men that were in the town to come up to the castle to sup with the Earl of Foix. Then these two squires made them ready and lighted up torches, and so we went up to the castle, and so did all other knights and squires that were lodged in the town.

Of the state or ordinance of the Earl of Foix, and how the town of Santarem rebelled for the great travail, damage and outrage that was done thereto. [Ch. 31]

OF the estate and order of the Earl of Foix cannot be too much spoken nor praised, for the season that I was at Orthez I found him such and much more than I can speak of. But while I was there I saw and heard many things that turned me to great pleasure.

I saw on a Christmas Day sitting at his board four bishops of his country, two Clementines and two Urbanists: the Bishop of Pamiers and the Bishop of Lescar, Clementines, they sat highest, then the Bishop of Aire and the Bishop of Roy on the frontiers of Bourdelais and Bayonne, Urbanists. Then sat the Earl of Foix, and then the Viscount of Roquebertin of Gascony and the Viscount of Bruniquel, the Viscount of Gousserant and a knight of England of the Duke of Lancaster's, who as then lay at Lisbon; the duke had sent him thither. The knight was called Sir William Willoughby. And at another table sat five abbots and two knights of Aragon called Sir Raymond de Montflorentin and Sir Martin de Roanès. And at another table sat knights and squires of Gascony and of Bigorre, first the Lord d'Anchin, then Sir Gaillart de la Motte, Sir Raymond of Castelnau, the Lord of Caumont, Gascon, the Lord of Caupene, the Lord de la Lane, the Lord of Montferrand, Sir William de Benac, Sir Peter of Curton, the Lord of Valencin, and Sir Auger named the Bascle, and at other tables knights of Béarn a great number. And the chief stewards of the hall were Sir Espang of Lyon, Sir Chiquart de Bois-Verdun, Sir Monaut de Navailles and Sir Peter of Beaulx of Béarn, and the earl's two bastard brethren served at the table, Sir Ernaulton Guillaume and Sir Peter of Béarn, and the earl's two sons Sir Yvain of l'Echelle was sewer and Sir Gracien bare his cup. And there were many minstrels as well of his own as of strangers, and each of them did their devoir in their faculties. The same day the Earl of Foix gave to heralds and minstrels the sum of five hundred francs and gave to the Duke of Touraine's minstrels gowns of cloth of gold furred with ermines, valued at two hundred francs. This dinner endured four hours.

Thus I am glad to speak of the Earl of Foix, for I was there in his house a twelve weeks and well treated in all things. And while I was there I might learn and hear tidings of all countries, and also the gentle knight Sir Espang of Lyon, in whose company I entered into the country, he caused me to be acquainted with knights and squires such as could declare to me anything that I could demand, for I was informed of the business of Portugal and of Castile, and what manner of war they had made, and of the battles and encounters between those two kings and their assisters, of which business I shall make just report. . . .

How Sir Henry Percy and his brother, with a good number of men of arms and archers, went after the Scots to win again his pennon that the Earl of Douglas had won before Newcastle-upon-Tyne; and how they assailed the Scots before Otterburn in their lodgings (1388).   [Ch. 138]

IT was showed to Sir Henry Percy and to his brother, and to the other knights and squires that were there, by such as had followed the Scots from Newcastle and had well advised their doing, who said to Sir Henry and to Sir Ralph, 'Sirs, we have followed the Scots privily and have discovered all the country. The Scots be at Pontland and have taken Sir Edmund Alphel in his own castle, and from thence they be gone to Otterburn, and there they lie this night. What they will do tomorrow we know not. They are ordained to abide there, and sirs, surely their great host is not with them, for in all they pass not there a three thousand men.' When Sir Henry heard that he was joyful and said, 'Sirs, let us leap on our horses, for by the faith I owe to God and to my lord my father, I will go seek for my pennon and dislodge them this same night.' Knights and squires that heard him agreed thereto and were joyous, and every man made him ready.

The same evening the Bishop of Durham came thither with a good company, for he heard at Durham how the Scots were before Newcastle and how that the Lord Percy's sons with other lords and knights should fight with the Scots. Therefore the Bishop of Durham, to come to the rescue, had assembled up all the country and so was coming to Newcastle. But Sir Henry Percy would not abide his coming for he had with him six hundred spears, knights and squires, and an eight thousand footmen. They thought that sufficient number to fight with the Scots, if they were not but three hundred spears and three thousand of other. Thus they departed from Newcastle after dinner, and set forth in good order and took the same way that the Scots had gone, and rode to Otterburn a seven little leagues from thence and fair way, but they could not ride fast because of their footmen. And when the Scots had supped and some laid down to their rest, and were weary of travelling and assaulting of the castle all that day, and thought to rise early in the morning in cool of the day to give a new assault, therewith suddenly the Englishmen came on them and entered into the lodgings, weening it had been the masters' lodgings, and therein were but varlets and servants.

Then the Englishmen cried, 'Percy! Percy!' and entered into the lodgings, and ye know well where such affray is, noise is soon raised. And it fortuned well for the Scots, for when they saw the Englishmen came to wake them, then the lords sent a certain of their servants of footmen to skirmish with the Englishmen at the entry of the lodgings, and in the meantime they armed and apparelled them, every man under his banner and under his captain's pennon. The night was far on but the moon shone so bright as an it had been in a manner day. It was in the month of August and the weather fair and temperate. Thus the Scots were drawn together and without any noise departed from their lodgings, and went about a little mountain, which was greatly for their advantage. For all the day before they had well advised the place, and said among themselves, 'If the Englishmen come on us suddenly then we will do thus and thus, for it is a jeopardous thing in the night if men of war enter into our lodgings. If they do, then we will draw to such a place, and thereby either we shall win or lose.'

When the Englishmen entered into the field, at the first they soon overcame the varlets, and as they entered further in, always they found new men to busy them and to skirmish with them. Then suddenly came the Scots from about the mountain and set on the Englishmen or they were aware, and cried their cries, whereof the Englishmen were sore astonished. Then they cried, 'Percy!' and the other party cried, 'Douglas!'. There began a cruel battle, and at the first encounter many were overthrown of both parties. And because the Englishmen were a great number and greatly desired to vanquish their enemies, and rested at their pace and greatly did put aback the Scots so that the Scots were near discomfited, then the Earl Douglas, who was young and strong and of great desire to get praise and grace, and was willing to deserve to have it and cared for no pain nor travail, came forth with his banner and cried, 'Douglas! Douglas!'. And Sir Henry Percy and Sir Ralph his brother, who had great indignation against the Earl Douglas because he had won the pennon of their arms at the barriers before Newcastle, came to that part and cried, 'Percy!'. Their two banners met and their men. There was a sore fight. The Englishmen were so strong and fought so valiantly that they reculed the Scots back. There were two valiant knights of Scots under the banner of the Earl Douglas called Sir Patrick of Hepburn and Sir Patrick his son. They acquitted themselves that day valiantly; the earl's banner had been won an they had not been; they defended it so valiantly and in the rescuing thereof did such feats of arms, that it was greatly to their recommendation and to their heirs for ever after.

It was showed me by such as had been at the same battle, as well by knights and squires of England as of Scotland, at the house of the Earl of Foix, for anon after this battle was done I met at Orthez two squires of England called John of Newcastle and John of Cantiron. Also when I returned from Avignon I found also there a knight and squire of Scotland. I knew them and they knew me by such tokens as I showed them of their country, for I, author of this book, in my youth had ridden nigh over all the realm of Scotland. And I was as then a fifteen days in the house of Earl William Douglas, father to the same Earl James of whom I spake of now, in a castle a five leagues from Edinburgh in the country of Dalkeith. The same time I saw there this Earl James, a fair young child, and a sister of his called the Lady Blanche. And I was informed by both these parties how this battle was as sore a battle fought as lightly hath been heard of before of such a number, and I believe it well. For English on the one party and Scots on the other party are good men of war, for when they meet there is a hard fight without sparing: there is no 'Ho!' between them as long as spears, swords, axes or daggers will endure, but lay on each upon other. And when they be well beaten and that the one part hath obtained the victory, they then glorify so in their deeds or arms and are so joyful, that such as be taken, they shall be ransomed or they go out of the field, so that shortly each of them is so content with other that at their departing courteously they will say, 'God thank you'. But in fighting one with another there is no play nor sparing; and this is true, and that shall well appear by this said encounter, for it was as valiantly fought as could be desired, as ye shall hear.

How the Earl James Douglas by his valiantness encouraged his men who were reculed and in a manner discomfited, and in his so doing he was wounded to death (1388).   [Ch. 139]

KNIGHTS and squires were of good courage on both parties to fight valiantly. Cowards there had no place but hardiness reigned with goodly feats of arms, for knights and squires were so joined together at hand strokes that archers had no place of neither party. There the Scots showed great hardiness and fought merrily with great desire of honour. The Englishmen were three to one, howbeit I say not but Englishmen did nobly acquit themselves, for ever the Englishmen had rather been slain or taken in the place than to fly.

Thus as I have said, the banners of Douglas and Percy and their men were met each against other, envious who should win the honour of that journey. At the beginning the Englishmen were so strong that they reculed back their enemies. Then the Earl Douglas who was of great heart and high of enterprise, seeing his men recule back, then to recover the place and to show knightly valour, he took his axe in both his hands and entered so into the press that he made himself way in such wise that none durst approach near him, and he was so well armed that he bare well of such strokes as he received. Thus he went ever forward like a hardy Hector, willing alone to conquer the field and to discomfit his enemies. But at last he was encountered with three spears all at once: the one struck him on the shoulder, the other on the breast and the stroke glinted down to his belly, and the third struck him in the thigh; and sore hurt with all three strokes so that he was borne perforce to the earth, and after that he could not be again relieved. Some of his knights and squires followed him but not all, for it was night and no light but by the shining of the moon. The Englishmen knew well they had borne one down to the earth but they wist not who it was, for if they had known that it had been the Earl Douglas, they had been thereof so joyful and so proud that the victory had been theirs. Nor also the Scots knew not of that adventure till the end of the battle, for if they had known it they should have been so sore dispaired and discouraged that they would have fled away. Thus as the Earl Douglas was felled to the earth, he was stricken into the head with an axe, and another stroke through the thigh. The Englishmen passed forth and took no heed of him, they thought none otherwise but that they had slain a man of arms.

On the other part the Earl George de la March and of Dunbar fought right valiantly, and gave the Englishmen much ado, and cried, 'Follow Douglas!' and set on the sons of Percy. Also Earl John of Moray with his banner and men fought valiantly and set fiercely on the Englishmen, and gave them so much to do that they wist not to whom to attend.

How in this battle Sir Ralph Percy was sore hurt and taken prisoner by a Scottish knight.
[Ch. 140]

OF all the battles and encounterings that I have made mention of herebefore in all this history, great or small, this battle that I treat of now was one of the sorest and best fought, without cowardice or faint hearts, for there was neither knight nor squire but that did his devoir and fought hand-to-hand. This battle was like the battle of Cocherel, the which was valiantly fought and endured. The Earl of Northumberland's sons Sir Henry and Sir Ralph Percy, who were chief sovereign captains, acquitted themselves nobly, and Sir Ralph Percy entered in so far among his enemies that he was closed in and hurt, and so sore handled that his breath was so short that he was taken prisoner by a knight of the Earl of Moray' called Sir John Maxwell. In the taking the Scottish knight demanded what he was, for it was in the night so that he knew him not, and Sir Ralph was so sore overcome and bled fast that at last he said, 'I am Ralph Percy.' Then the Scot said, 'Sir Ralph, rescue or no rescue, I take you for my prisoner. I am Maxwell.' 'Well,' quoth Sir Ralph, 'I am content. But then take heed to me for I am sore hurt; my hose and my greaves are full of blood.' Then the knight saw by him the Earl Moray and said, 'Sir, here I deliver to you Sir Ralph Percy as prisoner, but sir, let good heed be taken to him for he is sore hurt.' The earl was joyful of those words and said, 'Maxwell, thou hast well won thy spurs.' Then he delivered Sir Ralph Percy to certain of his men, and they stopped and wrapped his wounds. And still the battle endured not knowing who had as then the better, for there were many taken and rescued again that came to no knowledge.

Now let us speak of the young James Earl of Douglas, who did marvels in arms or he was beaten down. When he was overthrown, the press was great about him so that he could not relieve, for with an axe he had his death wound. His men followed him as near as they could, and there came to him Sir James Lindsay his cousin and Sir John and Sir Walter Sinclair and other knights and squires. And by him was a gentle knight of his, who followed him all the day, and a chaplain of his, not like a priest but like a valiant man of arms, for all that night he followed the earl with a good axe in his hands and still skirmished about the earl thereas he lay, and reculed back some of the Englishmen with great strokes that he gave. Thus he was found fighting near to his master, whereby he had great praise, and thereby the same year he was made Archdeacon of Aberdeen. This priest was called Sir William of North Berwick. He was a tall man and a hardy, and was sore hurt. When these knights came to the earl they found him in an evil case, and a knight of his lying by him called Sir Robert Hart; he had a fifteen wounds in one place and other. Then Sir John Sinclair demanded of the earl how he did. 'Right evil, cousin,' quoth the earl, 'but thanked be God there hath been but a few of mine ancestors that hath died in their beds. But, cousin, I require you think to revenge me, for I reckon myself but dead for my heart fainteth oftentimes. My cousin Walter and you, I pray you raise up again my banner which lieth on the ground and my squire Davy Collemine slain. But, sirs, show neither to friend nor foe in what case you see me in, for if mine enemies knew it they would rejoice and our friends discomforted.' The two brethren of Sinclair and Sir James Lindsay did as the earl had desired them and raised up again his banner and cried, 'Douglas!'. Such as were behind and heard that cry drew together and set on their enemies valiantly and reculed back the Englishmen and many overthrown, and so drove the Englishmen back beyond the place whereas the earl lay, who was by that time dead, and so came to the earl's banner the which Sir John Sinclair held in his hands, and many good knights and squires of Scotland about him. And still company drew to the cry of Douglas. Thither came the Earl Moray with his banner well accompanied, and also the Earl de la March and of Dunbar, and when they saw the Englishmen recule, and their company assembled together, they renewed again the battle and gave many hard and sad strokes.

How the Scots won the battle against the English-men beside Otterburn and there was taken prisoners Sir Henry and Sir Ralph Percy; and how an English squire would not yield him, no more would a Scottish squire, and so died both. And how the Bishop of Durham and his company were discomfited among themselves (1388).

[Ch. 141]

TO say truth, the Englishmen were sorer travailed than the Scots, for they came the same day from Newcastle-upon-Tyne, a six English miles, and went a great pace to the intent to find the Scots, which they did; so that by their fast going they were near out of breath, and the Scots were fresh and well rested, which greatly availed them when time was of their business, for in the last skirmish they reculed back the Englishmen in such wise, that after that they could no more assemble together for the Scots passed through their battles. And it fortuned that Sir Henry Percy and the Lord of Montgomery, a valiant knight of Scotland, fought together hand-to-hand right valiantly without letting of any other, for every man had enough to do. So long they two fought that perforce of arms Sir Henry Percy was taken prisoner by the said Lord of Montgomery.

The knights and squires of Scotland as Sir Malcolm Drummond, Sir Thomas Erskine, Sir William, Sir James and Sir Alexander Lindsay, the Lord of Fenton, Sir John of Sandilands, Sir Patrick of Dunbar, Sir John and Sir Walter Sinclair, Sir John Maxwell, Sir Guy Stuart, Sir John Haliburton, Sir Alexander Ramsay, Robert Collemine and his two sons John and Robert, who were there made knights, and a hundred knights and squires that I cannot name, all these right valiantly did acquit themselves.

And on the English party, before that the Lord Percy was taken and after, there fought valiantly Sir Ralph Lumley, Sir Matthew Redman, Sir Thomas Ogle, Sir Thomas Gray, Sir Thomas Helton, Sir Thomas Abingdon, Sir John Lilleburn, Sir William Walsingham, the Baron of Helton, Sir John of Copeland, the Seneschal of York and divers other footmen. Whereto should I write long process? This was a sore battle and well fought, and as fortune is always changeable, though the Englishmen were more in number than the Scots and were right valiant men of war and well expert, and that at the first front they reculed back the Scots, yet finally the Scots obtained the place of victory, and all the foresaid Englishmen taken and a hundred more saving Sir Matthew Redman, Captain of Berwick, who when he knew no remedy nor recoverance, and saw his company fly from the Scots and yielded them on every side, then he took his horse and departed to save himself.

The same season about the end of this discomfiture, there was an English squire called Sir Thomas Waltham, a goodly and a valiant man: and that was well seen, for of all that night he would neither fly nor yet yield him. It was said he had made a vow at a feast in England, that the first time that ever he saw Englishmen and Scots in battle, he would so do his devoir to his power, in such wise that either he would be reputed for the best doer on both sides or else to die in the pain. He was called a valiant and a hardy man and did so much by his prowess, that under the banner of the Earl of Moray he did such valiantness in arms that the Scots had marvel thereof, and so was slain in fighting. The Scots would gladly have taken him alive, but he would never yield, he hoped ever to have been rescued. And with him there was a Scottish squire slain, cousin to the King of Scots called Simon Glendinning, his death was greatly complained of the Scots. This battle was fierce and cruel till it came to the end of the discomfiture, but when the Scots saw the Englishmen recule and yield themselves, then the Scots were courteous and set them to their ransom and every man said to his prisoner, 'Sirs, go and unarm you and take your ease, I am your master.' And so made their prisoners as good cheer as though they had been brethren without doing to them any damage. The chase endured a five English miles and if the Scots had been men enough there had none escaped, but either they had been taken or slain. And if Archambault Douglas and the Earl of Fife, the Earl Sutherland and other of the great company who were gone towards Carlisle had been there, by all likelihood they had taken the Bishop of Durham and the town of Newcastle-upon-Tyne. I shall show you how.

The same evening that the Percys departed from Newcastle, as ye have heard before, the Bishop of Durham with the rear band came to Newcastle and supped, and as he sat at the table he had imagination in himself how he did not acquit himself well to see the Englishmen in the field and he to be within the town. Incontinent he caused the table to be taken away and commanded to saddle his horses and to sound the trumpets, and called up men in the town to arm themselves and to mount on their horses, and footmen to order themselves to depart. And thus every man departed out of the town to the number of seven thousand, two thousand on horseback and five thousand afoot. They took their way toward Otterburn whereas the battle had been, and by that time they had gone two mile from Newcastle, tidings came to them how their men were fighting with the Scots. Therewith the bishop rested there, and incontinent came more flying fast, that they were out of breath. Then they were demanded how the matter went. They answered and said, 'Right evil; we be all discomfited. Here cometh the Scots chasing of us.' These tidings troubled the Englishmen, and began to doubt. And again the third time men came flying as fast as they might. When the men of the bishopric of Durham heard of these evil tidings they were abashed in such wise that they brake their array, so that the bishop could not hold together the number of five hundred. It was thought that if the Scots had followed them in any number, seeing that it was night, that in entering into the town, and the Englishmen so abashed, the town had been won.

The Bishop of Durham, being in the field, had goodwill to have succoured the Englishmen and recomforted his men as much as he could, but he saw his own men fly as well as other. Then he demanded counsel of Sir William Lucy and of Sir Thomas Clifford and of other knights what was best to do. These knights for their honour would give him no counsel, for they thought to return again and do nothing should sound greatly to their blame, and to go forth might be to their great damage, and so stood still and would give none answer; and the longer they stood the fewer there were, for some still stole away. Then the bishop said, 'Sirs, all things considered, it is none honour to put all in peril nor to make of one evil damage twain. We hear how our company be discomfited and we cannot remedy it, for to go to recover them we know not with whom nor with what number we shall meet. Let us return fair and easily for this night to Newcastle, and tomorrow let us draw together and go look on our enemies.' Every man answered, 'As God will, so be it.'

Therewith they returned to Newcastle. Thus a man may consider the great default that is in men that be abashed and discomfited, for if they had kept them together and have turned again such as fled, they had discomfited the Scots. This was the opinion of divers. And because they did not thus, the Scots had the victory.

[The madness of King Charles the Sixth of France]
(1392).   [Ch. 184]

. . . . WHEN the French king had tarried the space of three weeks in the city of
Le Mans and the knights returned that he had sent into Brittany, then he said,
since he had heard the duke's answer, he would no longer tarry there, for he said
the tarrying there greatly displeased him, and would pass forth into Brittany to
see his enemies, that was the Duke of Brittany who sustained the traitor Sir Peter
of Craon. The intention of the king was that if any knights and squires came
against him, or that he found any towns closed, he would put down that duke
for ever and set a governor in the country till the duke's children were of lawful
age, and then render to them the heritage, and the duke never to have any part
thereof. This opinion the king held still and no man could put him therefrom.
And thus on a fair day about ten of the clock the king departed from the city of
Le Mans, and had commanded his marshals the night before to cause all his army
both before and behind to dislodge and to draw to Angers, and said that he would
not return till he had been in Brittany and destroyed the traitors that had put
him to so much pain and trouble. The marshals did the king's commandment.

The day that the king departed was marvellous hot, for the sun as then naturally
was in his chief force, and to the intent to declare the truth of everything, the
same season that the king lay at Le Mans he was sore travailed with daily sitting
in council, and also he was not perfectly whole nor had not been all that season.
He was feeble in his brain and head, and did eat or drink but little and nigh daily
was in a hot fever, so that he was greatly annoyed and pained. And also for the
displeasure that he had for the constable's hurt, he was full of melancholy and his
spirits sore troubled and travailed; and that his physicians spied well, and so did
his uncles, but they could not remedy it, for no man durst counsel him to break
his voyage into Brittany. And as it was informed me, as he rode forward in the
forest of Le Mans, a great signification fell to him, by the which, if he had done
well, he should have called his council about him, and well advised himself or
he had gone any further. Suddenly there came to the king a poor man, bare-
headed, bare-legged and bare-footed, and on his body a poor white coat. He
seemed rather to be a fool than wise, and boldly, suddenly he took the bridle of
the king's horse in his hands and stopped the horse and said, 'Sir king, ride no
further forward for thou art betrayed.' Those words entered into the king's head,
whereby he was worse disposed in his health than he was before so that his heart
and his blood was moved. Then the king's servants struck so the poor man that
he let the king's horse go, and made no more of his words than of a fool's speaking,
which was folly as divers men said, for at least they should have better examined
the man and to have seen if he had been a natural fool or no, and to have known
from whence he came. But they did not so, but left him behind, and he was never

seen after to any man's knowledge, but such as were near to the king heard him speak these words.

The king passed forth, and about twelve of the clock the king passed out of the forest and came into a great plain all sandy. The sun also was in his height and shone bright, whose rays were marvellously hot, whereby the horses were sore chafed and all such persons as were armed were sore oppressed with heat. The knights rode together by companies, some here and some there, and the king rode somewhat apart because of the dust. And the Duke of Berry and the Duke of Burgundy rode on his left hand talking together, an acre breadth of land off from the king. Other lords, as the Earl of March, Sir Jacques of Bourbon, Sir Charles d'Albret, Sir Philip d'Artois, Sir Henry and Sir Philip of Bar, Sir Peter of Navarre and other knights rode by companies. The Duke of Bourbon, the Lord Coucy, Sir Charles de Hangest, the Baron d'Ivry and divers other rode on before the king and not in his company, and they devised and talked together and took no heed of that fell suddenly on the chief personage of the company, which was on the king's own person. Therefore the works of God are marvellous and his scourges are cruel and are to be doubted of all creatures. There hath been seen in the Old Testament, and also in the New, many figures and examples thereof. We read how Nebuchadnezzar, King of Assyrians who reigned a season in such triumphant glory that there was none like him, and suddenly in his greatest force and glory, the Sovereign King our Lord God, King of heaven and earth, Former and Ordainer of all things, apparelled this said king in such wise that he lost his wit and reign, and was seven year in that estate, and lived by acorns and mast that fell from the oaks and other wild apples and fruits, and had taste but as a boar or a swine. And after he had endured this penance God restored him again to his memory and wit. And then he said to Daniel the prophet that there was none other God but the God of Israel. Now the Father, the Son and the Holy Ghost, three Persons in one God, hath been, is and ever shall be as puissant to show his works as ever he was, wherefore no man should marvel of anything that he doth. Now to the purpose why I speak all these words.

A great influence from heaven fell the said day upon the French king, and as divers said, it was his own fault, for according to the disposition of his body and the state that he was in, and the warning that his physicians did give him, he should not have ridden in such a hot day at that hour, but rather in the morning and in the evening in the fresh air; wherefore it was a shame to them that were near about him to suffer or to counsel him to do as he did. Thus as the French king rode upon a fair plain in the heat of the sun, which was as then of a marvellous height, and the king had on a jacket covered with black velvet which sore chafed him, and on his head a simple bonnet of scarlet, and a chaplet of great pearls which the queen had given him at his departure, and he had a page that rode behind him bearing on his head a chapeau of Montauban, bright and clear

P

shining against the sun. And behind that page rode another bearing the king's spear painted red and fringed with silk, with a sharp head of steel: the Lord de la Riviere had brought a dozen of them with him from Toulouse, and that was one of them. He had given the whole dozen to the king, and the king had given three of them to his brother the Duke of Orleans and three to the Duke of Bourbon. And as they rode thus forth, the page that bore the spear, whether it were by negligence or that he fell asleep, he let the spear fall on the other page's head that rode before him, and the head of the spear made a great clash on the chapeau of steel. The king, who rode but afore them, with the noise suddenly started, and his heart trembled and into his imagination ran the impression of the words of the man that stopped his horse in the forest of Le Mans, and it ran into his thought that his enemies ran after him to slay and destroy him. And with that abusion he fell out of his wit by feebleness of his head, and dashed his spurs to his horse and drew out the sword and turned to his pages, having no knowledge of any man, weening in himself to be in a battle enclosed with his enemies, and lifted up his sword to strike he cared not where, and cried and said, 'On, on upon these traitors!' When the pages saw the king so inflamed with ire they took good heed to themselves, as it was time. They thought the king had been displeased because the spear fell down, then they stepped away from the king.

The Duke of Orleans was not as then far off from the king. The king came to him with his naked sword in his hand. The king was as then in such a frenzy, and his heart so feeble, that he neither knew brother nor uncle. When the Duke of Orleans saw the king coming on him with his sword naked in his hand, he was abashed and would not abide with him: he wist not what he meant. He dashed his spurs to his horse and rode away, and the king after him. The Duke of Burgundy who rode a little way off from the king, when he heard the rushing of the horses and heard the pages cry, he regarded that way and saw how the king with his naked sword chased his brother the Duke of Orleans. He was sore abashed and said, 'Out, harrow! What mischief is this? The king is not in his right mind, God help him. Fly away nephew, fly away, for the king would slay you.' The Duke of Orleans was not well assured of himself and fled away as fast as his horse might bear him, and knights and squires followed after. Every man began to draw thither: such as were far off thought they had chased a hare or a wolf, till at last they heard that the king was not well in his mind.

The Duke of Orleans saved himself. Then men of arms came all about the king and suffered him to weary himself, and the more that he travailed the feebler he was, and when he struck at any man they would fall down before the stroke. At this matter there was no hurt but many overthrown for there was none that made any defence. Finally when the king was well wearied and his horse sore chafed with sweat and great heat, a knight of Normandy, one of the king's chamberlains whom the king loved very well, called Guillaume Martel, he came behind the king suddenly and took him in his arms and held him still. Then all other approached and took the sword out of his hands and took him down from his horse and did off his jacket to refresh him. Then came his brother and his three uncles, but he had clean lost the knowledge of them, and rolled his eyes in his head marvellously and spake to no man. The lords of his blood were sore abashed and wist not what to say or do. Then the Dukes of Berry and of Burgundy said, 'It behoveth us to return to Le Mans. This voyage is done for this time.' They said not as much as they thought, but they showed it right well after when they came to Paris, to such as they loved not, as ye shall hear after . . . . . .

How Sir John Froissart arrived in England, and of the gift of a book that he gave to the king (1395).   [Ch. 196]

TRUE it was that I, Sir John Froissart, as at that time treasurer and canon of Chimay in the earldom of Hainault, in the diocese of Liége, had great affection to go and see the realm of England, when I had been in Abbeville and saw that truce was taken between the realms of England and France and other countries to them conjoined and their adherents, to endure four years by sea and by land. Many reasons moved me to make that voyage. One was because in my youth I had been brought up in the court of the noble King Edward the Third and of Queen Philippa his wife, and among their children and other barons of England that as then were alive, in whom I found all nobleness, honour, largesse and courtesy. Therefore I desired to see the country, thinking thereby I should live much the longer, for I had not been there twenty-seven year before, and I thought, though I saw not those lords that I left alive there, yet at the least I should see their heirs, the which should do me much good to see, and also to justify the histories and matters that I had written of them. And or I took my journey I spake with Duke Albert of Bavaria, the Earl of Hainault, Holland, Zealand and Lord of Friesland, and with my Lord William Earl of Ostrevant, and with my right honourable Lady Jane, Duchess of Brabant and of Luxembourg, and with the Lord Enguerrand, Lord Coucy, and with the gentle knight the Lord of Gommegnies, who in his youth and mine had been together in England in the king's court. In likewise so had I seen there the Lord of Coucy and divers other nobles of France holding great households in London when they lay there in hostage for the redemption of King John, as then French king, as it hath been showed herebefore in this history.

These said lords and the Duchess of Brabant counselled me to take this journey, and gave me letters of recommendation to the King of England and to his uncles, saving the Lord Coucy: he would not write to the king because he was a Frenchman, therefore he durst not, but to his daughter, who as then was called Duchess of Ireland. And I had engrossed in a fair book well illumined all the matters of amours and moralities that in four and twenty years before I had made and compiled, which greatly quickened my desire to go into England to see King Richard, who was son to the noble Prince of Wales and of Aquitaine, for I had not seen this King Richard since he was christened in the cathedral church of Bordeaux, at which time I was there and thought to have gone with the prince the journey into Galicia in Spain; and when we were in the city of Dax the prince sent me back to England to the queen, his mother.

For these causes and other I had great desire to go into England to see the king and his uncles. Also I had this said fair book well covered with velvet, garnished with clasps of silver and gilt, thereof to make a present to the king at my first coming to his presence. I had such desire to go this voyage that the pain and travail grieved me nothing. Thus provided of horses and other necessaries I passed the sea at Calais and came to Dover the twelfth day of the month of July. When I came there I found no man of my knowledge, it was so long since I had been in England and the houses were all newly changed, and young children were become men and the women knew me not, nor I them. So I abode half a day and all a night at Dover. It was on a Tuesday, and the next day by nine of the clock I came to Canterbury to Saint Thomas' shrine and to the tomb of the noble Prince of Wales, who is there interred right richly. There I heard mass and made mine offering to the holy saint and then dined at my lodging. And there I was informed how King Richard should be there the next day on pilgrimage, which was after his return out of Ireland where he had been the space of nine months or thereabout. The king had a devotion to visit Saint Thomas' shrine, and also because the prince his father was there buried. Then I thought to abide the king there, and so I did. And the next day the king came thither with a noble company of lords, ladies and damosels, and when I was among them they seemed to me all new folks, I knew no person. The time was sore changed in twenty-eight year, and with the king as then was none of his uncles. The Duke of Lancaster was in Aquitaine, and the Dukes of York and Gloucester were in other businesses, so that I was at the first all abashed, for if I had seen any ancient knight that had been with King Edward or with the prince, I had been well recomforted and would have gone to him, but I could see none such. Then I demanded for a knight called Sir Richard Stury whether he were alive or not, and it was showed me, yes, but he was at London. Then I thought to go to the Lord Thomas Percy, great Seneschal of England, who was there with the king. So I acquainted me with him and I found him right honourable and gracious and he offered to present me and my letters to the king, whereof I was right joyful, for it behoved me to have some means to bring me to the presence of such a prince as the King of England was. He went to the king's chamber, at which time the king was gone to sleep, and so he showed me and bade me return to my lodging and come again, and so

I did. And when I came to the bishop's palace I found the Lord Thomas Percy ready to ride to Ospringe and he counselled me to make as then no knowledge of my being but to follow the court, and said he would cause me ever to be well lodged till the king should be at the fair castle of Leeds in Kent.

I ordered me after his counsel and rode before to Ospringe, and by adventure I was lodged in an house where was lodged a gentle knight of England called Sir William Lisle. He was tarried there behind the king because he had pain in his head all the night before. He was one of the king's privy chamber, and when he saw that I was a stranger and, as he thought, of the marches of France, because of my language, we fell in acquaintance together, for gentlemen of England are courteous, treatable and glad of acquaintance. Then he demanded what I was and what business I had to do in those parts. I showed him a great part of my coming thither, and all that the Lord Thomas Percy had said to me and ordered me to do. He then answered and said how I could not have a better mean, and that on the Friday the king should be at the castle of Leeds. And he showed me that when I came there I should find there the Duke of York, the king's uncle, whereof I was right glad, because I had letters directed to him, and also that in his youth he had seen me in the court of the noble King Edward his father, and with the queen his mother.

Then on the Friday in the morning Sir William Lisle and I rode together, and on the way I demanded of him if he had been with the king in the voyage into Ireland. He answered me, 'Yes'. Then I demanded of him the manner of the hole that is in Ireland called Saint Patrick's purgatory, if it were true that was said of it or not. Then he said that of a surety such a hole there was and that he himself and another knight of England had been there while the king lay at Dublin, and said how they entered into the hole and were closed in at the sun going down and abode there all night, and the next morning issued out again at the sun-rising. Then I demanded if he had any such strange sights or visions as were spoken of. Then he said how that when he and his fellow were entered and past the gate that was called the purgatory of Saint Patrick, and that they were descended and gone down three or four paces, descending down as into a cellar, a certain hot vapour rose against them and struck so into their heads, that they were fain to sit down on the stairs, which are of stone. And after they had sat there a season they had great desire to sleep, and so fell asleep and slept there all night. Then I demanded that if in their sleep they knew where they were, or what visions they had. He answered me that in sleeping they entered into great imaginations and in marvellous dreams otherwise than they were wont to have in their chambers. And in the morning they issued out and within a short season clean forgot their dreams and visions, wherefore he said he thought all that matter was but a fantasy. Then I left speaking any further of that matter because I would fain have known of him what was done in the voyage in Ireland, and I thought as then to have demanded what the king had done in that journey, but then company of other knights came and fell in communication with him, so that I left my purpose for that time.

Thus we rode to Leeds, and thither came the king and all his company, and there I found the Lord Edmund Duke of York. Then I went to him and delivered my letters from the Earl of Hainault his cousin and from the Earl of Ostrevant. The duke knew me well and made me good cheer and said, 'Sir John, hold you always near to us and we shall show you love and courtesy. We are bound thereto for the love of time past and for love of my lady the old queen my mother, in whose court ye were: we have good remembrance thereof.' Then I thanked him as reason required. So I was advanced by reason of him and Sir Thomas Percy and Sir William Lisle; by their means I was brought into the king's chamber, and into his presence by means of his uncle the Duke of York.

Then I delivered my letters to the king and he took and read them at good leisure. Then he said to me that I was welcome as he that had been and is of the English court. As on that day I showed not the king the book that I had brought for him; he was so sore occupied with great affairs that I had as then no leisure to present my book. The king was so sore busied there in council for two great and mighty matters: first was in determining to send sufficient messengers, as the Earl of Rutland his cousin-german, and the earl marshal,* the Archbishop of Dublin, the Bishop of Ely, the Lord Louis Clifford, the Lord Henry Beaumont, the Lord Hugh Spencer and many other, over the sea to Charles the French king to treat with him for a marriage to be had between the King of England and the French king's eldest daughter, named Isabel, of the age of eight years. The second cause was, the Lord de la Barthe, the Lord of Terride, the Lord of Puycornet, the Lord of Castelnau, the Lord of Lesque, the Lord of Caupene, and the councillors of Bordeaux, Bayonne and of Dax were come into England and had quickly pursued their matter since the king's return out of Ireland, to have an answer of the requests and process that they had put forth to the king on the gift that the king had given to his uncle the Duke of Lancaster of the lands, seignories, lordships and baronies in Aquitaine which they verified to pertain to the king and realm of England. They had alleged to the king and his council that his gift might not pass so, because it was unprofitable and inutile: for they said all those lands held of right and of the demesne of the crown of England, wherefore they said they would not disjoin nor dissever them from the crown. They alleged furthermore many other reasonable causes, as ye shall hear after in this process, but thus to have counsel of those two great matters the king had sent for the most part of the prelates and lords of England to be at the feast of Maudlintide at a manor of the king's called Eltham, a seven English miles from London. And when they had tarried at Leeds a four days, the king returned to Rochester and so to Eltham, and so I rode forth in the king's company.

* Thomas Mowbray.

GLOSSARY

Some of the words included here are also used in their modern sense.

A, *on*, as in 'a-horseback'.
Abusion, *deception.*
Abye, *pay for.*
Addition, *title.*
Advertise, *observe.*
Advise, *observe, consider.*
Affiance, *confidence.*
Amities, *friendly relations.*
An, *if.*
Archgaye, *lance.*
Arranged, *pitched* (battle).
Astonied, *stunned.*
Avail, *descend.*
Avoid, *leave, dismiss.*

Bails, *barriers.*
Barded, *equipped with armour* (of horses).
Bascot, *bastard.*
Bassenet, *helmet.*
Bastide, *fortress.*
Battle, *division, army.*
Behoof, *use, advantage.*
Behoveful, *advantageous.*
Believe, *trust.*
Ben, *be, are.*
Beseen, *furnished, arrayed.*
Bidaus, type of light-armed soldier.
Bombard, early form of cannon.
Boot, *help.*
Broach, *spit.*
Bruit, *noise, rumour.*
Brunt, *shock, violence.*
Bushment, *ambush.*

Camlet, a kind of light cloth.
Can, *know.*
Canayr, *kettledrum.*
Captal, *lord.*
Certain, *inform.*
Coast, *go by the side of, accompany.*
Compact, *compacted, bound.*
Complect, *embrace.*
Condign, *well-merited.*
Contemplation, *regard,* as in 'out of regard to'.
Continue, *contents.*
Convenable, *proper.*
Countervail, *atone for.*
Cure-boly, *boiled hide.*
Currour, *scout.*
Custos, *keeper.*

Damage, *loss, pity.*
Day, to 'give day' is to fix a future time for payment, to give trust.
Defend, *stop, repel.*
Despite, *outrage, offended pride.*
Devoir, *duty.*
Dime, *tithe.*
Dispense, *expense.*
Diverse, *perverse.*
Doubt, *fear.*
Douze-peers, *twelve peers.*
Dress, *direct one's course.*

Easily, *slightly.*
Eke, *also.*
Ensample, *example.*
Ensign, *teach.*
Extraught, *extracted, descended.*

Fail, *miss.*
Felly, *angrily.*
Felonous, *angry.*
Fewe, *deer's track.*
Foin, *thrust.*
Foot, *principle, basis.*
Franchises, *liberties.*
Fray, *fright, disturbance.*

Genetours, *mounted troups, i.e.* riding gene**ts,** small Spanish horses.
Gest, *exploit.*
Glaive, *spear.*
Glint, *glance.*
Grapper, *grappling-hook.*
Gre, *favour, goodwill.*
Grise, *grey fur.*
Gules, *red* (in heraldry).
Gurged, *collected.*

Harness, *baggage, armour.*
Harrow, *exclamation of distress.*
Herse, *harrow, triangle.*
Hosting pace, *rapid pace, i.e.* as of an army advancing.
Housel, *give communion to.*
Hight, *am called,* as in 'I hight'.
Humet, *fesse cut short at each end.*

Imagine, *consider.*
Incontinent, *immediately.*
Intend, *attend, endeavour.*
Inutile, *void.*

Journey, *day, battle, expedition.*

Kirtle, *petticoat.*

Let, *hinder, delay.*
Lightly, *usually, readily.*
Limit, *appoint.*
List, *desire.*
Louage, *praise.*

Malengine, *deceit, evil advice.*
Maltote, *tax.*
March, *region.*
Marching, *bordering.*
Martinet, *engine for casting stones.*
Mester, *craft.*

Naker, *kettledrum.*

Obeisant, *obedient.*
Only, *alone.*
Or, *ere.*
Ordain, *set in order.*
Oreiller, *pillow* (in heraldry).
Orison, *prayer.*

Pain, *endeavour.*
Pavis, *shield.*
Pavised, *covered with a shield.*
Pensel, *small pennon.*
Pight, *pitch, fix.*
Pike, *thrust.*
Pill, *plunder.*
Plain, *full.*
Poister, *weigh down.*
Prewe, *brave.*

Quit, *set free.*

Rack, *loss.*
Rash down, *pull down.*
Recule, *retire, drive back.*
Regaly, *royalty.*
Relieve, *lift, raise oneself up.*
Repoin, *feel sorry.*

Salet, *head-piece.*
Seethe, *boil.*
Sentence, *meaning.*
Servage, *bondage.*
Set .. by, *esteem.*
Sewer, *server of meat.*
Skrye, *sudden attack.*
Sodden, *cooked.*
Somer, *beast of burden.*
Sowter, *cobbler.*
Sparkle abroad, *disperse, scatter.*
Spial, *watch.*
Springalle, *siege weapon.*
Succours, *reinforcements.*
Surge, *wave.*

Tail, *fasten behind.*
Targe, *shield, buckler.*
Thereas, *where.*
Trandal, *camp-follower.*
Travail, *trouble* (verb).

Trespass, *transgress, die.*
Trow, *believe.*

Valiance, *valour.*
Vidame, title of feudal lord, as 'the Vidame of Chalons.'
Viage, *journey, expedition.*
Void, *leave.*
Volve, *turn over.*

Wage, in 'kept field and wage of battle', to give decisions on questions of chivalry.
Wealth, *benefit.*
Ween, *think.*
Winage, *duty on wine.*
Without, *unless.*
Withsay, *speak against.*
Wood, *mad.*
Wrye, *turn.*

INDEX